Reassessing the Role of Government in the Mixed Economy

Symposium 1982

Edited by Herbert Giersch
Institut für Weltwirtschaft an der Universität Kiel

Routledge
Taylor & Francis Group
LONDON AND NEW YORK

First published 1983 by Westview Press

Published 2019 by Routledge
52 Vanderbilt Avenue, New York, NY 10017
2 Park Square, Milton Park, Abingdon, Oxon OX14 4RN

Routledge is an imprint of the Taylor & Francis Group, an informa business

CIP-Kurztitelaufnahme der Deutschen Bibliothek

Reassessing the role of government in the mixed economy: symposium 1982 / ed. by Herbert Giersch. — Tübingen: Mohr, 1983.

ISBN 3-16-344674-4 kart.
ISBN 3-16-344675-2 Gewebe

NE: Giersch, Herbert [Hrsg.]

Library of Congress Cataloging-in-Publication Data
Reassessing the role of government in the mixed economy / edited by Herbert Giersch.
p. cm.—(Publications of the Institute of World Economics, University of Kiel)
Based on a symposium held by the Kiel Institute of World Economics, June 23–25, 1982.
Includes bibliographies.
ISBN 0-8133-0598-5: $17.89
1. Economic policy—Congresses. 2. Economic development—Political aspects—Congresses. 3. Mixed economy—Congresses. I. Giersch, Herbert. II. Universität Kiel. Institut für Weltwirtschaft. III. Series.
HD73.R43 1987
338.9—dc19 **87-20142**
CIP

ISBN 13: 978-0-367-28514-2 (hbk)

ISBN 13: 978-0-367-30060-9 (pbk)

Contents

Preface

The disappointing performance of our economies over the last ten years has been attributed to several factors. One of them is the growth of government. The inefficiency of increasing governmental production, the disincentive effects of rising taxation, transfers and social insurance, and the restrictive influence of proliferating government regulations are all said to have undermined our ability and willingness to adjust to innovations and exogenous disturbances. Are these claims well founded, and if so, how should the role of government be redefined?

To address these questions we decided to hold a symposium on the subject of "Reassessing the Role of Government in the Mixed Economy". It took place at the Institut für Weltwirtschaft in Kiel on June 23-25, 1982. The papers and comments that are contained in this volume were presented at the symposium.

In several foreign countries, notably in the United States and the United Kingdom, governments have been elected which are trying to reduce the economic role of government. Since it was our aim to learn from their experience, we have invited economists from those countries to report and evaluate the policies that have been adopted by their governments, and we have asked German experts to comment on these papers. Most of the German discussants are contributing papers to a corresponding German volume which is forthcoming[1].

The first eight papers are concerned with governmental production, the last three with governmental regulation.

The papers by Alan Peacock and Rudolph Penner analyze the British and American attempts to cut public expenditure growth and make suggestions for future action in this respect. Richard McKenzie's study shows how federal matching grants to lower-level governments can act as incentives to increase government expenditure and how President Reagan's proposal for a transition to block grants and, finally, to an intergovernmental separation of functions is designed to eliminate those perverse incentives and to lay the responsibility for spending decisions and for financing the spending in the hands of the same political decision-makers.

[1] Wie es zu schaffen ist. Agenda für die Deutsche Wirtschaftspolitik, Herbert Giersch (Hrsg.), Deutsche Verlags-Anstalt, Stuttgart, September 1983.

Walter Eltis' paper opens the discussion about the nationalized industries. He analyzes the British problems, notably the exploding budgetary cost of subsidizing inefficient governmental production, and discusses possible solutions. The following papers by Marc Blaug, Herbert Grubel, Roland Vaubel und Edgar Olsen look at specific lines of governmental production: education, social insurance and public housing. All of them conclude that there is no economic case for the public provision of these goods and services, but that some of those who buy them may perhaps have to be subsidized. In the field of social insurance, the problem is aggravated by the government's legal monopoly in the provision of the mandatory insurance protection and by its too far-reaching and rigid prescription of the extent and nature of the insurance coverage. The authors suggest ways of enlarging the citizen's freedom of choice. In education, as Marc Blaug shows, there may be an economic case for the governmental provision or guarantee of loans to students.

Olsen's contribution about the government's role in the housing sector marks the transition from governmental production to governmental regulation. Olsen discusses the U.S. experience with public housing, rent control, and housing subsidies (allowances) and argues that entitlement housing allowances for low-income earners are the least objectionable type of interference. He shows that rent controls are an extremely inefficient way of attaining redistributive aims, since their economic cost amounts to about half the implicit transfers which they generate.

Thomas Tietenberg appraises the U.S. experience with market approaches to environmental protection. He describes the transition from the original and inefficient policy of imposing rigid emission standards on each enterprise to the more flexible property-right solutions, such as the offset policy, the bubble policy and emissions banking, and he analyzes the comparative advantages of each of them. Michael Pustay demonstrates that the deregulation of U.S. air transportation has in fact delivered the improvements that were expected from it: lower prices and costs, higher capacity utilization and more competition than would have prevailed otherwise. He argues that even larger gains could be achieved in Europe if the collusive price fixing of state-owned airline companies were terminated as well.

I want to express my gratitude to all those who helped to organize the conference and to publish this volume, notably Klaus-Werner Schatz and Roland Vaubel. Thanks are also due to the Hanns Martin Schleyer-Stiftung for its financial support, the City of Kiel for its traditional hospitality and Dietmar Gebert, Patricia Jassmann and Bernhard Klein for shouldering the bulk of the editorial work.

Kiel, March 1983 Herbert Giersch

Alan Peacock

Reducing Government Expenditure Growth: A British View

I. Introduction

In seeking to devise ways of reducing government expenditure growth, the economist only possesses a limited range of skills which might enable him to put forward useful suggestions. Economists have not been backward in coming forward with schemes ranging from various constitutional changes to incentive devices and may be inclined to argue that it is not their business to comment on the operationality of these schemes. It is the business of bureaucrats - the experts in the art of the plausible - and of politicians - the experts in the art of the possible - to decide whether or not their schemes can be implemented. This "take it or leave it" approach, however, does nothing to improve the credibility of economists as advisers to governments or political parties. Anyone engaged in this end of our trade will know that the credibility of economic advice depends on how far one can produce constructive proposals without doing violence to economic logic; and that is not an easy matter.

I have interpreted my task as that of looking for proposals to reduce government expenditure growth which have at least some prospect of acceptance by those most likely to be affected by them, the electorate. Individual members of the electorate will presumably be interested in maximising the gains from their transactions with government, subject to the acceptance of a decision rule which governs the election of any political party or coalition in power. Economic analysis of the political decision-making process may therefore be of some assistance in identifying schemes for expenditure control which are feasible. It is for this reason that I have explored below the extent to which public choice theory can point us in the direction of feasible solutions for reducing government expenditure growth by considering what the theory has to tell us about its determinants. I cannot say that the results of my analysis are particularly convincing, but even if that is the case, it is interesting to know why.

I have also been asked to put forward "a British view". If this were taken to mean that British economists have a distinct approach to the question at issue, then I would be at a loss to know what to write. Views on the utility function of governments, the constraints on maximising it, and the efficiency of the instruments for maximising it subject to those constraints, differ widely. At the moment debate on the size of the public sector rather resembles a Turkish wrestling match in which all the contestants battle with one another until one is left the winner, but with the crucial difference that every contestant claims victory. The ideological split between economists is more pronounced than at any time in my professional career. That would not matter if there were broad agreement about the appropriate choice of policy instruments to use in maximising any given government utility function but, as the Monetarist debate indicates, this is far from being the case. Nor is this a private "dialogue of the deaf" but a cacophonous public free-for-all, which is hardly an inspiring sight. I can only detect one characteristic of government expenditure growth on which contending factions agree and this is on the "waste" and "inefficiency" associated with highly centralised government; but there is certainly no agreement on how to eliminate these (I have examined "Right" and "Left" views on this matter in Peacock [1981]).

I have therefore taken a "British view" as meaning that British experience in trying to reduce government expenditure growth has elements which will be of interest outside the United Kingdom. Certainly the United Kingdom has a government much more committed to reducing government expenditure growth than at any time since the 1930s and its relative successes and failures may warrant examination.

Before embarking on the economic analysis of government expenditure growth and the problems that this growth has created in the United Kingdom, it may be useful to look briefly at some of the characteristics of that growth which require explanation. Section II tabulates government expenditure trends in relation to GDP in a number of countries and in a number of different ways. Section III offers a critical examination of recent explanations of government expenditure growth which have tried to answer the intriguing question whether such growth approaches some equilibrium level or some equilibrium ratio of government expenditure to GDP. If the answer were clear-cut one way or the other, it should tell us something about the ease or difficulty of reducing government expenditure growth. Section IV gives a brief account of British attempts to create the conditions which will favour a reduction in that growth. Section V offers a few closing remarks.

II. Government Expenditure Growth: An Overview

Since the early 1960s, when a number of authors began to look closely at the statistics of long-term growth in government expenditure and to speculate on its determinants [see Peacock, Wiseman, 1961; 1979; Musgrave, 1969], governments and international organisations (notably the IMF) have invested quite heavily in improving our statistical knowledge of post-war trends in government growth as an instrument of fiscal planning. Some recent results, which place particular emphasis on the distinction between nominal and real growth in government spending, are of relevance to this contribution [see Beck, 1981; Heller, 1981]. A summary of Beck's calculations with some additions by Heller is given in the table on the next page. In this table, Government Consumption represents expenditure on current goods and services, and Total Government Expenditure adds Transfer Outlays to Consumption. GDP is the Gross Domestic Product as measured by UN statistical conventions.

The left-hand side of this table shows the shares of Government Consumption in GDP and the proportion of Total Government Expenditure (G) to GDP at current prices. The trends shown are familiar to us all, and though one might speculate on the variability of shares by cross-section and historical comparisons, I have no space to do so. I shall also not indulge in the favourite pastime of arguing about what should or should not be included in the numerator or denominator in the ratio G/GDP.

The middle columns of the table present a very different picture, for these show how the real share of government expenditure has changed in relation to real GDP. Consider first of all government consumption. This information is arrived at by calculating separate deflators to remove the effect of price changes for both government consumption and GDP. There is a particular problem about performing this operation with respect to government consumption. Price deflators of goods and services take into account changes in the quality of goods purchased and changes in the productivity of direct labour services. As government output is not marketed and therefore is not priced, there are immense difficulties encountered in measuring changes in productivity. In fact, the common convention is to assume that government services output is a linear function of labour input, which implies that the productivity growth of labour services in government is zero. It is claimed that such an assumption will bias the price deflators of

Comparison of Nominal and Real Shares of Government Consumption and Total Government Expenditure in GDP, 1950-1977 (percent)

	Nominal share				Real share from perspective of							
					government				taxpayer			
	1950	1960	1970	1977	1950	1960	1970	1977	1950	1960	1970	1977
	Government Consumption											
Austria	11.3	12.7	14.6	17.4	11.3	8.7	7.5	7.5	11.3	14.4	17.0	20.2
Canada	10.3	13.9	19.2	20.3	10.3	11.4	12.7	11.6	10.3	14.9	21.6	25.1
Denmark	10.2	12.7	19.8	24.0	10.2	11.1	13.1	14.4	10.2	13.1	21.8	26.1
Finland	11.1	12.7	15.9	20.3	11.1	10.2	11.0	12.7	11.1	12.8	17.7	23.2
France	12.8	12.9	13.4	14.9	12.8	10.9	9.6	9.2	12.8	13.4	14.4	16.2
West Germany	14.3	13.6	15.9	20.6	14.3	11.6	11.1	12.8	14.3	14.9	18.8	24.0
Greece	11.5	11.2	12.6	15.9	11.5	8.4	7.2	8.6	11.5	12.1	14.1	18.8
Ireland	13.7	12.4	14.8	18.6	13.7	12.3	13.2	15.5	13.7	12.7	16.7	21.3
Netherlands	12.2	13.4	16.3	18.3	12.2	11.7	9.3	9.6	12.2	14.5	19.0	21.1
Sweden	13.7	15.8	21.4	28.5	13.7	14.1	15.3	17.2	13.7	16.4	23.3	32.4
Switzerland	11.2	10.1	10.5	12.9	11.2	9.3	8.7	9.7	11.2	10.3	11.8	14.9
United Kingdom	16.3	16.5	17.7	20.8	16.3	14.2	13.3	14.4	16.3	17.5	19.1	22.2
United States	12.1	17.9	19.1	18.5	12.1	15.8	16.8	13.4	12.1	18.6	20.6	20.1
	Total Government Expenditure											
Austria	21.2	25.6	33.1	39.8	21.2	23.3	28.7	33.7	21.2	28.9	38.2	46.5
Canada	19.0	25.7	32.2	36.9	19.0	23.8	27.3	32.3	19.0	27.4	36.2	45.9
Denmark	18.1	21.7	34.6	40.0	18.1	20.5	29.2	31.9[a]	18.1	22.5	36.7	45.7
Finland	20.4	22.2	27.6	35.6	20.4	20.5	24.0	30.4	20.4	22.7	30.9	40.9
France	26.7	30.2	34.7	41.8	26.7	28.9	32.3	38.5	26.7	31.4	37.2	45.5
West Germany	28.3	28.2	31.6	41.3	28.3	27.6	29.6	38.3	28.3	31.0	37.2	49.6
Greece	19.6	17.8	22.4	29.0	19.6	14.2	18.3	24.6	19.6	17.9	25.2	34.2
Ireland	23.0	25.6	34.3	43.3	23.0	25.2	35.2	44.1[a]	23.0	25.6	38.8	49.8
Netherlands	23.9	27.8	39.6	52.3	23.9	26.6	36.4	48.3	23.9	30.0	46.0	60.4
Sweden	23.7	26.9	37.1	55.6	23.7	25.8	32.4	48.1	23.7	28.1	40.4	63.3
Switzerland	19.3	17.5	21.3	30.4	19.3	16.9	21.0	29.8	19.3	17.9	24.3	34.9
United Kingdom	30.2	29.0	33.3	40.8	30.2	27.8	29.8	35.8	30.2	30.8	35.5	43.6
United States	20.0	25.7	30.3	32.6	20.0	23.9	28.8	28.8	20.0	26.6	32.6	35.5

[a] Refers to 1976.

Source: Beck [1981]; Heller [1981].

government consumption in an upward direction [see Heller, 1981, p. 64] but this claim could only be substantiated if surrogate measures of output, such as performance indicators, could be identified and agreed upon, and this does not seem to be a likely development. The deflation of transfer expenditures should presumably be carried out by the use of a consumer price index, though in principle separate deflators for the expenditure of particular groups of transfer receivers, notably pensioners, may be devised. This is not to underestimate the difficulties of constructing such deflators for longish periods of time, but these difficulties are common to all consumer price indices and are not compounded by the kind of problems encountered in the case of government consumption.

The middle columns reveal striking disparities between the growth in the ratio of government consumption to GDP in nominal terms and this growth in real terms, even allowing for statistical problems. For example, in the case of both the United Kingdom and West Germany the ratio in constant price terms actually declines, whereas for the United States it increases, but only slightly. However, in all countries in the sample the faster rate of growth in transfers in nominal terms, plus the importance of the consumption component in the GDP deflator, means that the ratio of Total Government Expenditure to GDP in real terms rises between 1950 and 1977. There are several other interesting features of this growth which might be explored. For example, in the case of West Germany according to the data, there is a "dip" in the ratio between 1950 and 1960 and only in the 1970s does the ratio increase quite markedly.

In the right-hand columns of the table, Heller offers a new twist to the statistical presentation of government expenditure growth by seeking to measure the opportunity cost of the public services to the taxpayer. This is done in admittedly rough-and-ready fashion by using the private consumption deflator as a proxy for the deflator relevant to the position of the "average" taxpayer in an attempt to determine what the resources applied to public consumption expenditure would have purchased if taxpayers were "free" to use the proceeds for private expenditure. As expected, the opportunity cost of public services steadily increases, implying that the terms of trade between public and private consumption have steadily decreased over the period 1950 to 1977. This is reflected in ratios of Total Government Expenditure to GDP which become higher than the nominal ratios. This calculation could obviously be attacked in various ways, notably in its implicit assumption that the growth in the ratio necessarily represents a welfare loss to the "average taxpayer".

I consider that these disparities between the growth in nominal and that in real terms in the ratio of government expenditure to GDP have an important bearing on the question of reducing expenditure growth. Answers to the question whether it is feasible to reduce growth may turn on the explanations offered for this phenomenon. A number have been given and they are not mutually exclusive. It could be that the reason for this "adverse" growth in what is now labelled the Relative Price Effect lies in the creation of a statistical illusion. Secondly, it could be that public services are subject to Baumol's disease [see Baumol, Oates, 1975, and pp. 12 ff.] and that lower productivity growth in the public as compared to the private sector is inevitable.

Thirdly, it could be that the lack of market incentives in the public sector means that low relative productivity in that sector is a function of institutional rather than technological factors. The arguments are clearly complicated by the dependence of the ratios on the real value of transfers, and by the extent to which this value is a reflection of political pressure to index transfer benefits, at least in the later years covered by the data.

From the standpoint of governments anxious to remain in power and therefore required, at least to some considerable degree, to take into account voter reactions to the growth of the public sector, but at the same time ideologically committed to reducing the rate of growth in government expenditure, various possibilities present themselves. For such governments the existence of a statistical illusion is not of prime importance, though if anything they may be biased towards stressing the dangers of growing government intervention as evidenced by the growth in total government expenditure. (In the United Kingdom, the present government has been attacked by the Left for exaggerating the growth in government expenditure.) If it is believed that Baumol's law of unbalanced growth has a firm foundation, then perhaps attention will be concentrated on reassessing the tasks of government with a view to reducing their range. Alternatively, attention might be concentrated on selling to the electorate the proposition that the important range of social services provided by government should operate solely to guarantee minimum or even absolute standards of provision rather than to provide services whose growth is related to the general growth in living standards. If it is believed that productivity gains can be reaped in the public sector but that these are not obtained because of the existence of X-inefficiency in government services, then attention might be concentrated less on shedding services or on controlling the improvement in their standards, and more on introducing or simulating competitive conditions in the provision of government services. Such governments will look for opportunities to price government services, to turn government departments into public enterprises and to "privatise" them.

There is an implicit assumption in the last paragraph that governments may have difficulty in convincing taxpayers/voters that, if expenditure growth and by implication the growth in tax yields are reduced, welfare losses will not exceed welfare gains, to the extent that voter support will be in jeopardy. The existence in recent years of tax revolts and strong attacks on government waste in a number of Western industrial countries suggests the contrary. Whether such a climate of opinion makes governments' task any easier in seeking to reduce government expenditure growth is a moot point. To throw light on this matter seems to me to entail a close examination of the determinants of government expenditure growth.

III. Explanations of Government Expenditure Growth and Expenditure Control

The explanations for the trends outlined in Section II above have themselves been subject to a rapid rate of growth in recent years [for a taxonomy, see Cameron, 1978]. What I hope to do in this section is to indicate how far the current state of the debate about growth in government expenditure influences views on the choice of methods of control. In doing so I shall eschew any final judgment on the hierarchy of explanations.

Broadly speaking, two types of testable model have developed from the earlier literature. The first tries to devise some empirical law of government expenditure growth in the tradition of Adolph Wagner, whose name still stalks the footnotes of countless articles. The second type usually presents some public choice model of the political decision-making process which embodies choices about public tax and/or expenditure levels. I shall refer briefly to the first type but regard the second type as more relevant to the subject matter of this paper.

There are many variants of the first model but by developing a useful "Gleichschaltung" of these models by Peltzman [1980] one is able to make a particular point about their relation to the question of controlling expenditure growth. I write

$$(1) \quad G = G(Y, P, R_p, A)$$

where G = per capita government expenditure
Y = per capita GDP
P = population
R_p = relative price of a unit of public services
A = a "catch all" term representing all other influences on G.

The model would be developed in order to identify the elasticity of G with respect to the independent variables and this conveniently provides an equation linear in logs for applying the usual multi-regression techniques. Thus:

$$(2) \quad G = Y^a P^b R_p^c A$$

Usually we are interested in the growth of G/Y so that (2) may be written as

$$(2a) \quad G/Y = Y^a P^b R_p^c A/Y \quad \text{so that}$$

$$(3) \quad \text{Log } G - \text{Log } Y = a\text{Log}Y + b\text{Log}P + c\text{Log}R_p + \text{Log } A - \text{Log } Y$$

where a, b, and c are elasticities

- $a > 0$ reflecting, say, public goods as "normal"
- $b < 0$ reflecting, say, some "scale effect" associated with population growth
- $c = ?$ depends on the price elasticity of demand for public goods.

Following Peltzman, one can simplify the equation further by assuming that R_p reflects Baumol's Law so that this term increases over time in line with the real wage rate which itself is a function of Y.

Thus $\log R_p = h \log Y$

where h is a constant and $0 < h < 1$.

Then (3) can be re-written as

$$(4) \quad \text{Log } G - \text{Log } Y = (a + ch - 1)\text{ Log } Y + b\text{Log}P + \text{Log } A$$

I am not concerned with the results of testing this model except to say that the degree of explanatory power varies both by country and by time period and that not all those who have adopted this approach have been content with log-linear models. What is noteworthy about this model is that it does not specifically identify a political process analogous to a market situation in which the behaviour of those who supply public goods and those who demand them are explicitly recognised. If we were considering how far government could intervene in a market in order to control the expenditure on a particular good, the appropriate form of intervention could not be specified without knowing the motivation of the "buyers" and "sellers" which will determine their reactions to a change in any parameters controlled by government. Presumably any government influence on the progress of government spending in such models entails further specification of the "catch-all" term, A[1]. Of particular importance is the lack of any suggestion that there could be an equilibrium level or rate of government expenditure growth to which the system might converge. Thus with a static population, and (a + ch) > 1, G/Y would go on rising for ever, unless "other factors" intervene!

In line with the commendable trend of identifying the micro-foundations of macro-economic models, a much more fruitful approach can be derived from the application of public choice theory to the study of government expenditure growth. At the end of a stream of suggestive articles on this subject, we come to the recent contributions of Peltzman [1980] and Meltzer and Richard [1981]. Following some intriguing suggestions of de Tocqueville [already noted and discussed in Peacock, Wiseman, 1979] both contributions derive the growth of government expenditure from de Tocqueville's proposition that this growth is a positive function of (a) the extension of the franchise; and (b) the inequality of income distribution. I shall summarise the Meltzer/Richard extension of these propositions and then present a self-made simple diagrammatic version of it which will form the basis of later discussion of expenditure control.

The demand for government services is regarded as essentially the demand for income redistribution. This redistribution can take the form of both transfers and real government services (e.g. education), many of which are not pure public goods and which confer direct benefits on users from which other users can be excluded. This redistribution has to be financed by taxes, and initially a balanced budget is assumed. The case where the franchise matters is where majority rule determines the amount of redistribution, in which case it may be assumed that the decisive voter is the voter with the median income. Voters with incomes below the median income choose candidates who favour redistribution and voters with incomes above the median income prefer lower taxes and less redistribution. (Interde-

[1] In essence the kind of "ratchet" effect supposedly identified by Peacock and Wiseman [1961] and associated with government responses to the social and economic effects of war and other disturbances is taken care of by the introduction of dummy variables.

pendent utility functions are therefore firmly rejected.) The vote of the median income receiver is decisive. Now historically, the spread of the franchise increased the proportion of voters with relatively low income within an unequal income distribution (in the sense that more than 50 per cent of income receivers had below-average incomes), and thus the median income voter's position would shift down the income distribution scale, raising the number of voters in favour of redistribution.

Interest centers on what happens when the extension of the franchise is completed. It could be that redistribution could continue if economic growth is associated with rising inequality of incomes, as Kuznets has suggested. However, if taxpayers/voters can choose between consumption and leisure, then the reduction in the price of leisure resulting from the rising tax burden on the upper income voters may lower the growth in taxable income and put a brake on the growth in the size of government. Assuming a balanced budget, then the proportion of the tax "take" to GDP would remain roughly constant and so would the proportion of government spending on goods and services and transfers as a proportion of GDP.

A figure, which I shall label de Tocqueville's Cross, may be useful. The rectangle abdfh represents the initial "equilibrium" position. Starting at point a, where the franchise covers, say, 30 per cent of the adult population, the given income distribution identifies a given percentage of voters, denoted by oc, with incomes below the average. The combination of the extent of the franchise and the given distribution of income, identifies the appropriate median voter income oe, the median voter position being crucial for the determination of T/Y which is represented by the distance og. (All axes are positive, of course.)

Consider what happens when the franchise is extended. The percentage of adult population enfranchised moves, say, to oa', and the percentage of voters with $y < \bar{y}$ will increase, with the enfranchisement of poorer voters from, say, oc to oc'. It may be noted that the same effect would be achieved if the franchise were not extended but the distribution of income became more unequal in the sense described. The relative median voter income would fall, and the decisive vote would shift the T/Y ratio upwards. The final result is shown in the rectangle a'b'd'f'h'. It is not possible in this four-quadrant system to show explicitly the effect of T/Y on $\Delta Y/Y$, and the possibility that there is a limit to the growth in T/Y is crudely represented by the upper bound LM. Nor is close investigation made of the shape as well as the slope of the various curves, which need not be linear.

De Tocqueville's Cross

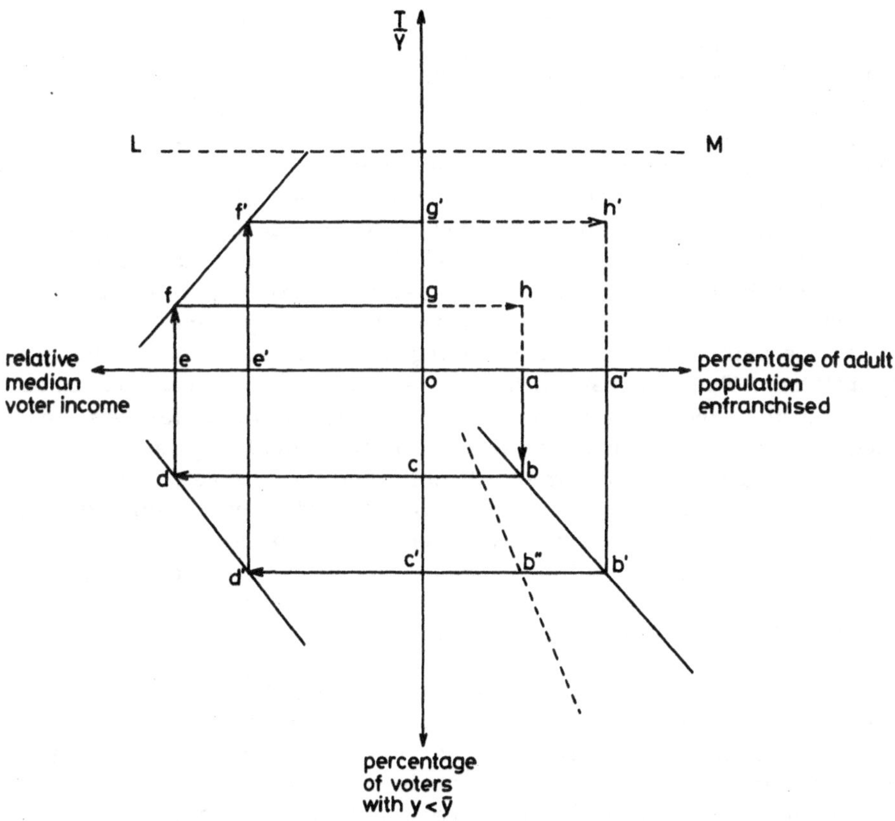

There are many questions raised by this model, as Meltzer and Richard realise, but the feature of most relevance to this contribution is the connection between T/Y and G/Y and the suggestion that there may be an upper limit to the size of these ratios. Clearly, the operationality of any device for control of expenditure is closely related to the demands of the electorate and the way in which these might govern the acceptance of some methods of control rather than others.

The first point to be made about limits to government expenditure growth relative to GDP is that G/Y can clearly rise faster than T/Y in money terms if governments increase the rate of borrowing. Meltzer and Richard specifically recognize this possibility and believe that it has been fully exploited in the 20th century as is evident from the growth in public debt. However, it seems to be assumed by them that voters, who throughout the analysis are assumed to have perfect knowledge, perceive that this policy imposes no costs on them but only on future generations of taxpayers. It is surely apparent to taxpayers/ voters that this is not so. If the proportion of G financed by borrowing increases and if governments issue interest-bearing debt to the private sector, then interest payments to present generations of taxpayers/voters are likely to make the pre-tax income distribution more unequal and at the same time may encourage the rich to substitute investment income for labour income. The translation of these complicated distributional and incentive effects into a demand for G becomes much more difficult. Likewise, if taxpayers/voters support governments that cover revenue deficits by money creation there is at least a prima facie case for holding that this will increase the rate of inflation. The interests of taxpayers/voters at any given initial position in the income distribution, before inflation accelerates, may then be very diverse and not identical as the model implies. Identifying the median voter becomes difficult, and the desire to "shift" the burden of current redistribution through the budget onto future generations may not be so clearly discerned. It seems reasonable to conclude that it is not established that the model unequivocally supports increasing the size of government for redistribution purposes by increasing the rate of growth in government debt.

The second point concerns the relation between T/Y and G/Y in real terms. If T/Y remains fixed, then to the extent that redistribution takes the form of differential access to services provided by the government, the real value of these services as a proportion of GDP (Y) may decline. It follows that if there is political pressure to provide a fixed proportion of output in real terms through the provision of government services, then T/Y must rise through time. The reason normally given for this proposition is that the opportunities for applying new technologies in service sectors (including government) are limited, whereas wages in these sectors are likely to rise at much the same rate as in manufacturing sectors if the normal forces of competition work in the labour market. This is the famous Baumol disease, and a simple proof of its application to the growth in government expenditure may now be given along similar lines to those by Baumol and Oates [1975].

(5) $$G_{ot} = a \cdot L_{gt}$$

$$(G_{ot} + P_{ot}) = Y_{ot} = a \cdot L_{gt} + bL_{pt} \cdot e^{rt}$$

i.e. Government output in period t is a linear function of labour input in the government sector, whereas GDP (Y) is a function of government output + private output, which is an exponential function of labour input in the private sector, reflecting productivity gains through time.

For simplicity assume $L_{gt} + L_{pt} = \bar{L}_t$

i.e. the labour force is fixed.

Now assume that the only cost of producing output is labour and that the wage rate is identical in both sectors. The wage rate (w) rises at the same rate as the growth in productivity, so that

$$w_t = w_o \cdot e^{rt}$$

(6) $$G_{et} = w_t \cdot L_{gt} = w_o \cdot e^{rt} \cdot (G_{ot}/a)$$

$$P_{et} = w_t \cdot L_{pt} = w_o \cdot e^{rt} \cdot (P_{ot}/b \cdot e^{rt})$$

where G_{et} represents government expenditure on goods and services in period t and P_{et} represents private sector expenditure on goods and services in period t.

It follows from (5) and (6) that

(7) $$G_{et}/P_{et} = e^{rt} \cdot [(G_{ot}/a) \cdot (b/P_{ot})]$$

Therefore G_{et}/P_{et} increases as t increases with G_{ot}/P_{ot} constant.

It follows that if there is a balanced budget so that

$$G_{et} = T_t, \quad \text{then}$$

$$T_t/Y_t = G_{et}/(G_{et} + P_{et})$$

where $T_t/Y_t = K$ which is the average tax burden.

Since G_{et}/P_{et} increases as t increases it follows that

$G_{et}/(G_{et} + P_{et})$ increases as t increases, if

$G_{ot}/(G_{ot} + P_{ot}) = G_{ot}/Y_{ot}$ constant

and therefore that

K increases as t increases.

We have already seen that a Relative Price Effect is evident in the comparison between government expenditure growth in current and constant prices (see Section II above) and this presents voters with a strong vested interest in the supply conditions governing the output of government services. If the supply conditions are fixed, as Baumol assumes, then resistance to increases in T/Y may be reinforced. This resistance, however, is unlikely to be translated into some automatic check on the growth in the ratio, given that taxpayers may be uncertain as to the effects on their tax burdens of foregoing increases in real benefits. As I have argued elsewhere [Peacock, 1979], the best one can do is try to interest voters in accepting some general rule of government expenditure growth while leaving open the question as to how that rule will be applied to particular services.

However, the Baumol argument seems to me to be suspect. There is growing evidence, at least in the United Kingdom, that the Relative Price Effect does not reflect simply technological but also principally institutional features of government production. If government output is not marketed and the government is a monopolist or quasi-monopolist in its production, then the majority of taxpayers/voters have a clear interest in supporting investigations into the prevalence of X-inefficiency, hoping thereby to find methods for its reduction. This follows from the supposition that efficiency gains could benefit those whose tax burden would otherwise be higher as well as those whose benefits through redistribution might otherwise have to be cut as tax resistance grows.

It is certainly true that a simple public choice model of government expenditure growth suffers from distinct limitations. All the usual caveats apply in the version presented, such as the omission of uncertainty in voters' perceptions of the precise effects of taxes and expenditures on their real incomes and the opportunity that uncertainty of budgetary impacts gives to bureaucrats and politicians to "rig" policy agenda. Nor is account taken of the possible influence of government employees as well as transfer receivers on the demand and the supply of government services. Their voting strength has grown pari passu with the growth of the public sector. Nevertheless, it must be true, if only in a tautological sense, that a necessary if not sufficient condition for government expenditure growth must be the willingness of the electorate to sanction the political programmes which determine the amount and pattern of both government expenditure and its finance. It also follows that effective limitation on that growth ultimately depends on the electorate's cooperation and how it is given expression through the relevant voting decision rule.

IV. The Approach to Reducing Expenditure Growth in the United Kingdom

1. Constitutional Reform

I have emphasised that taxpayers/voters are beset by the isolation paradox. A majority of them might prefer to see the rate of expenditure growth reduced, but they may be uncertain whether, if they so vote, the outcome of the political decision-making process, dependent on median voters, would produce a quid pro quo in reduced taxes. This has been one of the principal reasons for the revival of suggestions for financial reforms which would require constitutional changes.

Our de Tocqueville-inspired model offers some suggestions for change. The first does not look as if it has any chance for success, namely the narrowing or the modification in the franchise. Hugh Dalton, the famous public finance specialist and erstwhile Chancellor of the Exchequer, used to argue that the only solution to the reduction in public sector growth in the United Kingdom was to disenfranchise those who had reached pensionable age - like himself! The nearest thing to a practical suggestion has been a change in the voting system as applied to government employees who have a strong vested interest in the employment and promotion opportunities which growing government expenditure can provide. Tullock [1979] suggested that the United Kingdom might consider either disenfranchising civil servants or, perhaps a shade more practical, the creation of special constituencies for them and their families, separate from the normal geographical constituencies. This would still give them the power to vote but restrict the power exercised through the voting system, for the large majority of Members of Parliament would then represent constituencies in which there were no bureaucrats. The development of this proposal has attracted no takers, so far as I am aware.

Our model might suggest a different tack, which is to make the outcome of voting less dependent on the median voter. Two recent developments in political discussion in the United Kingdom have a particular bearing on the issue of public expenditure. The first is the growing support by "middle-of-the-road" politicians for changes in the voting rules, first in favour of proportional representation and, secondly, for devolution of government to regions. Both measures would help to reduce the deviation of individual voter preferences from the preferences governing the existing amount and pattern of government expenditure. The second measure is really a way of trying to curb the "tyranny of the (national) median voter" through the creation of alternative sources of supply of public services in "competing" regions.

There are two problems about these proposals. The first is the obvious one of implementation. The proposals could only be instituted as a result of legislation enacted by the central government legislature, the House of Commons, in which government is formed by the majority party, in which all members are elected by a first-past-the-post system and whose enactments cannot be challenged in a national constitutional court. Any legislative measures intended to reduce "voter alienation" would themselves entail a considerable surrender of the members' power to individual voters and to lower layers of government. Lord Hailsham, the Lord Chancellor, summed up the position in an informal remark: "the trouble with proportional representation is that when you are out of power you can't have it and when you are in power you don't want it", an observation which can be extended to cover the devolution of power as well. The second problem is that the only safe prediction that could be made about the effects of these constitutional changes on the size of government is that the composition of taxes and expenditure might be changed markedly, but not that government expenditure growth would necessarily be reduced. In the course of the debate on the devolution of government in the United Kingdom which has lasted nearly twenty years in its present phase, little reference has been made to reconsidering the balance between private and public provision of goods and services, and most of the statistical calculations develop models which simply reallocate existing functions between central and regional government [see Peacock, 1977].

The second major development pertaining to the problem of reducing expenditure growth has been the attempt to engender voter support by embodying in the constitution some general rule governing the growth of the public budget. Suggestions have ranged from a revival of the time-honoured suggestion that the central government should balance its budget to tax limitation or expenditure limitation proposals [for an excellent summary of the debate in the United States, see AEI, 1979]. There has been no counterpart to this debate in the United Kingdom in the sense that no bills have been seriously considered by the legislature which would impose limitations of this kind. Parliament has relied on its power to tax, on its control over the auditing system covering government expenditure, on the scrutiny powers of its Committee of Public Accounts and, latterly, on its Treasury and Civil Service Committee to achieve what control it thinks is necessary. Nevertheless, though not blessed by a constitutional code and not even embodied in any specific act of legislation, the "cash planning" system now operated by the U.K. Treasury is a rough-and-ready attempt to follow a general rule of expenditure growth. Its characteristics, effects and limitations may be of interest beyond the shores of the United Kingdom, and will now be separately discussed.

2. The Cash Planning and Control System

In principle, an expenditure rule which required that government spending at *current* prices (including capital spending) should not rise above some given ratio of GDP at current prices or should only fluctuate within a narrow ratio band might have certain distinct advantages over other macro-economic control measures designed to achieve the same end. A balanced-budget provision does not by itself promote control of government expenditure growth, for the budget can be balanced at widely different levels of expenditure and taxation. A tax limitation proposal still offers the possibility that government expenditure can be financed by borrowing.

Of course, macro-economic control of government spending growth may be judged not solely in terms of the contribution to the improvement of allocative and technical efficiency but also in terms of the contribution to economic growth and stability. So far as the objective of growth is concerned, one's view depends on what one regards as the appropriate role of the budget in growth promotion. Here I shall merely assert that the relationships between the size of the public sector, the methods of controlling its size and growth performance are not clearly established. So far as stability is concerned, an expenditure rule is clearly more flexible than a balanced budget rule, for it still leaves open the possibility of altering the tax/borrowing "mix". In an era of inflation, a current spending rule is clearly superior to a ratio fixed in volume terms, for it operates as a direct control on the amount of cash spent and it offers a clear signal to both spending authorities within government and to suppliers of government purchases that services will be cut back if prices and wages rise too much.

The U.K. Labour Government introduced "cash limits" into their budgetary planning system in 1976 primarily with stabilisation objectives in mind, at a time when it looked as if the Relative Price Effect would become so marked that stiff resistance to an increase in T/Y as a way of combatting inflation through control of private sector aggregate demand would be encountered. In any case, they were convinced by their economic advisers that direct tax increases which at that time might reduce r e a l d i s p o s a b l e i n c o m e s would destroy incomes policies based on movements in gross incomes. Limiting the growth of the public sector in current price terms would be the lesser of two evils. This system has been developed into a "cash planning and control system" by the Conservative Government in line with their belief in "supply-side" economics and in monetarism, which requires both a planned reduction in the relative size of the public sector in order to channel resources into the private sector and a reduction in pressure on the Public Sector Borrowing Requirement. In addition it has been claimed that such a system will contribute to greater efficiency in government spending through greater financial discipline.

The system is a "control system" in the sense that for the fiscal year ahead cash limits are placed on spending by each central government department, practically without exception, and on the grants paid to local governments. If for policy reasons this limit is exceeded, provision may be made for extra cash from a contingency reserve, but the reserve itself is a control figure for that year. (At the time of writing it had been announced that any extra defence expenditure during fiscal year 1982/83 as a consequence of the Falkland Islands dispute may have to be met from the reserve, but that it is not intended to increase the reserve itself.) The system is now a "planning system" in the sense that public expenditure plans for three years ahead are to be expressed in cash and no longer in volume terms, and these plans will be related to movements in GDP at current prices. This is a major departure in British planning procedures [for further details see Likierman, 1981].

The difficulties associated with cash planning and control are obvious and are well illustrated by United Kingdom experience:

(i) Strict cash limits cannot be applied in a truly comprehensive manner for two main reasons. The first is that the central government is not the sole spending authority. Alongside it there is a motley of local authorities, including local elected councils, police authorities, passenger transport executives, etc., as well as public corporations with a substantial degree of financial independence. Their operations can only be controlled by "cash-limiting" grants or subsidies received from central government. The second is that important segments of public expenditure are demand-determined, at least in the short run. For example, the government can only control the scope and the rates of payments to social security beneficiaries, but the volume of payments will depend on the number of qualified applicants. In fact, in the current fiscal year 1982/83 only 40 per cent of total government expenditure is cash-limited in the strict sense.

(ii) The current expenditure estimates adjust the volume estimates of expenditure by expected changes in prices. No government will willingly reveal price assumptions in case these will affect the price expectations of the private sector and through private sector reactions alter the assumptions on which the expenditure estimates have to be based. So far as cash-limited expenditure is concerned, price estimates may be disguised, at least in presenting data, but in the case of demand-determined expenditure it may not be too difficult for the outside investigator to work out the implicit movements in the price index. The U.K. Treasury have been able to get round this difficulty by revealing that projections of social security transfers are based on a positive but *declining* rate of inflation! Presumably no government using cash limits as a means of controlling the Public Sector Borrowing Requirement in the name of anti-inflationary policy could ever admit to assuming otherwise!

(iii) Cash limits by themselves can only be a blunt instrument in trying to improve efficiency. With all the problems associated with measuring the output of government services, it will be difficult to monitor performance in order to determine whether cash limits are met by reducing the quantity and quality of services or by increasing efficiency. This is illustrated by the United Kingdom government's attempt to prescribe limits on pay increases in public sector employment and targets for reduction in the number of government employees alongside the operation of cash limits.

(iv) With a considerable proportion of current expenditure goods and services incurred by local governments, the cash limits system has to extend its grip very firmly on other spending authorities. In the short run it has been possible for local governments to erode the cash limits policy by offsetting the decrease in the growth in grants from the central government with substantial increases in revenue from the local property tax, the local rate. In fiscal year 1981/82, for example, the cash expenditure target was exceeded by £ 1 1/2 billion which, although only a little over 1 per cent of total expenditure, was almost entirely the result of local government overspending. However, attempts to directly control local authorities' spending by penalising those who overspend, e.g. by reducing central government grants, are regarded as an unwarranted interference with local democracy.

3. Removing X-Inefficiency

Economists have devised a whole range of schemes designed to remove X-inefficiency in the provision of services provided by Government departments or agencies. These may be classified into two groups. The first concerns services which are identified as "pure" public goods, such as defence and law and order, where only very limited private production would be either possible or desirable. In such cases, some attempt must be made to simulate the market or at least to try to reform budgetary procedures so as to be able to facilitate quantitative assessment of performance. The second concerns services which, although perceived as having "publicness" attributes, might be produced in the private sector, subject to regulation, as an alternative to public provision. In such cases, the issue here is whether to recommend "privatisation" of the services, either by de-nationalisation or by greater public use of private contractors, e.g. for house building, garbage disposal, etc. or whether to keep the service within the public sector but to charge the public directly for its output.

Traditionally, politicians and administrators in the United Kingdom have concentrated primarily on the first range of schemes, and the tradition is strong. The Treasury and Civil Service Committee, including the evidence submitted to it by public officials, typifies this approach. Year after year, politicians criticise the lack of use of performance indicators and the need for much more investment in "value for money" studies to be conducted by the Comptroller and Auditor General and his staff; and year after year officials accept, with reservations, the conclusions of their masters. Nothing much happens, and it is easy to state why. So long as there is political disagreement about both the choice of performance indicators and trade-offs between them in the case of major public services, it is open to the bureaucracy to avoid making major organisational changes, and there are no built-in incentives to simulate competitive conditions in non-marketed services. Furthermore, members of Parliament on the various financial committees appear to believe that improving the "watch-dog" powers of the government auditing services would be the most effective method for improving efficiency. This is understandable, for the auditing services are outside executive control, and are closely linked to Parliamentary committees, but their particular skills, even if including management accounting, are better employed in detecting deficiencies in financial planning rather than in discovering remedies. An auditing service which itself produces an "output" which is not marketed may not be so conscious of the need to look for solutions which will simulate market pressures. (Recently, a motion by two members of the Treasury and Civil Service Committee to have the Government auditing services themselves subject to independent private audit was defeated!)

The possibility of charging for government services and possible privatisation of such services is being seriously considered by the present Government but the few changes made so far have little bearing on the problem of efficiency. There is a major obstacle which is readily apparent if we refer back to our public choice model. The areas in which turning services into "profit centres" or privatising them would be technically feasible are precisely those which are supported by voters because of their perceived redistributive impact - health, education and housing services. If these services were to be charged for, then this would stand a chance of being politically acceptable only if compensatory adjustments were made in the tax and transfer system. While there might be efficiency gains which would translate themselves into reduced growth in government expenditure, total government expenditure would be unlikely to undergo a radical reduction. It would only change in composition.

V. Concluding Remarks

The discussion on what to do about reducing government expenditure growth has gone beyond the point of offering a list of instruments which would achieve that end. That is not very difficult. What is much more difficult is to identify those instruments which are not excluded by the "boundary conditions" governing the choice of means to achieve acceptable political ends. Thus an economist who believes, for example, that it would be easy to solve the problem of reducing expenditure growth by "privatisation" of those services which are largely private goods in the technical sense either believes with the first Lord Halifax, Secretary of State to Charles II, that "Precepts, like fomentations, must be rubbed into us - and with a rough hand, too", or lives in a political vacuum, or believes that either he or those he advises have remarkable powers of persuasion if the implementation of policy measures requires the widespread consent of the governed.

I am conscious of the fact that all I have done is to illustrate this proposition and how difficult it is, even for a government as committed to discarding the role of Leviathan, to putting the engine of government expenditure growth into reverse, as that of Mrs. Thatcher. As I have indicated, the best chance seems to lie in some general rule by which government expenditure in current price terms should not exceed some fixed percentage of GDP at current prices. The problem of implementing such a rule ex ante would require that planned government expenditure should not exceed a given proportion of, say, the average of the last three years' GDP at current prices. A general rule of this kind still leaves room for considerable variation in the tax/borrowing "mix", in the composition of public spending, and in the delineation of the powers of various spending authorities. My conclusion is neither original nor particularly convincing but it will have to serve.

References

American Enterprise Institute (AEI), Proposals for a Constitutional Convention to Require a Balanced Federal Budget. Washington 1979.

Baumol, William J., Wallace J. Oates, with contributions by Vijay S. Bawa and David Bradford, The Theory of Environmental Policy: Externalities, Public Outlays and the Quality of Life. Englewood Cliffs, New Jersey, 1975.

Beck, Morris, Government Spending: Trends and Issues. Praeger Special Studies, New York 1981.

Cameron, David R., "The Expansion of the Public Economy: A Comparative Analysis". The American Political Science Review, Vol. 72, 1978, pp. 1243-1261.

Heller, Peter, "Diverging Trends in the Shares of Nominal and Real Government Expenditure in GDP: Implications for Policy". National Tax Journal, Vol. 34, No. 1, 1981, pp. 61-74.

Likierman, Andrew, Cash Limits and External Financing Limits. Civil Service College Handbook No. 22, London 1981.

Meltzer, Allan H., Scott F. Richard, "A Rational Theory of the Size of Government". Journal of Political Economy, Vol. 89, No. 5, 1981, pp. 914-927.

Musgrave, Richard A., Fiscal Systems. New Haven 1969.

Peacock, Alan, "The Political Economy of Devolution: The British Case". In: Wallace E. Oates (Ed.), The Political Economy of Fiscal Federalism. Lexington, Mass., 1977, pp. 49-63.

--, The Economic Analysis of Government and Related Themes. New York 1979.

--, "Government Expenditure and the Radical Left". The Journal of Economic Affairs, Vol. 1, 1981, pp. 145-149.

--, Jack Wiseman, The Growth of Public Expenditure in the United Kingdom. National Bureau of Economic Research, General Series, 72, Princeton 1961.

--, --, "Approaches to the Analysis of Government Expenditure Growth". Public Finance Quarterly, Vol. 7, No. 1, 1979, pp. 3-23.

Peltzman, Sam, "The Growth of Government". The Journal of Law and Economics, Vol. 23, No. 2, 1980, pp. 209-287.

Tullock, Gordon, "Bureaucracy and the Growth in Government". In: Institute of Economic Affairs (IEA), The Taming of Government: Micro/macro Disciplines on Whitehall and Town Hall. IEA Readings, 21, London 1979, pp. 21-43.

Comment

William Fellner

A brief discussion paper needs to be selective, and I will concentrate on what to me seems the most important part of Peacock's contribution. This is the further development of a hypothesis - or of a suggested explanation of observed trends - that moves along lines of the recent work of several authors, including that of Peacock himself[1]. The nontechnical origins of the basic insights involved in the analysis have repeatedly been attibuted to Alexis de Tocqueville who expressed these insights in 1835 in his famous book "De la démocratie en Amérique".

1. The hypothesis. When properly elaborated in a professionally constructed conceptual framework, as is done in Peacock's paper, the hypothesis can be summarized as follows. Define a frequency distribution of incomes limited to voters, and locate on the abscissa of the corresponding diagram the median income of voters. In a democracy you can expect the tendency toward the equalization of incomes by government activity, involving taxation and fiscal outlays, to be greater the higher that proportion of the aggregate income is which is earned by those income recipients whose income is located to the right of the median income of the voters. The reason is that those whose income is located to the left of the median plus those who earn the voters' median itself make up a group whose size is necessary and also sufficient to force redistributive political activity at the expense of all those located to the right of the median income of voters. Hence, the incomes earned by all those whose individual income is located to the right of the voters' median income represent the maximum "prize" (reward) obtainable by forming a viable spontaneous coalition of voters. The greater the prize, the more rewarding it is to form such a coalition. This latter proposition explains presumably also why, for forming a majority, the voters earning the median income of voters join the sector left of the median rather than the right-hand sector:

[1] Other recent contributions are listed in Peacock's paper and also in the like-minded article by Allan H. Meltzer and Scott F. Richard, "A Rational Theory of the Size of Government", Journal of Political Economy, Vol. 89, No. 5, 1981, pp. 914-927.

by joining the left-hand sector they greatly increase the reward obtainable by the majority.

It is generally recognized that redistributive pressures toward equalization are apt to approach a limit at some stage short of literal equality - a question to which I will return in a moment - but the main conclusion relates to a process that according to this hypothesis has contributed to *increasing* the redistributive pressures toward equality, and thus to *increasing* the volume of those governmental activities by which income is redistributed. The process that has this consequence is the gradual extension of the franchise to very much larger proportions of the population of democratic countries. The aggregate income earned by recipients whose incomes are located to the right of the median income of voters has thereby become increased significantly in relation to the aggregate income earned by voters whose incomes are located left of the median and at the median itself. Consequently, forming spontaneous voter coalitions directed against the recipients of incomes exceeding the median income of voters has gradually become much more rewarding. The voters earning incomes located to the left of the median plus those earning the voters' median income itself have had an increasingly powerful incentive to form such coalitions spontaneously.

2. *The distinctiveness of the hypothesis*. Note that the neatness and the simplicity of the proposition we are considering as well as its distinctiveness derive from its focusing on a single elementary property of a frequency distribution, namely, on the median income of voters. This median is made to serve as the criterion by which the population is partitioned into two sets with the suggestion that we thus obtain a partitioning of crucial significance. It is essential to keep this in mind because the mere proposition that, in a democracy, variously composed ad hoc majorities have opportunities for "ganging up" on minorities would, in contrast to the Peacock analysis, be trite. Except for tragic phases of history, the practical importance of the trite ganging-up proposition is presumably limited by the fact that if the ganging-up majorities need to be variously constituted for ad hoc purposes, then forming such coalitions is a dangerous practice - one never knows which group is the next victim - and in a well-functioning democracy there develops an esprit de corps that (we hope) sets narrow limits to this practice.

At any rate, Peacock and other authors have expressed a very much richer proposition than that in a democracy, particularly in one in which the suffrage is general, it is in principle possible to single out minorities successively for the purpose of dispossessing or otherwise damaging them, and that if a population is to be capable of maintaining democratic institutions, then it must be conditioned to developing resistance to such practices. The distinctiveness of the much more specific analysis we are considering results not from such a vague conception concerning gains obtainable by variously composed majorities at the expense of minorities, but from the emphasis on the median income of voters as the specific criterion for partitioning the population in a way that maximizes the reward of a viable coalition.

Convinced though I am that the results of the analysis are of substantial interest, I will now explain why, in my appraisal, essential modifying considerations reduce the significance of the well-defined criterion of partitioning suggested by the analysis.

3. Do even the limitations recognized by Peacock reduce the significance of the voters' median income? As I see it, one of the limiting factors recognized by Peacock and, generally, by the contributors to this approach, does not call for qualifying the role of the median. Another limiting force recognized by Peacock and other contributors does call for qualifying the role of the median, but perhaps to no very great extent. Let us first take a brief look in the next two paragraphs at these two generally recognized limiting factors, and then turn, in the following section, to what I regard as a more essential modifying consideration.

As redistribution toward equality progresses in a world described by this model, the aggregate income earned by recipients whose income is located above the median diminishes relative to the below-median incomes of voters. At some stage the negative effect of this on further redistributive pressures is apt to catch up with the positive effect of extended franchise on that pressure. This limiting factor of which it is unnecessary to remind the contributors does not require qualifying the role of the median.

Another counteracting force recognized by the advocates of this approach, including Peacock, does require qualifying the role of the median to some extent but perhaps not very much. If at some point any proportion of those in whose favor the redistribution is supposed to take place arrives at the conclusion that, as a result of the inefficiencies caused by the redistribution of relative shares, they are becoming net losers, then the below-median plus the median sector cease to have a majority. In that case forming a majority requires replacing the below-median dropouts with above-median recruits, and this in turn requires moving against a *smaller* set of *high-income* recipients which is a less rewarding undertaking. To the extent that this occurs, the pressure for redistribution is apt to become reduced. At the same time, to this extent the distinctiveness of the approach we are discussing becomes marred because the unwieldy problem enters of how to partition the population on successive occasions. - I will now suggest an additional qualification.

4. *The static outlook implied in the partitioning criterion.* It should be clearly recognized that the distribution measured in cross-sections of incomes during any period gives a misleading picture of what will turn out to be the lifetime income distribution of a population. The basic properties of the lifetime income distribution - such as its mode, or median or mean - can at best be guessed at by highly uncertain methods of projection with reliance on cohort profiles. These properties or parameters are not observable at any time in the sense in which the analogous properties are observable in distributions defined for any period's cross-section.

This is another way of saying that, aside from the few remarks I have made before about modifying or qualifying factors, we need to recognize the fact that the attitude of an income recipient to redistribution is apt to depend significantly on his expected but uncertain future income as well as on his present income. Where he stands at present relative to the ascertainable median income of voters will not by any means be the only determinant of his decision to vote against the interests of the right-of-the-median population or not to do so.

Consider a voter whose present income falls short of the median income of voters but who expects to earn an above-median income from some future period on. We should not overlook the fact that the more economically ambitious a population of given age structure is, the more individuals of this sort are likely to be present in the below-median sector of any period. Such an individual is presumably aware of the fact that any redistributive measure at the expense of the right-of-the-median sector makes it more difficult for him to get there. His decision will be influenced by the slope of the future time profile of his expected pre-tax income, by the variance about his mean expectation concerning that time profile, by his attitude to risk (that is, his utility function), and his time-preference function. I made no attempt to work this out in detail but no such attempt could lead to a simple solution comparable to that described by Peacock (that is, to partitioning at the median), and all solutions would be very likely to suggest ad hoc coalitions with changing composition over time. This is true all the more because, regardless of how ambitious and confident a population is, most upper middle-age individuals are likely to expect that thereafter their incomes will soon be declining.

In fact, many of the widely adopted redistributive measures - though, of course, not all - do have a pronounced life-cycle aspect. They tend to diminish the inequality between an individual's income when he is young, middle-aged, and old, *in addition* to redistributing at the expense of those whose income in successive cross-sections is high relative to the incomes of others. For reasons that are easy to appreciate, doubts are felt in many quarters about how well these measures are tailored to the intentions behind them and about how efficiently they are administered; yet the political support for subsidized education of the young and for old-age provisions is very wide and it remains strong. The nature of these measures is by no means fully described by stating that they mostly tax the right-of-the-median sector in order to channel income to below-median voters. Their orientation to life-cycles belongs among the essential characteristics of these measures; and to some extent these measures reflect also "interdependent utility functions", an aspect of the matter that should not remain unmentioned though here I will not discuss it further beyond a comment in a footnote[1].

At least for the United States it is safe to suggest that life-cycle-oriented transfers account for a large part of the story. For instance, according to the data listed in Peacock's table, total government expenditures in the United States rose in his latest period (1970 to 1977) from 30.3 to 32.6 percent of the GDP, that is, by 2.3 percentage points; for the same seven-year period I find in the available data a

[1] A large number of voters who by saving and investing individually could provide for their old age more efficiently than through the Social Security system nevertheless favor the existence of such a system. This is, in part at least, explained by the fact that very few would find it acceptable to see their improvident fellow citizens who have lost their earning ability starve or go without medical help. Interdependent utility functions play a role in this, as well as in the subsidization of education and in the acceptability to taxpayers of other transfer outlays. Peacock calls attention to the fact that analysis along his lines disregards utility interdependence, and the way he expresses this rightly suggests that this is to be considered a qualification.

1.7 percentage point increase in Social Security benefits relative to GDP and a 2.0 percentage point increase in the sum of Social Security benefits and of government employees' retirement benefits. These two life-cycle-oriented measures alone account for 2.0 out of 2.3 percentage points - a roughly 85 percent proportion of the increase. For earlier periods covered by Peacock's table this proportion is less high, but it still is in the neighborhood of one-half.

5. Conclusion and a brief remark on expenditure control. I consider the results reached along Peacock's line of analysis and along that of like-minded contributors significant in spite of the substantial importance I attribute to the modifications called for by lifetime incomes, for which we lack the measures placed in the center of the analysis I have tried to appraise. I see no contradiction in holding these judgments jointly because I prefer to go part of the way - Peacock's part - with reliance on a piece of well-developed analytical equipment, and to go the other part of the way by much less highly formalized adjustments, rather than have to go the whole way without the benefit of well-constructed tools applicable to observable data. But I do believe that in the present case much is left to the second part of the way, that is, to the adjustment to presumptive lifetime profiles. As I said, I believe that, given the age structure of a population, the question of how much is left to the lifetime adjustment depends in large measure on how economically ambitious a population is.

Let me make a brief final comment on the question of expenditure control on which Peacock expresses himself at the end of his paper. I, too, am convinced of the great importance of this problem. However, I am inclined to the view that we shall either succeed in developing the proper attitude to it when making our political decisions period after period, as I hope we shall, or shall not succeed at all. Only in countries with a written constitution is it worthwhile to distinguish, as a possible alternative, the method of subjecting legislatures to formalized long-run constraints in this regard. But even in such countries, including the United States, there would have to be enough escape clauses to render the constitutional constraints ineffective unless the attitudes developing in the country reflect the need to keep the path of government expenditures compatible with the efficient functioning of a market economy.

Rudolph G. Penner

How to Reduce Government Growth: An American View

I. Introduction

There is a strong public feeling in the United States that government is out of control. Having said that, it is not easy to give a precise meaning to the concept of being "out of control".

Part of the problem derives from the fact that it is rational for ordinary voters to remain ignorant regarding the details of government policy. They have no direct influence over that policy, and are kept busy enough gathering the information necessary to make efficient private decisions. Consequently, their attitudes toward government are not well defined and, as revealed in public opinion polls, often seem downright irrational. Poll after poll suggests that voters would like to see total spending and tax burdens reduced and yet, the same polls show a great reluctance to cut spending on specific programs such as defense, social security, education, etc. [see Dale et al., 1976, pp. 18 ff.; Public Opinion, 1981, p. 27]. There is, of course, a desire to cut waste and fraud but apparently little understanding that some waste and fraud is optimum, since it often costs much more than a dollar's worth of management resources to reduce waste and fraud by a dollar.

Some polls show hostility to specific program areas such as foreign aid and agriculture, but these two items typically constitute less than 3 percent of total outlays. More recently, there has been considerable hostility toward "welfare". Again, few seem to recognize that, at the Federal level, welfare is relatively unimportant. Outlays providing income-conditioned health, housing, nutrition, and cash assistance to the poor constitute less than 10 percent of total outlays and while there is some desire to cut these programs a bit, there is little support for altering them radically. Income-conditioned transfer payments are dwarfed by the cost of transfers and health services that are provided to rich and poor alike. Some of these, such as social security, have a redistributive element, but are not restricted to the poor. Such assistance constitutes about 30 percent of the total budget and its share is growing rapidly. The bulk of such assistance goes to the non-poor elderly and programs for the elderly are highly popular.

Defense spending constitutes about one-quarter of outlays, and with the disappearance of the hostility toward the military that was engendered by the Vietnam war and with the growing perception of the threat posed by the Soviets, increased defense spending has also gained strong public support.

In summary, attitudes toward total spending seem at best ambivalent and at worst confused. The generalized hostility toward government that aided the election of President Reagan may have its roots, as much or more, in the regulatory and tax policies of the government as in its spending policies. Since the early 1970s there has been an explosion of regulatory activity [Lilley, Miller, 1977]. Well-intentioned efforts to use regulation to improve the environment, to provide equal opportunity to minorities, and to insure worker health and safety have made government all intrusive and have imposed enormous costs on the private sector.

In tax policy, a combination of bracket creep and legislative action raised marginal tax rates on the middle and upper middle classes during the 1970s without significantly raising the revenue yield of the tax system. There was a growing perception that the income tax system was "unfair" and it made President Reagan's promise to cut marginal tax rates highly popular. Unfortunately, public hostility toward taxes, combined with public ambivalence toward spending, led American politicians to cut taxes vigorously in the summer of 1981 while making only minor changes in spending programs. The end result is the prospect of huge deficits unless spending is cut or taxes are raised significantly in the future.

This paper will focus mainly on the problem of cutting spending growth in the face of public ambivalence on the issue. While the voters often give contradictory signals to politicians on spending issues, there are other difficulties related to the manner in which democratic governments make spending decisions, and the result is very probably upwardly biased spending in the sense that the final outcome involves more spending than would be desired by the median voter. It is, in fact, the rational ignorance of the typical voter that opens the door to narrow-special-interest groups who lobby for spending on their own favorite programs even though those programs have low benefit-cost ratios judged from the interest of society as a whole. This is a common theme of the public choice literature and I have little doubt regarding its validity [Buchanan, Tullock, 1962].

However, its implications may often be exaggerated. Wasteful programs, specifically designed for narrow special interests, cannot become too visible or else they will provoke a reaction from the general taxpayer. This very fact restrains their growth. While the U.S. budget contains many such programs for farmers, home builders, the merchant marine, energy producers, etc., they have not been responsible for much of the growth of the Federal government relative to the GNP. This does not mean that they do not present problems, for they do involve much waste. But the real problem involves not *narrow* special interests but *broad* special interests, and, as already suggested, the most difficult budget control issue in the United States involves dealing with the growing elderly population. The American social security system has 36 million recipients. Millions of others, who are related to the recipients, also have a direct interest in the system insofar as they may have to bear greater financial responsibility for their elderly and disabled relatives if benefits are reduced. It is quite possible and in fact probable, that those with a direct interest in the system constitute a majority of the voting population. How, in a democracy, can this majority be prevented from exploiting the minority? I do not have a satisfactory answer, but the issue will be explored in the last section of this paper.

Dealing with defense spending is equally perplexing. There is majority voter support for a strong defense, but how is that to be achieved? The voter cannot possibly keep well informed on complex defense issues. Again, voter ignorance opens the door to narrow-special-interest groups who would like to sell whatever weapons systems they happen to produce. This difficult problem will be considered in the last section along with programs for the elderly. Since defense and elderly programs will constitute about 60 percent of the budget in the next few years, it is hard to imagine overall Federal budget control in the United States without contending with these two issues.

Prior to dealing with these two difficult areas in detail, more generalized budget control techniques will be examined. But prior to that, it is useful to examine recent trends in spending levels at all levels of government in the United States.

The table illustrates the experience of the last 26 years. There is a strong upward trend in total government outlays between 1955 and 1975 with some flattening since that time. That flattening is, in part, due to the effects of the business cycle, but the most dramatic development shown by the table involves state and local spending. In relative

U.S. Government Expenditures Compared to the Gross National Product, 1955-1981

Year	GNP[a]	Total government[b]		Federal		State and local	
		absolute[a]	relative[c]	absolute[a]	relative[c]	absolute[a]	relative[c]
1955	400.0	98.0	24.5	68.1	17.0	32.9	8.2
1960	506.5	136.4	26.9	93.1	18.4	49.8	9.8
1965	691.1	187.8	27.2	123.8	17.9	75.1	10.9
1970	992.7	313.4	31.6	204.3	20.6	133.5	13.5
1975	1549.2	534.3	34.5	356.6	23.0	232.2	15.0
1976	1718.0	574.9	33.5	384.8	22.4	251.2	14.6
1977	1918.0	624.0	32.5	421.5	22.0	270.0	14.1
1978	2156.1	681.9	31.6	460.7	21.4	298.4	13.8
1979	2413.9	753.2	31.2	509.2	21.1	324.4	13.4
1980	2626.1	869.0	33.1	602.0	22.9	355.0	13.5
1981	2925.5	979.7	33.5	688.4	23.5	380.5	13.0

[a]In U.S.$ billion. - [b]The sum of Federal plus state and local spending exceeds the total, since grants from the Federal to lower levels of government are included in the Federal budget and are also used to finance state and local spending. - [c]Percent of GNP.

Source: Council of Economic Advisors [1982, p. 320].

terms, state and local budgets grew much more rapidly than the Federal budget over the 1955-75 period. That relative growth came to a screeching halt in the middle 1970s. Between 1975 and 1981 state and local spending grew only 1 percent per year in excess of the GNP deflator.

One can only speculate on the causes of this drastic change. Demography probably explains a large part of the phenomenon. Between 35 and 40 percent of total state and local expenditures are related to education. The significant fall in birth rates during the 1960s greatly reduced this burden.

However, other factors also played a role. The tax revolt hit state and local governments before it affected the Federal government. It was manifested in the electorate passing constitutional limits on tax burdens in many states, but this was just a symptom of a more widespread movement which led politicians to restrain spending and tax burdens even in states in which no new constitutional limits were passed.

Control over grants-in-aid from the Federal to state and local government also played a role in curbing state and local spending. After growing from 0.7 percent of the GNP in 1955 to 3.5 percent in 1975, they leveled off, and many of the Carter Administration's budget-cutting efforts were concentrated in this area. By 1981, grants had fallen relatively to 3.0 percent of the GNP and can be expected to fall further in the Reagan Administration.

II. Institutional Responses to the Budget Problem

1. Planning Programming Budgeting Systems, Management by Objectives, Zero-Based Budgeting, and Sunset Laws

Various presidents since Lyndon Johnson have attempted to force more formal program evaluation on the bureaucracy. The goal is to provide information on the effectiveness of various programs, so that decision makers and through them, the voters, can identify particularly wasteful government activities.

Planning programming budgeting systems (PPBS) were used very effectively by Secretary of Defense McNamara in the early 1960s to identify waste in the Pentagon. Impressed with this accomplishment, President Johnson attempted to impose the same techniques on the non-defense bureaucracy. The goal of the effort was to identify the benefits and costs of entire programs defined with reference to their goals, regardless of how their costs might be spread across several budget line items. It soon became apparent that the success of PPBS in the Pentagon provided more testimony to the extreme inefficiency which existed in that agency than it did to the effectiveness of the technique.

The application of the technique to social programs illustrated profound weaknesses in the approach. By necessity, analysts engaging in cost-benefit analysis must make numerous rather arbitrary assumptions regarding unknowns. Evaluating goods and services that are not traded on private markets is particularly difficult. This opens the door for converting program evaluations into advocacy documents [Niskanen, 1972]. In other words, program evaluation is as much an art as a science. Theoretically, this problem could be reduced by forcing the production of competing evaluations from groups for and against the program, and decision makers and outside experts could make judgments about the quality and scientific basis of the various evaluations. But even one evaluation of each of the hundreds of Federal programs generates mounds of paper, and PPBS quickly suffered from information overload. It eventually collapsed under its own weight.

The Nixon Administration responded by introducing management by objectives (MBO). Managers of the bureaucracy were to identify goals clearly - something that is seldom done in the legislation creating programs - and to set out a schedule for meeting those goals. Program evaluation could be used to identify goals and costs. The Ford Administration attempted to give program evaluation a more formal role in the system by insisting that Cabinet Secretaries select several programs each year for priority evaluations. This was an attempt to increase the use of program evaluation without swamping the system with paper as occurred under PPBS.

Managing the MBO system became almost as cumbersome as managing programs themselves. But the approach was initiated late in the Nixon Administration, and the short duration of the Ford Administration prevented it from getting a fair trial. It does have considerable appeal. Although it can be gamed by the bureaucracy who can set limited objectives, promulgate an easy schedule for meeting targets, and select only efficient programs for evaluation, an energetic President and White House staff can, in theory, limit the worst abuses. It does, however, require constant attention from the President and this is difficult since he is constantly distracted by other matters, for example, in the foreign policy area. It is difficult to sustain his and the press' and public's attention to the problem of managing the bureaucracy. Compared to other issues, the problem of achieving good management seems totally without glamor.

President Carter, however, was able to make management efficiency a campaign issue in 1976. He promised to do wonders with zero-based budgeting (ZBB). Departments were forced to divide up programs into units. Objectives were to be defined for the units and the implications of adding or reducing spending on the unit were to be evaluated. For each program, a minimum budget level at which the program could be effective was to be specified. Options for increasing spending above the minimum were then ranked along with options for reductions or for eliminating programs entirely. A budget restraint was then established and Departments were to proceed down the ranking of options until their budgets were exhausted.

The approach was as cumbersome as PPBS. Mountains of paper were generated and a multitude of biased program evaluations poured forth. The system proved unworkable and was abandoned quietly.

Another approach toward inducing more careful program evaluation is the sunset law (SL). In this concept, all programs have a limited life. As their expiration date approaches, they are to be evaluated and are not supposed to be renewed unless they are proved to be effective. Although a number of sunset laws have been introduced into the Congress, no comprehensive approach has ever passed. Several states have experimented with the approach, but results have been modest at best and non-existent at worst. Although SL is not as cumbersome as PPBS or ZBB, it is still very demanding because of the large number of Federal programs. Even a requirement that programs be assessed only periodically, say, every five years, probably generates more of a paperwork burden than can be handled effectively by the bureaucracy and the Congress. Moreover, just as with PPBS and ZBB, the evaluations are likely to be advocacy documents rationalizing the continued existence of the program. The congressional committees who created the programs in the first place are unlikely to be very critical, and other decision makers are simply too busy to exercise oversight over the evaluation process.

In my own view, any comprehensive system that attempts to evaluate all government programs on a rigid schedule is unlikely to be effective. While program evaluations can play an important role in identifying inefficiency, our goals must be modest and only a very few evaluations can be handled effectively each year.

A President working through the Office of Management and Budget can force Departments to pick two or three programs for special attention each year. Cabinet Secretaries must be warned that the President will not regard them kindly if they pick only their best programs for evaluation or if their analysis is slipshod and biased. But a system of this type requires constant attention by the President himself. The Cabinet and bureaucracy will quickly assess the degree of interest of the President and if he is not really interested in the management of the bureaucracy, no system will work.

2. The Congressional Budget Process

In the early 1970s, President Nixon became frustrated by his inability to control spending through the Congress. To bring the matter to a head, he began to refuse to spend appropriated money on social programs. Such presidential impoundments had a long history even though it had never been clearly determined whether or not they were constitutional. However, President Nixon used this power more vigorously than previous presidents.

The impoundments were challenged in the courts, but before the issue could be settled, the Congress began to legislate restrictions on the President's power. Nixon effectively responded that the Congress had no mechanism for controlling spending itself and it was inappropriate for the Congress to restrict presidential power.

Since the late 19th century, the Congress had been making tax and spending decisions quite separately and spending was determined by a number of different committees without any vote ever taken on total spending, total receipts, or the implied deficit. The Congress knew that Nixon had the better side of the argument and they reacted by creating a new Congressional budget process in 1974 while, at the same time, creating explicit procedures through which a President could impound funds.

I shall not describe the complex details of these procedures since such descriptions are readily available elsewhere [Schick, 1981]. The important point is that the Congress had to vote on spending, tax, and deficit totals explicitly. It was hoped that legislators would no longer be able to vote for expanding particular programs while continuing to preach in favor of lower taxes and deficits.

It is difficult to assess the success or lack of success of the new procedures. Needless to say, they have not been overwhelmingly successful or else that success would be apparent. They have not greatly reduced the number of inconsistent votes by legislators. Their targets for total outlays and deficits have often been violated, and more and more frequently, the Congress has failed even to abide by the schedule for passing Congressional budgets.

Yet, it would be wrong to conclude that the procedure has been a failure. Inconsistent votes become very apparent and can, in theory, be used as evidence by opponents of incumbents. Because the process requires a five-year budget projection, the long-run implications of decisions are being made more explicit and the Congress has definitely lengthened its time horizon for making decisions. This has made the legislators more sensitive to the role of economic assumptions in determining future budget totals [Penner, 1981]. While this initially resulted in the adoption of overly optimistic economic forecasts, those forecasts became more realistic in 1982.

In addition, the Congressional Budget Office, created to provide technical information for the implementation of the process, has over the years greatly improved the quality of its analysis.

In summary, it cannot be claimed that the new process has significantly reduced the growth of outlays, but it has served an important educational function. It has provided analysis and data, making the legislator, press, and public better informed regarding the relative importance of various budget issues. More important, it takes time for a new process to become well established and for legislators to learn how to use it. I do believe, without being able to provide much evidence, that the process has the potential to become more effective in the future. It will, however, have to survive severe difficulties in the 1980s. The huge deficits created by the spending and tax legislation of 1981 have left the Congress with no easy options. Their only choice is to cut programs and raise taxes. Politicians hate doing both and since the relatively young process makes the unpleasant choices highly explicit, the process may be destroyed before the difficult decisions can be made.

3. Constitutional Restrictions

There are now powerful forces favoring a constitutional amendment that would impose limits on the government's ability to run deficits and to raise tax burdens. Most variants directly or indirectly limit spending as well. The movement is based on two intellectual foundations. First, it is believed that the current system is biased toward more spending than is desired by the median voter. Second, it is believed that the Keynesian Revolution destroyed the justification for balancing the budget without replacing it with any other fiscal norm which would impose restraints on the Congress. For that reason, most proposed constitutional amendments require some super majority, say 60 percent, to approve a deficit.

While it is easy to sympathize with the arguments and goals of those proposing a constitutional amendment, it is hard to accept the notion that the approach would be workable. A loosely written amendment, which only stated goals or simply stated that the Congress should plan for a balanced budget, would not be very effective. Budget totals are so dependent on economic forecasts that creative forecasting can almost always result in a planned budget balance. A more rigorous amendment which required a balanced budget or a certain tax burden on spending total as an outcome would be extremely difficult to administer. It could, in fact, do more harm than good.

There is, for example, a very high probability of legislative impasse in any system requiring a super majority. The Congress would often face a situation in which existing laws would lead to a deficit. It may be impossible either to get a majority vote to cut spending or raise taxes, or to get a 60 percent vote to approve a deficit. Such an impasse could only be broken through logrolling, and since program spending is the currency used by politicians to buy votes and since purchasing a large deficit is as easy as purchasing a small deficit under all of the proposed amendments, it is logically possible that spending and deficits would be larger than they are without the amendment.

Another danger is that a rigid budget amendment would push politicians into achieving their goals by using regulation, government-sponsored institutions, and credit programs instead of using their taxing and spending powers. It is generally agreed that non-budget devices for commanding resources are less efficient and subject to even less control than are budget aggregates. The whole government may become even less efficient as a result.

I believe that constitutional amendments that attempt to limit budget aggregates are misguided. If the constitution is to be amended, I think that it would be more practical to give the President more power to limit spending. This could be accomplished by increasing presidential impoundment powers. Presumably the President, who represents the entire nation, is less the victim of special interest pressures than is the typical legislator who represents a smaller, more specialized constituency. However, the current Congress is totally unwilling to sacrifice any of its own power and, at present, is vehemently opposed to considering such an amendment.

4. Limiting Spending by Limiting Tax Receipts

Milton Friedman and others have argued that the best way to limit spending is to limit tax receipts. Buchanan and Wagner [1977, pp. 103 ff., 134 ff.] have on the other side argued that deficits facilitate greater spending growth because the sale of bonds, being a voluntary exchange, represents a politically easy way to expand spending as opposed to levying compulsory taxes. The empirical evidence on the issue is murky, although the steady upward trend in deficits over the last two decades would seem to favor Buchanan-Wagner rather than Friedman [Niskanen, 1978]. In any case, cutting taxes before cutting spending represents a risky strategy. The resulting deficits create huge policy uncertainty. It is not clear to private decision makers whether the deficits will be tolerated in the long run, whether they will be monetized, whether personal and/or business taxes will be raised, or whether they will be successful in limiting spending. Even if this technique works in the long run, it could do much short-term harm.

5. Across-the-Board Cuts in Spending

It is sometimes proposed that all agencies should suffer equally during times of fiscal austerity. It is recognized that this approach is inefficient, but it is thought that by curbing everyone at once, the power of special interest groups can be thwarted since they often coalesce to back each other's favorite spending programs.

Unfortunately, this approach is simply not practical in the United States. Different agencies have different portions of their budgets tied up in long-run contractual commitments. For example, much of the budget of the Department of Housing and Urban Development (HUD) is dedicated to paying interest subsidies on 30-year mortgages, whereas the Department of Justice has few commitments of this type. A 10 percent across-the-board cut would therefore mean that many of HUD's non-contractual programs would have to be cut by far more than 10 percent whereas Justice could handle such cuts more easily. In other words, an approach that, at first sight, appears to be evenhanded is anything but that. Adjusting for such differences becomes very complicated and as soon as that happens the approach falls apart very quickly.

6. The New Federalism

President Reagan would like to place much more responsibility for non-defense programs at the state and local level. Cost-sharing grants for such programs would be initially replaced by block grants and eventually Federal assistance would be ended altogether [Barfield, 1981, pp. 23-46].

It has been suggested earlier that a reduction in grants may have already played a role in slowing state and local spending. When states and localities have to raise the funds for programs themselves, it is reasonable to believe that the programs will be examined more critically. Decentralization could also be expected to reduce the power of special interest groups. There are economies of scale in lobbying. Maintaining one office to influence Federal legislation is a lot easier than maintaining 50 lobbies in various states.

It may be countered that the Federal government has an interest in encouraging state and local activities that have beneficial impacts outside of their own geographical jurisdictions. This argument has merit, but it is hard to find evidence that the current Federal grant system has been influenced much by a desire to maximize beneficial externalities subject to a budget restraint.

I see the New Federalism as a very promising technique for limiting total spending. It has the beneficial by-product of reducing the number of issues that have to be settled by Federal legislators. It should allow them to specialize more on those issues that are truly Federal and thus to make better-informed decisions.

There are many inconsistencies in President Reagan's New Federalism proposal, e.g., some income redistribution programs such as Aid to Families with Dependent Children and food stamps are to be given to states and localities, while others such as Medicaid are to be federalized. It is, therefore, unlikely to be adopted in its entirety. A more gradual movement toward decentralization is likely and in fact there has been irregular movement in that direction ever since the Nixon Administration adopted general revenue sharing. I see it as one of the most positive developments in the American political scene.

III. Social Security and Defense

The previous section described various techniques for controlling spending and most were found to be wanting. There were, however, a few glimmers of hope. A policy of selective program evaluation, vigorously supported by the President, can provide information that helps counter the biased data often produced by narrow-interest groups. The new congressional budget process has added marginally to the rationality of congressional decision making and could make a more significant contribution in the future. Providing the President with stronger impoundment powers would also be helpful, and decentralizing decision making by devolving fiscal functions down to the state and local level would weaken the lobbyists and put the program decisions in the hands of those who are most directly influenced by program benefits and costs.

However, it is crucial to emphasize that none of these techniques will significantly reduce the relative burden of government in the United States over the next decade unless they make some impact on two huge and rapidly growing functions of government which pose very special problems. Those functions are caring for the elderly and disabled, and defending the country. Counting outlays on only the three main programs in the former category - social security, medicare, and supplementary security income, which provides aid to the indigent elderly and disabled - and adding them to defense outlays yields a spending total equal to 52 percent of the total outlays of fiscal 1981. If current spending policy is continued, these programs will constitute about 60 percent of total spending in fiscal 1987.

As already noted, the main political problem in contending with the elderly and disabled is the sheer size of the constituency. The constituency is not only large; it is extremely well organized. It represents the most powerful lobbying group in the United States and politicians live in abject fear of its power.

There is no shortage of efficient and equitable options for slowing the growth of the social security system [Levy, 1981], but none can get a reasonable hearing. To cite but one example, almost all experts agree that some portion of social security benefits should be included in taxable income. Benefits are now tax free. But when the taxation of a portion of benefits was recommended by a recent Presidential Commission, a resolution opposing the recommendaton was immediately introduced in the House of Representatives. Only one Member of Congress voted against the resolution, although a more recent commission advocated some taxation of benefits and it now has wider supa hope of being effective against such overwhelmingly powerful political forces.

It is not easy to be optimistic about our prospects for dealing with this situation. As I see it, the only hope lies in convincing the members of the constituency itself that by blocking reasonable reforms, they are in danger of killing the taxpaying goose that is laying their golden eggs.

The possibility of dampening the demands of the elderly is not quite as preposterous as it sounds. First, it is necessary to emphasize that there is no need to reduce the real benefits of those already retired. The big problem involves the rise in real average benefits for each successive cohort of retirees that is promised by current law. Slowing that rise by even one-half of one percentage point per year could save massive amounts of money in the long run. Second, convincing the elderly of the need for a reduced rate of growth of real benefits will become easier as the elderly become better off. As recently as the early 1960s, the elderly as a group were among the poorest groups in American society. Since that time their economic status has improved more rapidly than that of any other group and if in-kind benefits are counted, the incidence of poverty among the elderly is now lower than that in the population as a whole. Since the middle 1970s, the relative improvement in the status of the elderly has been especially rapid, primarily because real wage rates have fallen in the rest of the economy.

I do not want to seem overly optimistic about persuading the elderly to dampen their demands, but they should at least become less frantic about protecting their benefits as their economic status improves. Recent attempts to curb the social security system's growth may have failed miserably, but it is significant to note that options for slowing benefit growth are now being debated openly by politicians, and the proposals of a recent bipartisan commission have more chance for success than any in past history. They may not yet be ready to vote for reform, but ten years ago the issue could not even be raised in public. The only issue open to debate was how fast to expand the system.

The problem of enhancing the efficiency of defense spending is easier to handle politically, but very difficult to analyze conceptually. Much spending is directed at protecting ourselves from events that have a tiny probability of occurring but which would have disastrous consequences if they did emerge. The question, "How much is enough?" is not easy to answer when we are discussing the survival of a nation.

While there is a fairly broad consensus among social security experts regarding the efficiency and equity implications of various options that would slow the growth of social security benefits, there seems to be less consensus among defense experts regarding the worth of complex, highly expensive weapons systems such as the MX missile, the B-1 bomber, and nuclear carrier task forces. The high casualty rate among war ships during the Falklands War is now being used as evidence that (a) large ships are obsolete or (b) only task forces centered by large carriers can protect themselves against missile attacks.

How can the non-expert legislator or voter decide who is right? He probably cannot. However, military spending like all other spending should be rationed. Currently, in the United States the military are having virtually every wish fulfilled. It may be necessary to impose rationing using very crude rules of thumb.

Although it is totally unsatisfactory intellectually, the issue tends to be debated using the crudest possible quantitative criterion. Should real defense spending grow at 7 percent per year between now and 1987 or at 5 percent? Should the United States devote 6 percent of the GNP to defense or 8 percent?

Note that all of these numbers imply a much larger U.S. defense effort than occurred during the last decade. There is a broad consensus favoring that course. The debate is only about how much greater the effort should be.

It may not be possible to improve the quality of the debate very much beyond using crude aggregate rules of thumb. However, I would make one strong suggestion. It was noted earlier that PPBS techniques were effectively applied in the Pentagon in the early 1960s. After years of financial stringency, it is probably safe to say that the Pentagon of the 1980s is more efficient than that of the 1950s. But there is still a need to enhance the intensity and quality of program analysis. The Reagan Administration has been moving in the opposite direction. The role of program analysis has been downgraded because program analysts are hated by the military professionals who are now in the ascendency.

There is room for reversing past trends by placing somewhat more emphasis on analysis. In the longer run, such a reform should serve the interests of those wanting a stronger defense. Politicians who oppose the military will be constantly searching for examples of extreme waste and with the current U.S. defense program such examples will be easy to find. There is a danger that examples of waste will provoke a public reaction that will cause the pendulum of public opinion to swing in a vehemently anti-military direction. Obviously, better program analysis cannot prevent waste entirely but it can reduce the probability of fiascos. It is, therefore, my strong conclusion that while reducing the power of the analysts may serve the short-run interests of the Reagan Administration, it represents a grave error relative to their long-run interests.

IV. Conclusions

The analysis of this paper has not been very reassuring. It has primarily been about techniques that have not worked in the past or are unlikely to work in the future. Yet, there are glimmers of hope. Decentralization of decision making to state and local levels appears promising. The congressional budget process shows signs of becoming more and more effective if it can survive the extreme pressures of the last few years. A President who gives high priority to better management can have an impact on the bureaucracy and intensified program analysis in the Pentagon may lead to more effective military spending.

But the overwhelming conclusion is that better budget control is not easy to obtain. It is an arduous step-by-step process requiring much effort. It will not be obtained by simple-minded blunderbuss techniques such as constitutional amendments, across-the-board cuts, etc. Processes have to be judged by the information they provide. Ultimately, it is the ordinary voters who must control spending. They must be willing to punish any politician who tries to exploit them.

References

Barfield, Claude E., Rethinking Federalism: Block Grants and Federal, State and Local Responsibilities. American Enterprise Institute Studies, 349, Washington 1981.

Buchanan, James M., Gordon Tullock, The Calculus of Consent: Logical Foundations and Constitutional Democracy. Ann Arbor 1962.

--, Richard E. Wagner, Democracy in Deficit: The Political Legacy of Lord Keynes. New York 1977.

Council of Economic Advisors, Economic Report of the President 1982. Washington 1982.

Dale, Edwin L., Jr., Donald R. Lesh, Lloyd A. Free, Priorities in an Uncertain Economy: Inflation, Recession and Government Spending. Washington 1976.

Levy, Mickey D., Achieving Financial Solvency in Social Security. American Enterprise Institute, AEI Special Analyses, 81-6, Washington 1981.

Lilley, William III, James C. Miller III, "The New 'Social Regulation'". Public Interest, 1977, No. 47, pp. 46-61.

Niskanen, William A., "Why New Methods of Budgetary Choices? - Administrative Aspects". In: Nouvelles Méthodes de Choix Budgétaires. Congrès de Nuremberg, Sept. 1971, 27. Session, l'Institut International de Finances Publiques, Budapest 1972, pp. 97-105.

--, "Deficits, Money and Inflation: What is the Evidence?". Journal of Monetary Economics, Vol. 4, 1978, pp. 591-602.

Penner, Rudolph G., Budget Assumptions and Budget Outcomes. The AEI Economist, Washington, August 1981.

Public Opinion, "Opinion Roundup". American Enterprise Institute, Vol. 4, No. 1, Washington 1981, pp. 19-42.

Schick, Allen, "The First Five Years of Congressional Budgeting". In: Rudolph G. Penner (Ed.), The Congressional Budget Process After Five Years. American Enterprise Institute, Washington 1981, pp. 3-34.

Comment

Gerhard Fels

1. I must confess that I am much in sympathy with Penner's paper, which highlights most of what an economist can contribute to the pressing question of how to reduce public spending. When I was asked to comment upon this paper I had planned to contribute some comments on the German experience with the control of public spending. But when I read through Penner's paper on American experience and also through Peacock's paper on British experience, I felt that this would bring me too much into a situation of competition with two excellent papers on other countries. This would have been too risky for me. So I decided to choose a more complementary approach in my comment. I shall concentrate on those aspects of Penner's paper which in my opinion deserve a different view. Only marginally will I touch upon some German experience.

2. High tax burdens and high public deficits have made expenditure cutting one of the most urgent businesses of many governments in the world. Penner gives two main explanations of the problem:

- First, due to rational ignorance of the typical voter there is "upwardly biased spending in the sense that the final outcome involves more spending than would be desired by the median voter" (p. 32).
- Secondly, there are broad special interests on the side of the majority of the voting population, which in the United States is increasingly formed by older people.

Of course, these are important factors behind government growth. The first explanation, rational ignorance, is a well founded argument of public choice theory. Penner states that its implications are often exaggerated, except perhaps in the field of defence expenditure, the necessity of which can in many cases hardly be assessed by the voters. Penner seems to give more weight to the second explanation, which is redistribution from the active population to the non-active population - ultimately a problem of power distribution in a democracy. The two explanations give Penner guidance for the expenditure reduction strategies which he discusses. But since both explanations refer to structural factors of decision making in a democracy he can not be very optimistic with regard to achieving a rapid solution.

3. Although I have no difficulties with these two explanations of government growth, I hesitate to accept them as a sufficient explanation of the present level of government activity, which is much higher than was the case fifteen or twenty years ago. Rational ignorance of the median voter is not a recent phenomenon, and there have always been broad interests within the majority and the attempt to exploit the minority. Is it plausible that these normal features of public choice and democracy are responsible for present difficulties? In my view the answer is no. The main cause of excessive spending seems to lie more in a conscious and deliberate economic and social policy based on a paradigm in which government was deemed to hold the key to full employment and social equity. This policy was started in the United States during the first half of the 1960s - the Kennedy-Johnson era - and had its main budget effects in the period from 1965 to 1975 when total government spending rose from 27.2 to 34.5 per cent of GNP (p. 34). I would admit that the factors mentioned by Penner have contributed to the rapid growth of government spending. But I cannot imagine that it would have taken place on such a scale without the momentum of a policy of full employment and social equity - the unresolved heritage of which now burdens the government. During the second half of the 1970s the costs of this policy became increasingly visible - in terms of a rising and discouraging tax burden and two-digit inflation. What is now at stake is the way back to more fiscal rationality. It will not be an easy path, but the insight has grown that past economic and social policy was largely misguided. Perhaps this permits a slightly more optimistic view than Penner holds on the basis of the evaluation of past institutional responses to the budget problem and the electoral situation in the United States.

4. Adherents of the previous paradigm may have reasons to justify the economic and social policy which has made government expenditure a third of GNP. As compared with European countries, social security was (and still is) at a low standard. The explosion of ideas of social equity and the revolt of the blacks during the 1960s were met by welfare programmes so that the American society became pacified again. During the 1970s, 19 million jobs were created in the American economy. One may argue how far rapid government growth has favoured job creation or has impeded it. (At least the rapid employment increase must be seen in the context of unchanged real wages over the last decade.) But there is a broad consensus now that overshooting took place with the old kind of policy, that the rate of saving is too low, that too small a part of saving goes to business investment, and that all this has primarily to do with the tax system. An only recent

lesson, at least for the most outspoken supply siders, is that tax cuts have to be paralleled by expenditure cuts. When the Reagan administration began to implement its economic program, it was the naive belief in the mechanics of the Laffer-curve which caused the administration to take a more or less relaxed attitude toward larger expenditure cuts. Since then the learning process has been progressing. But a drastic expenditure cut has been on the agenda only for several months.

5. In his paper, Penner provides us with a comprehensive survey of the various institutional responses to the budget problem which were tried in the past. What we can learn from the analysis of all these budgeting and planning procedures is that they have not worked well enough. Penner sees only two promising institutional approaches to a better control of government spending. The first is a constitutional amendment that gives the President more power to control expenditure. The second is the New Federalism, which places more responsibility at the state and local level.

I feel overtaxed in embarking upon a discussion of the institutional framework of government in the United States. Instead, I shall pick up three points from.the German scene which serve to underline Penner's analysis.

6. One of the main sources of discontent with public spending in Germany is the high and increasing share of subsidies to private producers and consumers. It was already in 1968 that the Law on the Promotion of Stability and Growth committed the Federal government

- to report periodically on financial assistance and tax allowances granted to the private sector, and
- to submit proposals as to the period in which and the extent to which these subsidies can be reduced or removed.

The experience with this institutional attempt of expenditure control was that it has not prevented a rapid increase in expenditure in the time since 1968. There was no educational effect. The government presents the reports which list the subsidies (not all, but most), mentions the purpose of individual measures, and states in many cases that the volume of assistance is likely to increase.

7. A second relevant experience: The German Council of Economic Experts uses a budget concept to evaluate the effects of budget policy

which breaks down the total budget deficit into three components: (1) a kind of "normal" deficit, which is defined by standards realized in years in which the economy operated without severe tensions, (2) a cyclical part which is supposed to disappear when full capacity utilization is achieved, and (3) a structural part which has to do with too high an expenditure level in relation to the tax revenue which can be expected with full capacity utilization. If we rule out tax increases, the expenditure path which brings the structural deficit to zero can be considered the path which brings the economy to a situation without adverse supply effects (or crowding-out effects) from the overall public budget. Although this concept is designed to deliver a guideline for public expenditure control, the government always refused to accept it, nor was any other concept of expenditure limitation employed. The reason seems to be that government does not like conceptual constraints. It wants to preserve its freedom for discretionary action.

8. The third point refers to the mixed financing of public expenditure, which Penner also discusses under the topic New Federalism. In Germany most spending on the local level and a large part of spending on the state level is not funded solely by that level's own tax revenue but also by grants and contributions from the states or the federal government, respectively. Thus there is not a sufficient correspondence between revenues and expenditures, a situation which weakens a critical examination of spending by the authorities. If one looks at news reports on local government decision making, there is always the argument that the local authority only has to bear 20 or 30 per cent of a specific spending project, the rest being contributed by state and/or federal authorities. Moreover, in recent years such mix financing proliferated with various federal programs whose aim was to combat unemployment and which supported this kind of irrational decision making.

9. Let me come back to my argument that misguided policies and overshooting in the political system are the main causes of excessive government today. When the Reagan administration started with a new paradigm of economic policy determined to control government growth it was originally also the victim of too naive a concept of supply policy, and it also had to cope with a burden of the past. For instance, defense spending had been neglected after the Vietnam war, and there is now a strong belief that there is a backlog of projects to be undertaken. And there is also an increasing majority of the elderly population, claiming support. This makes governing difficult. But cuts in spending seem to be a solvable task if it is widely recognized that government is the problem, rather than the solution.

10. What can we conclude from this for a strategy to be pursued in order to cut spending in a way which minimizes the resistance of pressure groups? It is too unrealistic to believe in a mechanism which will do the job automatically. Penner's analysis, as well as Peacock's, supports this view very strongly. Deriving techniques for controlling spending is more a matter of political determination and political leadership than of scientific ingenuity. But I agree with Penner that some kind of institutional reform and precaution may be necessary and helpful. A clear correspondence between funding and spending on all levels of government activity would be a precondition for more rational budgeting. And more analysis which produces evidence as to who really benefits from the programmes designed for the poor would also be useful in addition to research on institutional innovations. Some constraints in the form of a medium-term target for overall public expenditure growth set up with the aim of constructing a budget with no adverse supply effects would also seem necessary. But most important is the paradigm which government follows.

Richard B. McKenzie

Restructuring Fiscal Federalism

I. Introduction

Has federal aid to states and localities increased the burden on local taxpayers? The evidence, surprisingly, seems to argue that it has. Instead of funds from Washington permitting states and localities to reduce their taxes, these funds have led to local tax increases. What has been intended as aid, therefore, has become a burden. It is this burden, in part, that the Reagan Administration's New Federalism could lighten.

Federal aid in the form of categorical and block grants and general revenue sharing grew in real terms at a compound annual rate of 8.1 percent between 1960 and 1980. On a per capita basis, the real growth for the two decades was, of course, at a lower but still striking rate: 6.9 percent. Representing about one tenth of state and local government revenues in 1960 (as well as 1950), federal aid by 1980 had practically doubled its contribution to state and local revenue coffers.

This dramatic growth in the dependence of subordinate governments on the federal treasury occurred at a time of steady growth in the revenues collected by state and local governments from their own sources (relative to the growth in revenues of the federal government). Between 1960 and 1980, real per capita taxes collected by state and local governments (excluding federal aid and charges) grew at a yearly compound rate of nearly 3 percent. During the same period, federal taxes per capita increased at a compound rate of 2.4 percent. The extraordinarily strong positive association between growth in state and local taxes from own sources and federal aid raises intriguing questions concerning the interplay between federal and state fiscal authority. One of the more important is: Does a cause-and-effect relationship exist between the rise in federal aid and the rise in state and local taxes?

Arguing that economic power should be returned to the people through tax cuts and reductions in federal social programs, including aid to state and local governments, the Reagan Administration has sought to restructure fiscal federalism, first by reducing the federal aid level, second by creating block grant programs out of former categorical grant programs, and third by eventually having state governments assume full financial responsibility for more than 40 aid programs. These shifts also raise questions concerning the interaction of federal and subordinate government fiscal powers. Many commentators assume that the transfer to the states of the funding of the aid programs, previously funded in part by the federal government, will entail increases in state and local taxes.

The purpose of this paper is limited to sorting out the theoretical and working relationship between federal aid and the tax levels of subordinate governments. More specifically, the analysis contained herein provides the basis for predicting the effects of both reducing the funding level of fiscal federalism and shifting from categorical to block grants. Additional research, now under way, will involve empirical tests of the predictions developed here.

A central conclusion of this institutional and theoretical analysis is that, by design, federal aid has been an important positive force behind the growth in state and local tax collections over the past two decades. Further, compared to categorical grants, block grants reduce the ability of subordinate governments to grow in response to an expansion of the federal funding. Therefore, contrary to popular presumption, a reduction in the level of federal aid and a greater use by the federal government of block grants can be expected to lead, ceteris paribus, to a reduction in state and local taxes from their own sources. The "New Federalism" of the Reagan Administration is a subtle means of controlling growth in government at all levels. These conclusions are supported by empirical studies that are currently being finalized by the author and that will be reported in a later paper.

II. Current Policy Proposals

The issue of the interdependence of federal aid and state and local taxes undergirds the theory of fiscal federalism in a "compound republic" and of current presidential policy. The Reagan Administration, acknowledging that by 1982 the federal aid system had become an unwieldy bureaucratic maze of hundreds of grant programs with thousands of rules and mandates for state and local governments, has proposed cuts of as much as 60 percent in the total funding level for the aid programs, which are to be phased out by 1991[1]. These proposed current dollar cuts would simply accelerate the decline in real dollars of aid begun in 1978 under the Carter Administration.

In 1981 President Reagan proposed that under the fiscal 1983 budget, 83 categorical grant programs be combined into six block grants to the states, and that the funding level of the block grants be reduced by 25 percent below the total of the 83 categorical grants in fiscal 1981. Congress passed legislation that combined only 56 categorical grants. Given the restrictions Congress placed on the new broader block grant programs, there is serious question whether or not the measures will achieve greater flexibility for state and local governments in their use of federal funds [Ascik, 1981].

In early 1982, the Administration unveiled a more comprehensive program for reshaping fiscal federalism. The final version of the new federalism is, at this writing, highly unpredictable, but an examination of the Administration's first federalism proposal is instructive of the type of program that may well emerge. Its key features are as follows [Office PPS, 1982a; 1982b]:

- Program Swaps. Under the Administration's first federalism package submitted in 1982, the federal government would, beginning in 1984, assume full financial responsibility for Medicaid, while the states would assume full funding of Aid to Families with Dependent Children (AFDC) and food stamps. The Administration estimates that in 1984 the states will save approximately $19 billion in Medicaid payments and incur between $15 and $16 billion in additional expenditures on AFDC and food stamp programs. (In a later version of the "swap" component of the program, the federal government retained responsibility for food stamps.)
- Program Turnbacks. The Administration's first federalism program mandated that between 1984 and 1991 responsibility for 43 categorical grants would be returned to the states. The additional cost of these programs to the states would be about $30 billion in 1984. (The second proposal developed by the Administration increased the number of "turnbacks" to 50.)

---

[1] For a description of the federal aid system, see Barfield [1978; 1981a; 1981b]. For a breakdown of the way the monies are allocated by the different departments, see U.S. Department of the Treasury [various issues].

- Declining Trust Fund. By setting aside excise taxes on tobacco, alcohol, gasoline, and windfall profits, an annual trust fund of $28 billion would be provided to the states. Each state's share of the trust fund "will be based on its 1979-1981 share of specified federal grants now slated for 'turnback' ..., with an adjustment for any gains or losses for individual states resulting from the Medicaid-welfare swap" [Office PPS, 1982a, p. 5].
- Program participation. Finally, between 1984 and 1987, states would have a choice whether they would continue to receive categorical grants or change to funds (called "super revenue sharing") from the trust funds. After 1987, the assumption of responsibility for the categorical grant programs would be mandatory. Between 1988 and 1991, allocations from the trust fund would be reduced to zero.

If the view tendered in this paper is correct, these cuts in real dollar aid may, ceteris paribus, lead eventually to even greater reductions in real state and local expenditures. A $10 billion reduction in federal aid, for example, can be expected to lead to more than a $10 billion decrease in state and local expenditures[1]. Although it may seem somewhat counterintuitive, given popular analysis of federal aid programs, tentative empirical analysis supports such a conclusion.

III. Perspectives on Federal Aid

A positive relationship between federal aid and state and local taxes can be deduced from operational and institutional as well as theoretical perspectives. The reasons for the anticipated positive relationship should therefore be explored in both the institutional and the conceptual setting.

[1] This does not mean that total state, local, and federal spending will actually be reduced under the Reagan proposal. The reductions in state and local tax collections may be offset by greater federal tax collections brought about by the federal government's need to finance the growing Medicaid. The point of this paper is that, given a more or less even swap in fiscal responsibilities, state and local tax collections will go down. The categorical grant programs will not be maintained by state and local governments at the same level as would have been the case under federal stewardship.

1. The Institutional Setting

From an institutional perspective, a positive link between federal aid and state and local taxes can be tentatively established by considering the operational complexity and built-in incentives of the system. The grants system involves more than 500 programs (the exact number depends on what programs are counted and who does the counting), administered by scores of agencies and bureaus, many of which have overlapping and conflicting authority [Barfield, 1981a, pp. 18-19]. The number of grant programs by category are listed in the table. In 1978 there were, for example, 35 pollution control programs, 36 transportation programs (not all administered by the Department of Transportation), 78 health programs, and more than 100 education programs. In 1980, 25 percent of the approximately $80 billion in aid went directly to local governments, up from 8 percent in 1960. All in all, by 1980 four-fifths of the local governments, or 65,000, received federal aid, either directly from the federal treasury or indirectly through state governments charged with the responsibility of dispersing federal aid [Barfield, 1978, Ch. 4].

State and local taxes can be - must be - used to search through this bureaucratic maze for programs in which the probability of successfully securing grants warrants the time devoted to completing applications, many of which end up encompassing hundreds of pages of justification for the requested monies. These search costs impinge on state and local budgets.

The Advisory Commission on Intergovernmental Relations (ACIR) found, through a survey of 442 grant programs in existence during 1975, that two-thirds of the grants, amounting to 60 percent of the total grant funds for the year, were "project grants", meaning the funds were distributed predominantly by administrative discretion. An additional 8 percent was based partially on formulas and partially on administrative discretion, and a sizable percentage of the formula and formula/project grants was based on formulas constructed by the administering bureau [Barfield, 1978, Ch. 4].

State and local taxes can be - must be - used to lobby for the discretionary government grants. The grants system, in other words, induces state and local governments to become classic rent seekers. Of course, the net effect of the grants system on state and local taxes depends on the ability of state and local governments to cover their searching and lobbying costs with additional federal dollars. The often-

Categorical Grant Programs of the U.S. Federal Government, 1978

Budget subfunction	Number of programs
Department of defense-military	5
General science and basic research	1
Energy	6
Water resources	7
Conservation and land management	13
Recreational resources	10
Pollution control and abatement	35
Other natural resources	4
Agricultural research and services	9
Mortgage credit and thrift insurance	2
Other advancement and regulation of commerce	2
Ground transportation	36
Water transportation	2
Mass transportation	8
Air transportation	3
Other transportation	1
Community development	5
Area and regional development	36
Disaster relief and insurance	9
Elementary, secondary, and vocational education	70
Higher education	10
Research and general education aids	21
Training and employment	23
Other labor services	1
Social services	47
Health	78
Public assistance and other income supplements	27
Hospital and medical care for veterans	5
Criminal justice assistance	13
General property and records management	1
Other general government	2
Total	492

Source: ACIR [1981].

made assumption that such costs are readily and fully compensated by federal grants must be questioned because of the dynamics of any grants system. The lobbying of one or several state and local governments (which may eventually be fully compensated for their lobbying and searching costs) can influence other governments to enter the competitive game for grant favors. In the two-party competitive case, this can be illustrated by reaction curves that project outward and cross at an ever higher equilibrium as the total federal aid increases[1].

Further, as Tullock has shown, when the number of game players, or rent seekers, is "large" (and there were 80,000 governmental units in the United States in the late 1970s) and the slope of the marginal cost curve of rent-seeking is "low", the rent-seeking expenditures summed across all rent seekers (state and local governments) can, in rent-seeking equilibrium, exceed the total value of the rent (federal aid) that is sought[2]. Granted, competition for grants is restricted by the use of formulas and minimums and maximums on the amounts that can be distributed to governmental units. Nevertheless, to establish a positive relationship between federal aid and state and local taxes, such an extreme equilibrium condition as illustrated in Tullock's work need not exist. All that is required is that a portion of the rent-seeking expenditures be a "tack-on" to the level of government revenues that would be collected in the absence of fiscal federalism. To the extent that a portion of the state and local governments' rent-seeking costs are absorbed by the federal government, the rent-seeking cost curves of state and local governments are lowered, increasing the probability that the rents will be absorbed by the collective rent-seeking expenditures.

Of the 442 programs in the ACIR's 1975 survey, 64 percent of the formula-based categorical grants included matching provisions, under which state and local governments under most programs were required to finance a portion, and sometimes a major portion, of funded projects from their own tax sources [Barfield, 1978, p. 99]. 61 percent of the project grants required a nonfederal match [ibid., pp. 106-107][3]. How these matching provisions affect total state and local tax collections depends on (1) the elasticity of demands for the subsidized goods and services, (2) the extent to which only marginal units are subsidized, and (3) the degree to which the grants system induces a reallocation of state and local tax monies away from nonfederally subsi-

[1] For a description of how reaction curves can be usefully employed in game theoretical situations, such as that which probably exists in the grants economy, see Congleton [1980].

[2] According to Tullock's calculations, when the exponent on the rent-seeking cost functions is 3 or greater and the number of rent seekers is 2 or more, the sum of the investment across all rent seekers will exceed the rent that is to be achieved [Tullock, 1980].

[3] For a delineation of the distribution of the matching requirement, by the extent of the nonfederal match, see Barfield [1978, p. 108, Figure IV-1].

dized to federally subsidized programs. A federally subsidized good with an elastic demand can lead to greater state and local expenditures even if all marginal and inframarginal units are subsidized; the lower price (net of federal subsidy) combined with the proportionally greater quantity will result in greater expenditures. Of course, if the federal government subsidizes goods and services not provided originally by state and local governments, then any state and local expenditures must come either from greater tax collections or other state and local programs, or both.

Although nothing certain can be said a priori about the impact of federal grant matching provisions on state and local taxes, there are several institutional reasons for expecting a positive relationship. First, empirical studies have tended to show that publicly provided goods and services have low elasticity coefficients[1]. However, with an expansion in the scope and magnitude of state and local government through the grants system, an expansion of state and local governments into product and service markets that have private substitutes might be anticipated. This would imply, over time, a general increase in the elasticity of demand for state and local products and services along with the growth in the grants system. The greater the number of private alternatives, the greater the elasticity of demand. One prominently cited study on the impact of federal aid on state and local expenditures found that in the ten survey areas 51 percent of local projects with federal and state aid would not have been undertaken in the absence of the partial federal aid. Eleven percent would have been undertaken only partially [Lovell et al., 1979]. Of all the categorical grants that the ACIR classified by purpose, 57 percent were in part or total designed to stimulate activities that otherwise would not have been taken on by state and local governments; one-third of the formula grants were also "stimulative" in nature; and many grant programs were designed to "add to" state and local governments' capacity to provide goods and services [Barfield, 1978, pp. 108-109; ACIR, 1981]. Admittedly, these observations do not mean that state and local taxes are driven upward of necessity by federal aid. (Programs funded partially by the federal government may replace other programs in state and local government budgets.) However, it certainly should not be concluded, as is often the case, that federal aid necessarily supplants the need for state and local taxes. Obviously, the matter must be submitted to empirical tests.

---

[1] For a review of much of the empirical literature on the subject of elasticity of demand, see Gramlich [1977].

Second, given the discretion which bureaus and agencies have in allotting their funds, state and local governments are forced to compete for federal aid in terms of the types of projects undertaken, the level at which the programs are funded, and the state and local governments' shares of the project costs. Such competition can drive up the taxes that state and local governments are required to collect. Although the rents may not be fully dissipated with the competition, the competitive process, over time, can lead to greater taxes imposed on state and local constituencies.

Third, revenue sharing explicitly introduces "tax effort" (i.e., state and local taxes as a percent of state and local incomes) as a factor in the formula used to distribute any given amount appropriated by Congress. The higher the tax effort, the greater the federal aid. Thirty-two other formula grants are founded partially on some factor representing "financial need", most often per capita income. In some of the cases, however, "need" is left undefined [Barfield, 1978, p. 101]. Supposedly, high income states and localities experiencing severe financial exigencies would still qualify for aid on the basis of "need", even though the "need" may or may not have been self-inflicted, as in the case of many urban areas. From previous research, "tax effort" is known as one of the most prominent positive determinants of the distribution of federal aid across states, significant at the 0.0001 confidence level [McKenzie, Yandle, 1982][1].

Such tax effort provisions, explicitly written into the formulas or implicitly employed by grant administrators in the use of their discretionary authority, effectively reduce the marginal price of state and local government goods and services (since a dollar of state and local taxes can buy more than a dollar's worth of goods and services). And they convert a portion of the federal budget into a common access resource, giving rise to expenditures to use, and possibly overuse, that resource. By raising its own taxes in light of the way in which tax effort is employed, a state can tap into the tax bases of other states and externalize its own production costs. An incentive inheres in such a scheme for all states to install new taxes or increase old ones and to avoid tax decreases (since a cut in state and local taxes would lead to an increase in the effective tax prices of goods and services by way of a reduction in federal aid).

---

[1] When broken down, per capita state and local taxes are consistently positive, while per capita state income is negative in explaining the allocation of per capita federal aid across states.

The creation of the existing brand of fiscal federalism forces state and local governments into a classic prisoner's dilemma: On the one hand, if they individually raise taxes, they acquire access to the federal treasury, enhancing their budget totals. On the other hand, if they don't raise taxes, then their share of the federal aid budget can slip as other state and local governments raise their taxes to gain a competitive edge. To the extent that area growth is dependent on the distribution of federal aid, state and local governments that stay out of the competitive struggle can suffer relatively lower growth rates[1]. Such a noncompetitive response to the emergence and growth of fiscal federalism may lead only to an increase in a state's or local government's "fiscal residuum" (total tax collections minus the value of the public goods and services provided). This increase in fiscal residuum can occur because states that do not respond competitively to the tax effort factors in grant programs will shoulder, through the federal tax system, a greater share of the costs of goods and services produced in other states and localities.

Finally, in the ideal public sector setting, fiscal federalism would be designed to pursue general public purposes, not narrow interests reflected in redistributive programs. The present grants system, however, has all the markings of special-interest legislative efforts. Grant programs can be counted for almost every conceivable purpose, reflecting the particular interests of the congressional committees supervising the programs and blocks of congressional votes. It appears that grant programs have been heaped on top of grant programs.

Growth in the number and scope of programs over the years may have been a consequence of the federal government's attempts to raise state and local taxes. When the federal government provided the first matching grant program, say in education, state and local governments may have responded by drawing the state and local match requirement from, say, the police budget, which became "deficient". A matching grant program may then have been devised to overcome the deficiency in the police budget, which may have given rise to a deficiency in health expenditures. The grant system could have, in other words, effected budgetary deficiencies at the state and local levels, giving birth to the further expansion of the grant system (to the extent that, as noted at the start, more than 500 programs are in-

[1] How much state and local taxes are raised depends on the comparison of the positive effect of greater government aid due to the tax increase, and the negative effect of the tax rate increase, on economic development.

volved). In short, one consequence has been a considerable expansion in the scope of state and local programs - and in the process, an increase in state and local taxes.

2. Conceptual Perspective

Conventional public finance discussions of fiscal federalism are concerned with how federal grants can best be used to overcome externalities in the production of state and local goods and services. Breton [1965] develops an "economically optimum constitution" that divides government responsibilities according to the spatial coverage of the benefits from the governmentally provided goods and services. Under such a constitution, the national government would produce "national" goods, regional governments would produce "regional" goods, and so forth. A "perfect mapping" of government responsibilities would exist when the benefits of the goods extended only to the boundaries of the government producing the goods. In a similar manner, Olson [1969] develops the concept of "fiscal equivalence" for identifying the optimum distribution of government responsibilities. The system of governments established with complete fiscal equivalence would be one in which only those who benefited from a particular government's activity paid for those benefits and those benefits only.

Both authors devise their organizational structures based on the inefficiencies created by the existence of externalities in state and local government production and taxing decisions[1]. In both externality cases, public goods and services are underproduced. When, for example, external benefits flow into another governmental jurisdiction, the government producing the goods cannot collect for all benefits received. It must therefore fail to produce all units for which total marginal benefits exceed the total marginal cost of production. Similarly, underproduction can occur because of the limited taxing power of local governments: if tax rates are raised independently by one locality, a part of its tax base will be induced to migrate to some point just across the jurisdictional boundary, creating what is known in the literature as the "border effect". Again, local governments are unable to raise their taxes sufficiently to cover the total cost of the optimum production level. To achieve the optimum, Breton and Olson recom-

[1] Olson goes further and discusses the identical inefficiencies created by "internalities", benefits received by only a part of any government's citizenry.

mend adjusting the boundaries to "internalize the externalities". The grants economy developed at the federal and state levels is a device for moving closer to, if not fully achieving, a "perfect mapping" or complete "fiscal equivalence".

A federal government interested solely in achieving greater efficiency in production, as implicitly envisioned in Breton and Olson's work, would be largely indifferent to the method by which extended production was to be financed - whether all marginal and inframarginal units were subsidized, just marginal units were subsidized, or the necessary revenue were raised by higher federal tax rates or federally induced higher state and local tax rates. Under such a benevolent, altruistic government, the tax revenues of state and local governments may go up or down with an extension of the grants economy. What happens depends on the method of financing employed and, as noted above, on the elasticities of demands for the subsidized goods and services.

However, predictions regarding the directional influence of federal aid on state and local taxes can be garnered from a maximizing model of government. Conventional public finance theorists tend to assume implicitly that the federal government is a nonmaximizer, i.e., it is more or less unconcerned with how it can best use its fiscal powers to its own advantage [Gramlich, 1977]. Hence, the elasticity of demand is important in addressing the question of whether state and local tax collections go up or down. A federal government interested in maximizing its own influence, given its own limited budget resources and the necessity for the political goodwill of members of Congress, will seek, to the extent possible, (1) to subsidize only marginal units (in which case the elasticity of demand for the individual publicly provided goods and services does not matter) and (2) to finance only a part of the additional units, which can be accomplished by using federal aid to pull up state and local tax rates. Tax increases across all states uniformly reduce the elasticity of demand faced by individual government units. Either of these methods minimizes the cost to the federal treasury, which may seek to maximize its influence, and the political operatives in Congress, who may seek to maximize their political fortunes.

In terms of the accompanying figure, expansion of a locally provided good from Q_1, the equilibrium quantity in the absence of federal aid, to Q_2, the social optimum, can be achieved with minimum expense to the federal treasury by grants covering slightly more than the difference between the marginal cost curve (MC) and the demand curve (D), or the shaded triangular area. The local government would have to raise additional taxes to cover the remaining area between Q_1 and Q_2 under the demand curve. State and local taxes would have to go up even if highly inelastic goods were subsidized, on the margin, by the federal government. Of course, when the aid is withdrawn, production will return to Q_1 and local taxes will contract.

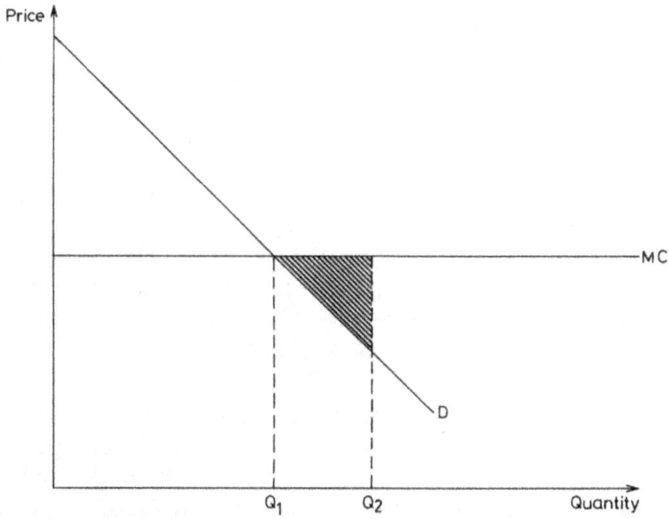

Further, as argued by McKenzie and Staaf [1979], state and local officials have an interest in supporting a grants economy that induces upward pressures on all state and local tax rates. Under their model of monopoly government, revenue sharing (as well as other grant programs) is a device by which state and local governments seek to cartelize the government market, overriding their competitive dilemma and the relatively low elasticities of demand they confront. When governments are forced to operate independently of one another, their tax rates are held in check by the ability of people and industry to "vote with their feet". One means of going beyond the competitive tax equilibrium is for the federal government to apply uniform tax rates across the country and to distribute the proceeds to state and local governments in the form of aid. Another means of accomplishing the same objective is for the federal government to induce subordinate governments to raise their tax rates. From this perspective of government, the matching requirements are effectively quid pro quo's between the different levels of government, each intent on shifting a greater portion of the nation's income into the public sector.

Whether efficiency rises or falls with an extension of fiscal federalism is unclear. Production may be extended up to or beyond the optimum level. Clearly, from this maximizing government perspective, state and local government taxes should be induced upwards. The maximizing revenue level of the federal government, however, may be unaltered by the introduction of fiscal federalism. On the other hand, the government can, through the grants system, spread its revenues over a greater quantity of goods and services in its objective function, whatever its objective function happens to be.

IV. Categorical versus Block Grants

Categorical grants, by definition, are quite restrictive, leaving state and local officials little leeway in determining how federal funds are spent. A categorical grant for patrol cars may spell out in some detail what types of cars can be purchased. Block grants offer state and local governments considerable freedom in determining spending allocations. Funds may be provided, for example, "to improve police readiness", a sufficiently general objective that allows the subordinate government the freedom to spend the funds on officers or equipment, or even fire power. Categorical grants do not, therefore, give subordinate governments as much freedom to use federal funds for the needs that might otherwise have been financed by state and/or local taxes.

As noted, left to their own devices in raising revenue, states will seek an equilibrium level of taxation consistent with competition from other states. If funds are handed over to the states in lump sum form, the competitive drive of states for a greater tax base will, in equilibrium, induce states to respond to the availability of federal funds by lowering their own tax collections. The penalty to the states for lowering taxes under lump sum grants is zero. The very distinction between categorical and block grants implies that the penalty for substituting federal for state funds is greater under categorical grants. It follows that the distinction implies greater opportunity for substitution of federal for state funds under the block grant programs. Further, a shift of a given number of dollars from categorical to block grants will lead to a reduction in state taxes. The commonly voiced concern that "block grants reduce federal control of state and local government" speaks to this prediction.

V. Conclusion

The exact effect of President Reagan's "New Fiscal Federalism" on state and local taxes is not completely clear. It will depend ultimately on the rules for allocating federal funds under the new system, if a new system is ever enacted. Although fewer federal funds may be involved and a greater share of the funding level will be made in the form of block grants, the importance of state and local taxes in determining the distribution of federal aid may eventually be enhanced.

Presently, the Reagan Administration has only provided the broad outline of its programs; and because of the immediate opposition to the program that developed among state and local governments, the "new federalism" may not take final shape until 1983. State and local officials' opposition to the Reagan Administration's program, however, may be construed as tentative confirmation of the central proposition of this paper: across-the-board reductions in federal aid will result in a reduction in state and local taxes from their own sources, perhaps not immediately but eventually, when state and local governments are able to rid themselves of the fixed costs of current programs. State and local officials sense the competitive bind that the new program imposes on them[1]. While these officials may balk at the program, many state and local taxpayers stand to benefit.

---

[1] Empirical tests of this proposition support the central argument of this paper. When state and local revenue from their own sources are regressed against federal aid to states, as well as a number of other standardizing variables, federal aid is always positive and statistically significant at the 0.0001 confidence level [Frye, McKenzie, forthcoming].

References

Advisory Commission on Intergovernmental Relations (ACIR), The Federal Influence on State and Local Roles in the Federal System. Washington, November 1981.

Ascik, Thomas R., The Reagan Block Grant Proposal and Congressional Revisions. The Heritage Foundation, Backgrounder No. 145, Washington 1981.

Barfield, Claude E., Categorical Grants: Their Role and Design. Advisory Commission on Intergovernmental Relations, Washington 1978.

-- [1981a], Rethinking Federalism: Block Grants and Federal, State, and Local Responsibilities. American Enterprise Institute Studies, 349, Washington 1981.

-- [1981b], Significant Features of Fiscal Federalism: 1980-1981 Edition. Advisory Commission on Intergovernmental Relations, Washington 1981.

Breton, Albert, "A Theory of Government Grants". The Canadian Journal of Economics and Political Science, Vol. 31, 1965, pp. 175-187.

Congleton, Roger, "Competitive Process, Competitive Waste, and Institutions". In: James M. Buchanan, Robert D. Tollison, Gordon Tullock (Eds.), Toward a Theory of the Rent-Seeking Society. Texas A & M University, College Station 1980, pp. 153-179.

Frye, Berrier E., Richard B. McKenzie, "The Impact of Federal Aid on State and Local Taxes". The Heritage Foundation, Washington, forthcoming.

Gramlich, Edward M., "Intergovernmental Grants: A Review of the Empirical Literature". In: Wallace E. Oates (Ed.), The Political Economy of Fiscal Federalism. Lexington, Mass., 1977, pp. 219-239.

Lovell, Catherine H., et al., Federal and State Mandating on Local Governments: An Exploration of Issues and Impacts. University of California-Riverside, Riverside 1979.

McKenzie, Richard B., Robert J. Staaf, "Revenue Sharing and Monopoly Government". Public Choice, Vol. 33, 1979, pp. 93-97.

McKenzie, Richard B., Bruce Yandle, The Impact of Delegation Size on the Distribution of Federal Aid across State Governments. Clemson University, Department of Economics Working Paper, Clemson, S.C., 1982.

Office of the President's Press Secretary (Office PPS) [1982a], Federalism Initiative. Fact Sheet, Washington 1982.

-- [1982b], The President's Federalism Initiative: Basic Framework. Washington 1982.

Olson, Mancur, "The Principle of 'Fiscal Equivalence' : The Division of Responsibilities among Different Levels of Government". American Economic Review, Papers and Proceedings, Vol. 59, 1969, pp. 479-487.

Tullock, Gordon, "Efficient Rent Seeking". In: James M. Buchanan, Robert D. Tollison, Gordon Tullock (Eds.), Toward a Theory of the Rent-Seeking Society. Texas A & M University, College Station 1980, pp. 97-112.

U.S. Department of the Treasury, Fiscal Service Bureau, Federal Aid to States. Washington, various issues.

Comment

Klaus-Dirk Henke

According to McKenzie the restructuring of fiscal federalism by the Reagan Administration refers mainly to

- the reduction of the federal aid level (Verringerung von Bundeszuweisungen)
- the switch of federal aid from categorical grant programs[1] with matching requirements to block grant programs without matching requirements (Übergang von projektgebundenen Zuweisungen mit Selbstbeteiligung des Empfängers zu aufgabengebundenen Zuweisungen ohne Selbstbeteiligung des Empfängers) and
- the transfer of more financial responsibility to the state governments for some 40 aid programs.

Critics argue that this new federalism, which is part of the economic philosophy in favor of giving economic power back to people, will lead to higher taxes and other revenue increases by local and state governments. McKenzie wants to predict the effects of the above mentioned elements of new federalism on the tax levels of subordinate governments. His central thesis is - contrary to popular presumption - that "a reduction in the level of federal aid and a greater use by the federal government of block grants can be expected to lead, ceteris paribus, to a reduction in state and local taxes from their own sources" (p. 54). McKenzie maintains a clear and puzzling connection between public sector growth and the way a society organizes its fiscal structures. Overall reductions in federal aid and changes in the intergovernmental grant system[2] will lead, according to McKenzie, to a decline of local and state expenditures which is some multiple of the reduction in federal aid. If McKenzie is correct, his results may be applicable to the level and the structure of federal grants in West Germany, too. [For a survey on the federal grants to the states in West Germany, see tables 2 and 3 in the Appendix.]

---

[1] These are also referred to as project grants or specific purpose grants.

[2] See the chart in the Appendix for a survey on the different forms of intergovernmental grant systems.

The various connections between public sector growth and structures of fiscal federalism may be summarized as follows. There are four different strategies that change fiscal federalism:

A. Overall reduction in the level of federal aid (Verringerung von Bundeszuweisungen) to subordinate governments - leaving the grant system constant.

B. Changing categorical to block grants (Übergang von eng definierten Zweckzuweisungen zu weit definierten Zuweisungen) - leaving the matching system constant.

C. Changing matching to non-matching grants (Übergang von Zuweisungen, die die Mitfinanzierung des Empfängers erfordern, zu solchen ohne Mitfinanzierung) - leaving the broadness and purpose of grant constant.

   1. In the case of categorical grants
   2. In the case of block grants

D. All three changes taken together.

For each of these four strategies, there are four possible effects on the size of the public sector. It may keep constant (this expectation tends to reflect popular belief), or it may decline in a less than proportional manner, in a proportional manner, or in a more than proportional manner. The last effect is that expected by McKenzie.

To begin with strategy A, McKenzie expects a reduction in the so-called search and lobbying costs, because state and local government rent seekers will go out of business. This development might be questioned, however, since the competition for less money by more governments makes search costs likely to go up. Furthermore - at least in a German setting - the civil servants who devoted their time to completing applications and searching through the bureaucratic maze, will not become unemployed if rent-seeking activities lose their importance[1]. They will switch to other activities, e.g. to working on the problem of how to adjust to reductions of federal aid. The administration of "cutback management" may be one of their new tasks. In the long run, however, McKenzie may be right.

---

[1] Apart from public search and lobbying costs there may arise private search and lobbying costs, too, in case fiscal federalism is characterized by complete tax separation (freies Trennsystem).

Strategy B means an increase in the autonomy of the recipient of the transfer. Two main adjustments are possible:

(a) If the receiving government unit has spent the same amount for the type of expenditures as it did without the categorical grant, the restructuring strategy will not change the situation. The granting (federal) level did not induce additional state/local expenditures due to the substitution effect (Mitnahmeeffekt). The size of the public sector stays constant.

(b) If the receiving government unit used the categorical grant to fund projects which it otherwise would not have chosen (Zusätzlichkeitsthese), the restructuring strategy will lead to a higher utility of the receiving level, while the granting government will lose in importance and influence. Whether the growth of the public sector is affected will be an empirical question. It is plausible, however, that it will decline in a proportional or a less than proportional manner.

As is the case in West Germany, most of the American grants from the federal level include matching requirements. This means that state and local governments are required to finance a portion of the projects from their own tax or other sources. The knowledge of the adjustment process of the recipient is again decisive for the evaluation of such a switch from matching to non-matching grants. Given the same amount of the grant (differential incidence) this restructuring strategy (C) is twofold. First, the federal level may change from categorical grants with a matching requirement to the same system without state or local financial participation. Second, the federal level may give block grants without matching requirements instead of those with financial participation.

If the receiving unit obtained a categorical grant with a matching requirement in the past and the new strategy does not require such a payment, then the receiving unit has more freedom to choose. It may spend the same amount as before or just the received sum for the required purpose. If it chooses to use its original financial participation for other purposes, it may choose other government functions and/or reduce expenditures. This budgetary behavior of lower levels of government will determine the public sector growth. It seems to be realistic, in a democratic setting, to expect that the public sector will remain constant.

A similar situation will arise if block grants become available without matching requirements. Again more fiscal autonomy is given; the adjustment will affect the public sector growth accordingly.

Finally, there is the case of decreasing federal aid (A) while at the same time restructuring the system from categorical to block grants (B) and from a system with matching requirements to one without financial participation (C) within the project and block grant system[1]. It is this type of change (D) from which McKenzie expects a positive relationship between the reduction of federal aid and the decline in the size of the public sector, assuming that the tax volume of subordinate levels will decline by more than the original reduction in the level of federal aid. In my opinion the main influence in strategy D will stem from the overall reduction in the level of federal aid, with strategies B and C being of less importance.

It is open to empirical tests whether the taxes of state and local levels increase when federal aid decreases, whether state expenditures decline or whether McKenzie is correct that "across-the-board reductions in federal aid will result in a reduction in state and local taxes from their own sources" (p. 67). In any case one has to distinguish carefully between the fiscal adjustment of subordinate government levels only and the overall effect on the size of the public sector.

What is urgently needed then - and I strongly agree with McKenzie - is more empirical work on fiscal adjustment under budgetary stringency[2]. His reference on page 60, however, to American studies, showing that "in the ten survey areas 51 percent of local projects with federal and state aid would not have been undertaken in the absence of the partial federal aid" [for a similar experience see Nathan, Adams, 1977] is not yet a sufficient proof of his presumption, because the preferences of the federal agencies are most likely to be different from the preferences of subordinate government levels. Assuming matching requirements the state and local governments could have used the money without the grants for other purposes, so that the overall reduction of the public sector would only be proportional. Only in a (realistic?) case where subordinate levels do without this money from the financial participation would the McKenzie effect occur. Furthermore, the normative question arises whose preferences should

[1] There is also a case of restructuring possible which is characterized by a switch from categorical grants with matching requirements to block grants without matching requirements. Furthermore, it is possible that strategies that combine A and B or C are chosen.

[2] Empirical evidence in the past presented neither tax-increasing nor tax-declining effects as a sequence of different grant systems [Gramlich, 1977, p. 232; ACIR, 1977].

be fulfilled - federal, state or local - when tax money is spent. According to the new philosophy of the Reagan administration, probably those preferences that are closest to the people have the highest value, whereas in the theory of fiscal federalism one would dispute this - depending on the function - on the basis of the geographic size of the benefit areas.

In my opinion McKenzie is correct when he argues that just the very fact that the federal level participates in financing certain programs may induce activities by subordinate governments. "The grants system ... induces state and local governments to become classic rent seekers" (p. 57). A good example is the German Hospital Financing Act of 1972, according to which investment and certain operating costs are partially (about 30 percent) reimbursed by the federal level. This mixture of financing responsibilities (Mischfinanzierung) has certainly increased the number of hospitals and in particular the number of hospital beds, which, according to different standards, are much too high. By centralizing the financing structure and by switching to categorical grants instead of other financing mechanisms, the public sector growth in health care has been increased. This example fits McKenzie's assertion that changing categorical grants to block grants will reduce total public activity[1]. In addition, the particular German example is characterized by the (too) many levels of competence and particular features in the voting process in a federal/state commission which is in charge of investment decisions. The higher the number of institutions which are responsible for financing, the less is the inducement to save, would be my hypothesis, or in other words: the higher the fiscal illusion of the level which is in charge of investing the money, the more likely this level will spend larger amounts of money. If this is correct, there are good reasons for separating vertically the responsibilities in financing public functions between different levels of governments. Breton's "economically optimum constitution" and Olson's "fiscal equivalence" point in the same direction. In such a system the function of grants is reduced to fully achieve only this objective.

A typical American problem is dealt with when McKenzie refers to a kind of revenue sharing that explicitly introduces "tax effort" as a prerequisite for receiving federal aid. He states that "the higher the tax effort, the greater the federal aid" (p. 61). In this case the marginal price of state and local public goods is reduced and a state "can ex-

[1] A closed-ended block grant would be a more adequate alternative to the current Hospital Financing Act in West Germany.

ternalize its own production costs" (p. 61)[1]. McKenzie compares this situation to the classic prisoner's dilemma: the moderate government units will lose money and will perhaps suffer from lower growth rates, and the more aggressive units acquire access to the federal treasury and tap the tax bases of other states by raising their own tax rates.

Raising taxes to present a high tax effort and thus to receive more federal money leads not necessarily to more revenue from the unit's own tax bases. Instead, factor outmigration due to tax increases, i.e. lower fiscal residua can be the consequence of the fiscal behavior that McKenzie describes, and the more tax bases leave a region the higher must be the tax rates. This tax spiral may be adverse to the objectives of regional development and should be observable in the United States, if McKenzie's observation of the described prisoner's dilemma is correct. This kind of fiscal behavior can be regarded as an instrument to achieve a competitive tax equilibrium, a system in which the tax rates of different governments are held in check by the ability of enterprises and people to "vote with their feet" (p. 65). This concept depends on the actual mobility of labor and capital which is determined by many factors apart from the tax costs. In case of high immobility of factors of production one might argue that total tax yield may even be higher compared to a system with uniform tax rates across the country.

An argument that stems from the German type of tax sharing is to be seen from Table 1 in the Appendix. It shows the proportions which different levels of governments receive. "Tax effort" in McKenzie's sense plays no role in such a system of tax sharing, the details of which are either prescribed by the constitution or are the subject - as in the case of the value added tax - of annual negotiations. While tax sharing in this (German) sense will not lead to tax effort on the local and state level[2] the opposite, however, is possible. The inducement to save decreases because the tax money stems from sources that flow even without efforts of the receiving level of government. If more fiscal autonomy is desired in the German system one either has to change the system of revenue sharing and allocate total revenue tax by tax to different levels

[1] This may also be the case for categorical grants without a tax effort clause [for more detail, see McDougall Commission, 1977, p. 207-212: Specific Purpose Grants in four Federations].

[2] An exception may be the case of the "Hebesätze" in the business tax and the potentially but so far not used "Hebesätze" in favor of the local level in the income tax according to the constitution (Art. 106 (5), 3 Grundgesetz).

and/or give the right to state/local units to tax certain tax bases (value added, income etc.) in addition to the existing taxes.

One argument that one may add to McKenzie's observation is the question of distribution (regional disparities, fiscal equalization) in the "New Federalism"[1]. My question refers to its role in the United States context. I wonder whether - e.g. - there are complaints when the living conditions are completely different in a rural setting in Alabama compared to urban areas where the access to infrastructure (schools, hospitals, theaters, swimming pools, etc.) is probably much better. This argument is in the center of the German discussion, though perhaps somewhat overemphasized. An explanation for this may be that the Federal Republic is such a small country compared to the United States and that regional and social closeness makes income differences more visible[2]. Finally, it should be stressed that objectives or criteria are necessary for an overall judgement of federal grant programs, i.e. to evaluate whether they are in line with the purpose they are supposed to serve [for more detail, see Musgrave, Musgrave, 1980, pp. 560 ff.]. On this McKenzie is very short, probably because he is mainly interested in the analysis of fiscal federalism and its allocative effects on the size and structure of the public sector in the United States. In a German setting with its completely different structures of fiscal federalism, McKenzie's predictions are not totally valid.

---

1 Macroeconomic effects of the New Federalism would be another additonal subject.

2 In a distributional sense there is a direct connection between the tax yield of state taxes (Landessteuern) and the part of the value added tax that the states receive. 25 percent of the tax yield of the value added tax (Länderanteil) will go to states with a low fiscal capacity. The lower - ceteris paribus - the tax yield from state taxes compared to the federal average per head, the higher will be the amount per head from the value added tax (Art. 107 (1) Grundgesetz und § 1 des Gesetzes über den Finanzausgleich zwischen Bund und Ländern in der Fassung des Beschlusses des Bundestages vom 02.07.1969 und des Bundesrates vom 10.07.1969, Bundestags-Drucksache V/4481).
A similar connection applies to the state financial compensation (Länderfinanzausgleich) according to §§ 5, 6, and 7 of the law cited just above, and to the general grants from state to local governments (Gemeindefinanzausgleich) [for more detail, see Advisory Commission, 1981, Chapters 2 and 3].

Appendix

Chart - Intergovernmental Grant Systems

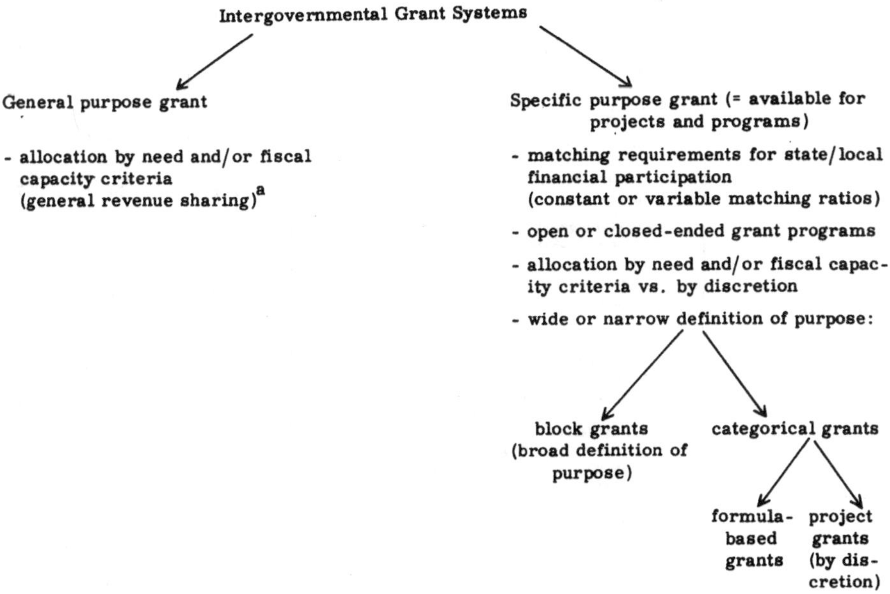

[a]In the United States "tax effort" is used as a factor in the formula used to distribute the money appropriated by Congress for different levels of Government.

Table 1 - Tax Sharing in West Germany, 1981 (percent)

	Federal	State	Local
Income tax	42.4	42.4	15.0
Corporation profits tax	50.0	50.0	-
Value added tax	67.5	32.5	-
Business tax[a]	13.3	13.3	73.3

[a]"Gewerbesteuer" on the basis of an average "Hebesatz" of 300 percent.

Source: Zimmermann, Henke [1982, p. 100].

Table 2 - Ausgaben des Bundes zur Mitfinanzierung von

Zweckbestimmung	1976	1977	1978
			Ist
I. Gemeinschaftsaufgaben (91a GG)			
Neubau und Ausbau von Hochschulen	1.190	990	1.015
Regionale Wirtschaftsstruktur	315	311	376
Agrarstruktur und Küstenschutz	1.271	1.392	1.582
Insgesamt	2.776	2.693	2.973
II. Bildungsplanung und Wissenschaftsförderung (91b GG)			
Leistungen an Länder	90	86	96
Leistungen an Dritte im Rahmen gemeinsamer Finanzierungen[a, b]	731	838	901
Insgesamt	821	924	997
III. Geldleistungsgesetze (104a Abs. 3 GG)			
Gasölbetriebsbeihilfe	538	570	575
Einmaliger Heizkostenzuschuß	-	-	-
Ausbildungsförderung	1.585	1.638	1.836
Wohngeld	808	734	894
Wohnungsbauprämien	1.121	926	935
Graduiertenförderung	23	15	15
Sparprämie[a]	2.508	4.367	2.390
Unterhaltsvorschüsse	-	-	-
Kindergeld für Bedienstete[a]	-	1.658	1.868
Investitionszuschußgesetz	153	518	155
TB-Hilfen nach § 66 BSHG	5	1	2
Sozialversicherung für Behinderte	43	57	62
Entschädigung an Opfer von Gewalttaten	-	1	1
Insgesamt	6.784	10.484	8.733
IV. Investitionshilfegesetz (104a Abs. 4 GG)			
Kommunaler Straßenbau/ÖPNV	1.939	1.801	1.978
Städtebau	190	217	197
Fernwärmeversorgung in städtischen Schwerpunktbereichen	-	12	28
Städtebauliche Vorhaben in Sanierungsgebieten (ZIP)	-	8	132
Sozialer Wohnungsbau[a]	1.025	1.001	1.032
Studentenwohnraumförderung	89	44	50
Modernisierung von Wohngebäuden	61	79	102
Krankenhausfinanzierung	983	915	785
Strukturhilfe Saarland	20	20	20
Ausbildungskapazitäten für berufliche Bildung	43	88	157
Schutz gewerbl. Anlagen v. Sturmfluten	-	73	110
Bau regionaler Erdgasleitungen	-	-	-
Förderung energiesparender Maßnahmen	-	-	6
Eisenbahn Kreuzungs-Ges. (Gemeinden)[a]	-	2	3
Konjunkturprogramm Sept. 74 u. Aug. 75	1.107	108	25
Bau von Kohleheizkraftwerken	-	-	-
Insgesamt	5.457	4.368	4.625
I.-IV. insgesamt	15.837	18.469	17.328
V. Sonstige Zahlungen an Länder			
Ergänzungszuweisungen an finanzschwache Länder	883	939	1.099
Bundeshilfe für Berlin	6.295	6.910	7.638
Sonstige Zahlungen (z.B. Erstattung aufgrund Bundesentschädigungsgesetz, G 131)	3.783	4.078	4.144
I.-V. insgesamt	26.798	30.396	30.209

[a] Zahlungen nicht oder nur teilweise über Länderhaushalte. - [b] Ohne Großforschungseinrichtungen.

Länderaufgaben, 1976-1985 (Mill. DM)

1979	1980	1981	1982	1983	1984	1985
			Soll	Finanzplan		
812	822	798	900	800	800	800
432	440	314	235	235	235	235
1.627	1.596	1.076	1.050	1.050	1.050	1.050
2.871	2.858	2.187	2.185	2.085	2.085	2.085
101	116	105	102	103	104	104
963	1.038	1.115	1.196	1.272	1.332	1.395
1.064	1.154	1.220	1.298	1.375	1.436	1.499
636	676	467	460	460	640	640
28	97	11	-	-	-	-
1.982	2.383	2.402	2.390	2.350	2.150	2.150
923	912	1.211	1.234	962	912	866
963	987	984	950	600	590	580
15	15	12	10	-	-	-
1.351	1.270	1.408	1.930	2.000	1.350	1.100
-	38	55	55	30	30	30
2.135	2.248	2.482	2.201	2.126	2.056	1.996
47	17	3	-	-	-	-
1	1	1	1	1	1	1
84	103	117	150	180	195	210
1	2	3	4	5	6	7
8.166	8.746	9.155	9.385	8.714	7.930	7.580
2.144	2.010	1.930	2.041	1.997	2.068	2.069
222	257	284	306	262	285	220
50	95	87	92	13	-	-
258	187	208	74	10	-	-
1.312	1.253	1.711	1.714	1.798	2.058	2.259
38	64	40	20	10	-	-
120	136	167	205	194	144	113
740	750	817	820	880	940	960
20	20	-	-	-	-	-
199	76	27	10	10	-	-
64	21	5	-	-	-	-
-	5	18	32	36	-	-
207	196	259	173	277	190	150
2	2	2	7	7	7	7
3	5	-	-	-	-	-
-	-	-	55	150	200	175
5.379	5.076	5.554	5.549	5.644	5.893	5.952
17.480	17.832	18.116	18.417	17.818	17.344	17.116
1.278	1.366	1.479	1.533	1.620	1.731	1.85
8.285	9.180	9.747	10.200	10.650	11.120	11.61
4.612	4.495	4.418	4.141	4.234	4.093	4.01
31.655	32.873	33.760	34.291	34.322	34.288	34.59

Source:
Der Bundesminister der Finanzen, Die Finanzbeziehungen zwischen Bund, Ländern und Gemeinden aus finanzverfassungsrechtlicher und finanzwirtschaftlicher Sicht, Bonn 1982, pp. 611 f.

Table 3 - German Federal Categorical Matching Grants to the States (Länder) by Program and Functional Area, 1982[a] (Mill. DM)

Bildung		Gesundheit		Verkehrswesen		Wohnungsbau		Regional- und andere Strukturpolitik	
Neubau und Ausbau von Hochschulen	900	Krankenhausfinanzierung	820	Kommunaler Straßenbau/ÖPNV	2.041	Wohnungsbauprämien	950	Regionale Wirtschaftsstruktur	235
Ausbildungsförderung	2.390	TB-Hilfen nach § 66 BSHG	1			Wohngeld	1.234	Agrarstruktur und Küstenschutz	1.050
Graduiertenförderung	10					Sozialer Wohnungsbau[a]	1.714	Gasölbetriebsbeihilfe	460
Leistungen an Dritte im Rahmen gemeinsamer Finanzierung[b,c]	1.196							Städtebau	306
Insgesamt	4.496	Insgesamt	821	Insgesamt	2.041	Insgesamt	3.898	Insgesamt	2.051

[a]Die sonstigen Zuschüsse, die nicht weiter aufgeschlüsselt werden, betragen 6.915 DM. - [b]Zahlungen nicht oder nur teilweise über Länderhaushalte. - [c]Ohne Großforschungseinrichtungen.

Source: Bundesministerium der Finanzen (unpublished data).

References

Advisory Commission on Intergovernmental Relations (ACIR), Federal Grants: Their Effects on State-Local Expenditures, Employment Levels and Wage Rates. Washington 1977.

--, Studies in Comparative Federalism: West Germany. Washington 1981.

Gramlich, Edward M., "Intergovernmental Grants: A Review of the Empirical Literature". In: Wallace E. Oates (Ed.), The Political Economy of Fiscal Federalism. Lexington, Mass., 1977, pp. 219-239.

MacDougall, Sir Donald, et al. (MacDougall Commission), Report of the Study Group on the Role of Public Finance in European Integration, Vol. II. Brussels 1977.

Musgrave, Richard A., Peggy B. Musgrave, Public Finance in Theory and Practice. 3rd Ed., Tokyo 1980.

Nathan, Richard P., Charles F. Adams, Jr., with the assistance of André Juneau and James W. Fossett, Revenue Sharing: The Second Round. The Brookings Institution, Washington 1977.

Zimmermann, Horst, Klaus-Dirk Henke, Finanzwissenschaft: Eine Einführung in die Lehre von der öffentlichen Finanzwirtschaft. 3rd Ed., Munich 1982.

Walter Eltis

Policy for the Nationalised Industries: The British Problem

I. Introduction

The policy that the state should follow with regard to nationalised industries is important for many European countries. In Britain, this is especially the case because the recent economic performance of the nationalised industries has given considerable cause for concern. While they produce only 8 to 10 per cent of the net national product at factor cost, they have - as will become evident below - obliged the government to guarantee borrowing of as much as 3.5 per cent of the national income to finance their investment and losses in some years, and in addition to provide current subsidies of 1.5 percent of the national income. This extra 3.5 percentage points on the public sector borrowing requirement has been a matter of great concern to monetarists who believe that a fraction of the excessive total of government borrowing that may result is financed through monetary expansion. The recent performance of the nationalised industries has also worried those more inclined to analyse the economy in Keynesian terms. Their prices have been rising much faster than those of the private sector. Since 1974, for instance, British nationalised industry prices have risen 25 per cent more than prices in general[1] and thus added to the pace of the wage-price spiral in Keynesian analyses of inflation - especially as coal, gas, electricity and rail transport, which are all nationalised in Britain, very clearly affect costs of production throughout the economy. There is also a widespread belief for which there is difficulty in providing an empirical basis that these industries are microeconomically inefficient, and relatively indifferent to the needs and demands of consumers - largely as a consequence of lack of competition.

The present paper will begin with an account of the pricing and investment policies of these industries in Britain since 1963, and it will

[1] Series for the prices charged by the nationalised industries, and for prices in general are published in the Department of Employment Gazette, London.

provide a statistical comparison of their economic surpluses and financing needs with those of private sector companies. After this, the implications for policy which follow from the analysis will be discussed.

II. The Financial Surpluses of the Nationalised Industries and of Private Sector Companies in Britain, 1963-1980

In Britain, detailed statistics are available for the financial accounts of the "public corporations", which include all nationalised industries and government-owned corporations such as the British National Oil Corporation, the former National Enterprise Board and such bodies as the Development Board for Rural Wales [CSO, 1978, p. 124]. These statistics for the public corporations are dominated by the nationalised industries.

The disastrous deterioration in the accounts of the public corporations from 1963 to 1980 is extremely clear from Table 1, which is derived from their financial accounts. Here the wage costs, interest costs, investment, necessary subsidies, etc. of the British public corporations are presented as percentages of their value-added net of the capital consumption of their assets as estimated by the British Central Statistical Office. Capital consumption is intended to measure the investment which would be needed each year to sustain the capital of these industries at a constant real level, and it is well known that this is exceedingly difficult to measure, especially in periods where the rate of inflation is rapid and changing. Nevertheless, capital is used up in the process of production; it does become obsolete and require replacement in due course, and that part of gross value-added which is needed to make good the depreciation of the capital stock is not a true value-added.

The derivation of this table and of Tables 2 and 3 below is explained in the Appendix. Table 1 brings out that the value-added by the British public corporations net of capital consumption has failed to cover even wages since 1973. The table underestimates if anything the deficit of value-added in relation to wages and interest because a great deal of the debt of the public corporations has been written off by successive governments, including £2,652 mill. from 1968 to 1975 [CSO, 1978, p. 129]. The interest on this part of total government debt, due

Table 1 - Deficits over Costs[a] of the British Public Corporations, 1963-1980

	1963-67	1968-72	1973-76	1977-80
Costs and deficits				
(1) Wage costs	89.9	93.6	107.3	103.2
(2) Interest	18.3	23.4	28.7	22.7
(3) deficit of value-added over (1) and (2)	- 8.2	-17.0	-36.0	-25.9
(4) Net investment	26.5	14.2	16.3	2.7
(5) deficit of value-added over (1), (2) and (4)	-34.7	-31.2	-52.3	-28.6
Financing of deficits				
(6) Non-trading income	2.0	2.9	5.5	4.9
(7) Subsidies (less taxes paid)	2.9	4.3	15.2	8.3
(8) Government-guaranteed borrowing	29.8	24.0	31.6	15.4

[a]In per cent share of value-added net of capital consumption.

Source: See the Appendix.

initially to the public corporations, is not shown in the table, which partly explains why interest costs are a lower fraction of value-added after 1976 despite the huge borrowing that continued throughout the period. Interest costs are also understated because the public corporations borrowed large sums in foreign currencies such as the deutsche mark at low nominal interest rates, but at a sterling cost which rose as the pound fell in relation to the deutsche mark. Any increase in interest costs due to alterations in the exchange rate is carried by the central government and this is not shown in the table. But what the table does show is extremely disturbing; it brings out that, from 1973 to 1976, the public corporations produced a net value-added which fell short of their wages by 7 per cent. When interest costs are also taken into account, their wages and interest together exceeded their net value-added by 36 per cent of the latter and governments had to pay subsidies or guarantee public sector borrowing to cover the approximately 3.5 per cent of the national income that this represented. That 3.5 per cent had to be found before investment by the nationalised industries could be taken into account. That amounted to 16.3 per cent of their net value-added in 1973-1976; thus a sum amounting altogether to over 52 per cent of their net value-added had to be found from outside to sustain them economically. 5 percentage points of these 52 were found from their own non-trading income and the remainder came from government-guaranteed borrowing and subsidies. It is startling that the public corporations had to turn to the government for finance amounting to as much as one half of their total value-added. The table indicates that their need for outside help fell slightly in 1977-1980 but this was mainly because they virtually ceased after 1976 to make net investments. They had therefore reached a point by 1980 where they either imposed a heavy burden on the remainder of the economy in the form of necessary borrowing or subsidies as in 1973-1976, or were more nearly self-financing as in 1977-1980 but could no longer invest.

The sharp contrast with the private sector is brought out in Table 2 which presents similar data for the same period for British private sector companies. It will be seen that these produced enough value-added to cover wages, interest and dividends throughout the period 1963-1980. Their surpluses of value-added over wages, interest and dividends fell as the British economy became less competitive internationally - the most plausible explanation of the slight fall in the surplus from the period 1963-1967 to the period 1977-1980. Despite this fall, investment net of capital consumption was remarkably stable at around 10 per cent of net value-added. Their value-added fell short of wages, interest, dividends and investment by 7.7 per cent during the period 1973-1976, which includes the deep recession of 1974-1976. However, for the final period of 1977-1980, their value-added almost sufficed to cover wages, interest, dividends and investment, to restore approximately the position of 1963-1967. There is no evidence of any trend deterioration from 1963 to 1980 apart from the 6 percentage point rise in the ratio of wages to net value-added which is best explained, as has been suggested, by the real increase in the sterling exchange rate.

It is now time to say something about the precise periods, 1963-1967, 1968-1972, 1973-1976 and 1977-1980 for which the data has been shown. In the ordinary way, economic data should be presented in cycles which go from peak to peak or from trough to trough, so that successive periods are comparable in the sense that they do not involve comparing one period dominated by slump conditions with another which is predominantly one of expansion. This course has not

Table 2 - Surpluses over Costs of British Private Sector Companies[a]: 1963-1980

	1963-67	1968-72	1973-76	1977-80
(9) Wage costs	77.2	79.5	88.5	83.0
(10) Interest and dividends	11.6	9.5	8.1	7.8
(11) surplus of value-added over (9) and (10)	+11.2	+11.0	+3.4	+9.2
(12) Net investment	9.5	10.0	11.1	9.7
(13) surplus (+) or deficit (-) of value-added over (9), (10) and (12)	+1.7	+1.0	-7.7	-0.5

[a]In per cent share of value-added net of capital consumption.

Source: See the Appendix.

been followed here because the accounts of the nationalised industries are best examined over periods where the attitude of government to their investment and pricing has had particular characteristics.

The first period 1963-1967 was one of expansion; British governments' predominant approach to economic problems during this time was Keynesian. Inflation did not exceed 5 per cent in this period while unemployment was 2 per cent or less, and Britain's fundamental economic weakness was diagnosed quite widely as an insufficient rate of economic growth in relation to the more successful OECD economies such as West Germany, France, Italy, Japan and even the United States (which has not had a particularly high rate of economic growth in the post-war period). The cause of the comparatively slow rate of growth was diagnosed to be partly one of attitudes to productivity change, and partly - and interdependently - a comparatively low rate of investment in industrial structures and equipment [see e.g. NEDO, 1963; 1964]. That was the main reason why in this period the public corporations were allowed to invest (as Table 1 shows) a net amount equivalent to 26.5 per cent of their net value-added and to borrow an approximately equivalent sum to do so. At that time their value-added sufficed to cover about nine-tenths of wages and interest. Private companies had surpluses over wages, interest and dividends of 11.2 per cent of value-added while the public corporations had deficits of 8.2

per cent; this discrepancy is best explained by the consideration that, at that time, the nationalised industries were expected merely to break even financially - which they nearly did - while private companies, of course, normally earn net profits and finance some of their net investment internally.

The immense investment of the period 1963-1967 was permitted because there was very little screening by the Treasury of investment projects by these industries. More investment in general was seen as a major national desideratum, and any projects which purported to cover the low nominal interest rates of that period were approved. Purported to cover is the right term, because prospective accounts of what capital should yield were naturally presented by the industries themselves, with in many cases unrealistically favourable assumptions that were not carefully scrutinised.

From 1968 to 1972 the main economic objective was to take advantage of the opportunity to correct the balance of payments which the sterling devaluation of 1967 offered. The devaluation was a factor in the wage explosion of 1969 which took inflation to about 10 per cent, and a containment of inflation became an important economic goal, both in its own right, and of course in order to contribute to a successful exploitation of the devaluation which would be completely vitiated if an increase in home costs removed the entire competitive advantage that was temporarily obtained in 1967. The predominant economic philosophy was still entirely Keynesian, and this called for an increase in saving relative to investment if the balance of payments was to be improved[1]. Investment by the nationalised industries was therefore scrutinised far more critically, especially while Mr. Jenkins was Chancellor of the Exchequer in 1967-1970. The nationalised industries were asked to invest only where projects could expect to earn a real rate of return of 8 per cent (formerly a return equivalent to the nominal interest rate had sufficed) which was seen as the rate of return the private sector earned on its assets. It is evident from Table 1 that the ratio of net investment by the public corporations fell by 12 percentage points of their net value-added from the period 1963-1967 to the period 1968-1972 and that this was associated with a considerable fall (though not of 12 percentage points) in the borrowing of these industries.

[1] See Black [1959] for one of the clearest available accounts of a Keynesian analysis of the relation between savings, investment and the effectiveness of devaluation.

The following period of 1973-1976 was dominated by Mr. Heath's dash for growth which was based entirely on Keynesian analysis. It was believed that growth would be achieved as a result of massive increases in effective demand brought about in the first instance by tax cuts and public expenditure increases. The consequent inflation would be contained through price and wage controls. The prevailing analysis of the British authorities at that time was that inflation was mainly a product of a wage-price spiral, and that if prices could be held down in one year, that would reduce the expected rate of inflation and therefore the rate of wage increases needed to compensate for price inflation in the following year. This would make future prices and costs lower than they otherwise would have been and so justify, ex post, the initial holding down of prices. Similarly, any holding down of wages which would appear unjust at first would lead to lower prices and therefore be justified after the event. It was this kind of ultra-Keynesian thinking that led Mr. Heath to promise to halt inflation "at a stroke" in the 1970 election campaign, and it led him to seek to hold down the prices of the nationalised industries below cost after the election. That is the main reason why wage costs were 93.6 per cent of the net value-added of the public corporations in 1968-1972, and 107.3 per cent of this in 1973-1976. Neglecting raw material costs, this is the result that would have been produced if prices had been 13 per cent lower in relation to wage costs in the second period than they were in the first.

The large deficits in 1973-1976 and the huge borrowing and subsidy requirements of the nationalised industries which were also due to the authorisation of large expansions of the capital stock in 1973, 1974 and 1975, were the product of the Keynesian diagnosis of economic problems, and of the solutions that Mr. Heath and his Ministers and advisers favoured. Mr. Wilson, who took over after the February 1974 general election, continued the same Keynesian policies as a result of a very similar economic appreciation of how the economy functioned. His Chancellor, Mr. Healey, actually cut the rate of VAT in April 1974, despite the presence of a large deficit in the balance of payments and in the budget, in order to reduce the rate of inflation. This tax cut brought the annual rate of inflation down to 8 per cent over a three-month period (which helped to win the October 1974 election for Labour) but inflation soon soared to 28 per cent as the growing deficits and collapsing pound produced more lasting effects on the inflation rate than the temporary once-for-all tax cut which lowered the cost of living for only a few months. In addition to holding taxes down in a vain effort to stem inflation, the government naturally wished to continue to hold down the prices of the nationalised industries, which is why 1973-1976 is tabulated as a single period in Table 1. Mr. Heath's government and Mr. Wilson's applied similar policies to the nationalised industries until 1976.

The disastrous effects of these ultra-Keynesian policies - together with developments in monetary theory in both Britain and North America, but of course especially North America - produced a climate of opinion in which official British economic orthodoxy changed. During 1976 there was a change of Prime Minister and it is generally recognised that Mr. Callaghan, the father-in-law of Mr. Peter Jay, diagnosed economic problems in essentially monetarist terms. His statement to a Labour Party Conference on 28 September, 1976 that: "We used to think that you could just spend your way out of a recession and increase employment by cutting taxes and boosting government spending. I tell you now in all candour that that option no longer exists, and that in so far as it ever did exist, it worked by injecting inflation into the economy." has become justly famous. He was succeeded as Prime Minister in 1979 by Mrs. Thatcher, who was more rigorously monetarist and, unlike Mr. Callaghan, appointed monetarist economic advisers - Professor Burns of the London Business School, and Professor Walters of Johns Hopkins University. But the real policy change occurred in 1976; it was assisted by the International Monetary Fund (IMF), which was called into Britain in the midst of the 1976 balance-of-payments crisis and which insisted on public expenditure cuts.

According to a rigid monetarist analysis, an increase in nationalised industry prices has no influence on the long-term rate of inflation, which is entirely independent of the wage-price spiral. Instead, inflation is influenced by the rate of growth of the money supply, which, according to the analysis of the London Business School, depends strongly and directly on the ratio of public sector borrowing to the National Product[1]. With this view of the working of the economy, the rate of inflation will be minimised if nationalised industries price and invest in order to minimise the ratio of their borrowing to the National Income. The high price increases needed to minimise the borrowing of the nationalised industries will raise the rate of inflation in the first instance, but the lower inflation resulting from less public sector borrowing and therefore slower growth of the money supply will counter-

[1] See, for instance, Beenstock et al. [1981] for an exposition in which it is argued that "unbalanced finance" involving an increase in the ratio of bonds to money cannot be used for very long.

act this initial rise in inflation and produce prices lower than they would otherwise have been in due course. This basic approach to the problem of how the nationalised industries should price became orthodox by 1979, and it began to become important in 1977 and 1978 as Mr. Callaghan's government, with Mr. Healey now cutting public expenditure as if he were a monetarist, began to apply entirely new policies.

These policy changes after 1976 are reflected in the reduction in investment by the public corporations from 16.3 per cent of their net value-added in 1973-1976 to 2.7 per cent of net value-added in 1977-1980. Mr. Callaghan's government did not go on to implement the full monetarist analysis of raising nationalised industry prices relative to other prices substantially in order to reduce borrowing further, but from 1979, when Mrs. Thatcher took over, to 1981 - the most recent year for which statistics are available - nationalised industry prices rose 15 per cent more than prices in general, so the full monetarist policy of raising nationalised industry prices and reducing investment in order to reduce public sector borrowing was applied.

The statistics of Table 1 show data for 1977-1980 as a whole; in this period wages still exceeded net sales by the public corporations, but by only 3 per cent instead of the 7 per cent of 1973-1976. This occurred despite the Conservative government's efforts to raise prices in relation to wages; in fact, according to data published in [CSO, 1981] wages exceeded net value-added by 8 per cent in 1980 when value-added may have begun to be influenced by the recession of 1979-1982. The worrying possibility the data raises, however, is that these industries may in total have become economically unviable by 1980. Their productivity may by then have become so low that sales revenues in excess of wage costs were just not obtainable at any pricing level - recession or no recession. As prices are raised, markets are lost to international competition in the case of British Steel and British Leyland, two British nationalised industries. They are lost to domestic competition from road transport in the case of British railways. Only the Post Office and the fuel industries have near monopoly powers, provided that the fuel industries act together, but price rises by the latter make British fuel-using industries uncompetitive in relation to European industry. In February 1981 the Energy Task Force of the National Economic Development Office produced a report which showed that British industry was paying between 20 per cent and 40 per cent more for gas and electricity than large fuel users on the continent of Europe [NEDC (81)15]. The fuel industries were in consequence instructed to offer British industry competitive prices; by the time the Energy Task Force produced its next report in November 1981 this had been broadly achieved, partly as a result of the substantial fall of the sterling exchange rate between February and November 1981 [NEDC (81)59]. The fuel industries were therefore boxed in. They were not allowed to raise prices because this would make the price of British fuel uncompetitive and prejudice the competitiveness of fuel-using industries in the European Common Market. However, if their prices were kept down, they offered insufficient surpluses over wages to finance investment without excessive borrowing.

The government's prime desire was to restrict nationalised industry borrowing because its wish to achieve its monetary and borrowing targets overrode all other considerations. It therefore set the nationalised industries *cash limits* to their borrowing. Because of their low productivity and the impossibility of achieving surpluses of prices over wages, the cash limits were used almost entirely to pay wages with the result that little was left over for net investment. This has undoubtedly been the case with British Rail, which has not been able to afford electrification because wages exhaust all the funds available, including the maximum borrowing the government will permit; British Steel, which has had losses exceeding what the government has been willing to tolerate; and the coal industry, where investment has been restricted because of the wage bill the miners' unions have forced on the government. The inability of the nationalised industries to earn significant surpluses over wages has therefore faced the authorities with a choice between borrowing, which they consider intolerable, or a cessation of investment, which is bound in the long term to make these industries technologically uncompetitive and therefore unviable.

The possibility that nationalisation has slowed the growth of productivity to the point where surpluses over wages cannot be obtained from market sales is the most worrying element in the story that has unfolded. The fact that their investment and pricing has been subject to the macroeconomic fashions of the day so that net investment has soared under Keynesian policies and been cut virtually to zero in the period of monetarism is disturbing. The fact that prices have reacted equally to the vicissitudes of short-term economic management has obviously led to great departures from the welfare optima on which text-book nationalised industry pricing is based. But the possibility that these industries have had to conform with Keynesian policies when they should have been monetarist or vice versa, when they should really have been aiming for Paretian prices, pales to insignificance when it is considered that their productivity may have become so low that there are now no prices at all at which they can earn large enough surpluses over wages to finance the fraction of necessary investment which cannot be financed through government borrowing.

It might be naively argued that it is government borrowing which should be allowed to give way because the need to have nationalised industries which can invest is paramount. That great Keynesian, Sir Roy Harrod, saw the difficulty with this approach as early as 1958 when he wrote that the nationalised industries "... floated their programmes gaily forward on a rush of Treasury Bills" (because the government could not sell enough bonds to finance their investment), that this encouraged the banks to increase their lending with serious inflationary effects in periods of boom, and that the excess of supply over demand for government stock presented "... much the most serious obstacle to efficient monetary management". He concluded with remarkable prescience, "... so long as the problem of financing the nationalised industries is unsolved, there is real danger that in another boom things might slip further, leading to the destruction of sterling and of our world interests that depend on its maintenance" [Harrod, 1958, pp. 188 ff.]. Clearly the nationalised industries cannot be allowed to force unlimited borrowing upon the government because this could indeed lead to a great and further acceleration of inflation. At the same time it is intolerable that British industry should have to pay substantially more for fuel, transport and telecommunications than producers on the continent of Europe and it is also intolerable that industries as important as these should cease to make net investments, which is the present situation in Britain.

So what solutions are there to the crisis that has arisen? Before these are set out, an alternative account of the fundamental problem will be presented.

III. The Inadequate Surpluses in Marketed Output of the Nationalised Industries

The argument has so far been presented in terms of the financial accounts of the public corporations. A most important consequence of these has been their influence on government borrowing which persuaded both Mr. Callaghan's and Mrs. Thatcher's governments to severely restrict the amount of investment they were allowed to undertake.

An alternative approach is to examine the contribution they make to a country's requirements of marketed output. All private consumption is marketed, all investment is marketed and all exports are marketed, so a nation's marketed output has to supply its entire private consumption, investment and export needs. Marketed output, the production of goods and services which are sold, comes from companies in the public and the private sectors of the economy, from the self-employed and from partnerships. These need to produce more marketed output than they themselves consume and invest, because about 40 per cent of a nation's total marketed output is nowadays purchased by those who produce no marketed output at all - workers in the public services such as health and education who do not market their services, pensioners who consume marketed output and produce none, members of the armed services, and so on. If these groups purchase more marketed output than the workers and companies of the market sector make available to them, as a surplus over the latter's own requirements, the difference will be imported and produce a deficit in the current account of the balance of payments[1]. If we write Y^* for net marketed output, C^* for the consumption of marketed output by those who produce it and I^* for the investment of marketed output by the companies of the market sector, then these will produce a surplus of marketed output of $Y^* - C^* - I^*$ which is available to the remainder of the economy. If G^* of this is consumed from government-financed incomes and invested in the non-market sector, that is in roads, defence projects, and other public investments for which no charges are made, the marketed output that will be available to the rest of the world will be $Y^* - C^* - I^* - G^*$. What goes to the rest of the world is

[1] The full implications of a division of the economy into market and non-market sectors, and the relevant equations, are set out by Bacon and Eltis [1978]. See also Johnston [1975] where this division is first set out.

exports less imports of marketed output, for which we can write B^* or the current account trade balance. It follows that

$$B^* = Y^* - C^* - I^* - G^*, \text{ or alternatively that } B^*/Y^* = (Y^* - C^* - I^*)/Y^* - G^*/Y^*$$

In simple terms, $(Y^* - C^* - I^*)/Y^*$ is the surplus of marketed output made available by the market sector expressed as a ratio of marketed output, G^*/Y^* is the ratio of government-financed purchases of marketed output to total marketed output, while B^*/Y^* is the balance-of-payments surplus on current account as a ratio of marketed output. It is therefore being suggested that the ratio of the current account balance-of-payments surplus to marketed output will equal the proportion of marketed output that is made available as a surplus by the market sector, less the ratio of market output that is purchased with government-financed incomes and by the government directly. Thus, if market sector companies and the self-employed consume 50 per cent of their net output and invest 10 per cent, the surplus they can make available to the remainder of the economy, $(Y^* - C^* - I^*)/Y^*$, will be 40 per cent. If 45 per cent of marketed output is consumed and invested from government-financed incomes by public service workers, recipients of social transfers, and in the form of non-market investment, G^*/Y^* will be 45 per cent, and the fact that market sector workers and companies themselves use up 60 per cent of their output, leaving just 40 per cent over for others, and that government-financed workers, etc., consume 45 per cent means that the current account balance-of-payments deficit, B^*/Y^*, will necessarily be 5 per cent of output. The extra 5 per cent of government-financed consumption and investment can only come from overseas in the form of an excess of imports over exports. The simplest way of presenting this relationship is to write e^* for $(Y^* - C^* - I^*)/Y^*$, the rate of surplus of the market sector, g^* for G^*/Y^*, the proportion of marketed output consumed and purchased by government and with government-financed incomes, and b^* for B^*/Y^*, the ratio of the current account surplus to marketed output. This gives the following result:

$$b^* = e^* - g^*$$

This equation can be estimated quite simply for the United Kingdom from the official data available, and this is done in Table 3. In this table, e^*,the rate of surplus of the market sector, is made up of the weighted average of the surpluses of private companies, public cor-

Table 3 - British Surpluses in Marketed Output[a], Government Demand for Marketed Output and the Balance of Payments, 1963-1980

	1963-67	1968-72	1973-76	1977-80
Rate of surplus of:				
(14) private companies	34.6	37.8	35.8	41.0
(15) public corporations	5.9	17.0	8.3	29.0
(16) the self-employed	29.9	32.3	41.3	44.9
(17) weighted average (e^*)	30.8	34.5	34.5	40.8
(18) Marketed output purchased by government and with government-financed incomes (g^*)	33.0	35.7	40.1	40.5
Balance of payments[b]				
(19) predicted ($b^* = e^* - g^*$)	-2.2	-1.2	-5.6	+0.3
(20) actual (at factor cost)	-1.8	-0.6	-5.1	+0.1

[a] Percentage of net marketed output. - [b] Surplus (+) or deficit (-) on current account.

Source: See the Appendix.

porations and the self-employed. It will be evident from the table that the public corporations have made smaller surpluses of marketed output available to the rest of the economy than private sector companies and the self-employed; this has important implications which will be discussed.

It may appear surprising after the information set out in Table 1 that the public corporations produced surpluses of marketed output of any kind. Table 1, however, set out their surpluses of value-added over wages and interest; for these the entire wage bill is deducted from their value-added to determine how much net revenue is surplus to their wage payments. The workers' entire wages, however, are not expended on marketed output. Of each £100 of wages and salaries in the 1970s about £30 was paid in taxes to the government and about £10 was saved, so only about £60 was actually spent on marketed output. A public corporation with a net value-added of £100 which paid £100 of wages and had no other costs would earn no financial surplus over wages. It would, however, produce a marketed output surplus of £40 because it produces £100 of marketed output, of which only £60 is bought back by its workers, with the result that £40 of marketed output remains to be purchased by pensioners, workers in the public services, or by consumers overseas.

The table shows that the balance-of-payments surpluses and deficits on current account are extremely close to the actual ones.

What emerges from Table 3 is that in the periods 1963-1967 and 1973-1976 the public corporations provided rates of surplus of marketed output which fell massively short of those necessary to meet the needs of the state. The required surpluses were provided in these periods almost exclusively by private sector companies. While the public corporations provided an adequate rate of surplus in 1977-1980, this was only achieved by cutting their net investment to less than 3 per cent of the marketed output they produced, as was shown in the previous section. Over the entire period 1963-1980, the average needs of the state amounted to 37.0 per cent of marketed output; private sector companies provided during this time an average rate of surplus of 37.2 per cent, and the self-employed a rate of surplus of 36.4 per cent. Private sector companies and the self-employed, therefore, provided a rate of surplus which was commensurate with the need to provide for social services, pensions, roads and defence. In contrast, the public corporations provided a rate of surplus which averaged just 14.6 per cent. This means that if the whole economy had priced and invested like the public corporations, it would only have been possible for government to make use of about 15 per cent of marketed output in the form of consumption by its employees, social transfers, and non-market capital projects. If government absorbed 37 per cent of marketed output in these ways, while the market sector only made 15 per cent available because it priced and invested entirely like the British public corporations, a balance-of-payments deficit on current account of some 22 per cent of marketed output would rapidly emerge. This might be financeable for a few months by international borrowing, but as soon as this proved impossible the exchange rate would collapse to produce rapid inflation, and the introduction of all-embracing foreign exchange controls, but these would be futile so long as the government attempted to absorb vastly more than the market sector's surplus of marketed output. It is a rule of arithmetic that the market sector surplus of marketed output has to be large enough to cover the marketed output requirements of government, if resort to foreign sources for marketed output is to be avoided, and that any shortfall must be made good from overseas with all the inevitable consequences.

In Britain the public corporations produce only around one-tenth of marketed output, so the fact that they produced surpluses which averaged only 15 per cent against the necessary 37 per cent did not produce devastating adverse effects. However, in the period 1973-1976 the Keynesian analysis that led to underpricing by the nationalised industries spilt over into the private sector. In their attempts to establish wage and price controls that were effective, both Mr. Heath's and Mr. Wilson's governments attempted to administer the prices of private sector companies. These had to refer price increases to a price commission which had the right to postpone the increases while the case for them was being investigated, and to forbid them. It will be seen from Table 3 that in this period only the self-employed provided surpluses which were adequate to meet the needs of the state, which required 40.1 per cent of marketed output. The private sector companies provided a rate of surplus of 35.8 per cent and the public corporations a rate of surplus of only 8.3 per cent, with the result that there was an overall rate of surplus of only 34.5 per cent. This produced a current account deficit of the balance of payments of over 5 per cent of marketed output, which obviously added to the weakness of sterling and the inflation in that period[1]. The year when the combination of underpricing by the nationalised industries and price controls leading to underpricing in the private sector had the most pernicious effects was 1974. The methods of estimation used to derive Table 3 show that, in that year, the state required 39.6 per cent of marketed output and the self-employed provided a rate of surplus of 41.0 per cent, but private sector companies, as a result of the strictness of the price controls which were then being applied, could

[1] It is to be noted that changes in raw material and especially oil prices which must obviously influence the balance of payments do so by influencing the rate of marketed output surplus: a higher oil price, for instance, squeezes the rate of surplus if companies cannot widen their profit margins sufficiently to produce the same net percentage margin on value-added as before. The rate of surplus in the market sector will also be reduced if workers consume a higher fraction of income as a consequence of higher oil and raw material prices. In practice, the higher import prices after 1973 may well have contributed to the squeeze in percentage profit margins which occurred, but there is no indication that it raised the proportion of workers' incomes consumed - rather the contrary, as the savings ratio rose after 1972.

provide a rate of surplus of only 29.0 per cent, while the public corporations which were both underpricing and investing heavily provided no surplus at all. The result was that the market sector itself absorbed over 70 per cent of marketed output, leaving just 30 per cent for the government (and for consumption from government-financed incomes). As the government actually absorbed almost 40 per cent of marketed output, a 10 per cent shortage had to be met from overseas. The predicted deficit in the current account of the balance of payments from the formula $b^* = e^* - g^*$ was 10.0 per cent and the actual deficit 8.8 per cent of marketed output. The lesson is that the underpricing of final outputs in relation to costs, which governments that use a wage-price spiral model to explain inflation sometimes impose on their economies, is one of the most certain recipes for balance-of-payments collapse and a great acceleration of inflation. Nationalised industries produce only a modest fraction of output in Britain and most West European economies, so underpricing by nationalised industries alone is likely to impose a burden of no more than 2 to 5 per cent of output on the rest of the community - or the world economy. However, where governments also force a considerable fraction of the private sector to underprice in a vain effort to slow down the wage-price spiral as in Britain in 1973-1974, the adverse effect on price inflation and on the balance of payments can be very severe indeed[1].

The present analysis of the pricing of the nationalised industries by examining its effect on their surpluses of marketed output confirms several of the conclusions of the previous more conventional analysis of their financial accounts. There were evidently very different policy approaches by the British authorities in the periods 1963-1967 and 1973-1976 from those of 1968-1972 and 1977-1980. We have already seen that in the former periods these industries forced heavy borrow-

---

[1] This is one crucial reason why the opportunities which were offered to new Left governments to transform Chile and Portugal led to such severe balance-of-payments collapse and, in the case of Chile, hyperinflation. The new governments attempted to run entire economies like British nationalised industries with high investment, underpricing, and a tolerance of overmanning. This necessarily produced a severe reduction in the rate of surplus of the market sector precisely when non-market state expenditures were being greatly increased. The accompanying budget deficits which were partly financed by monetary expansion were an interdependent element in the monetary collapse that followed. For some of the relevant Chilean statistics, see Eltis [1979a, pp. 136 ff.].

ing onto the government. It is clear from the present analysis that they also undermined the balance of payments through their small marketed output surpluses. In contrast, during the periods 1968-1972 and 1977-1980, the nationalised industries imposed less need to borrow, and they made larger marketed output surpluses available to the remainder of the economy. The two kinds of analysis give complementary accounts of the pressures they imposed. However, the effects of large government borrowing which underpricing shows in the traditional approach are perhaps less precisely predictable than the effects of inadequate marketed output surpluses. It is as clear-cut as anything in economics can be that aggregate marketed output surpluses which fall short of the absorption of marketed output by the government must produce balance-of-payments deficits on current account, and that these will destroy the international value of the currency if they are sufficiently severe and prolonged.

IV. The Government Policies That Are Needed

The above account of the pricing and investment of the British nationalised industries in the period 1963-1980 has brought out that these have been strongly influenced by considerations which bear no relation to any text-book account of how the state should price. They have been entirely subject to the need to further the macroeconomic balance of the economy. Unfortunately, British governments and the economists who influenced them have been extremely unsuccessful at diagnosing what the appropriate macroeconomic policies are. The microeconomic balance of the economy between nationalised and non-nationalised prices has therefore been sacrificed to a series of macroeconomic approaches which, while they appeared sensible at the time, appear eccentric in retrospect. The British economy had to live through the successive nostrums of investment at any price to further growth which dominated policy until 1966, underpricing to slow inflation which dominated policy from 1973 to 1975 and underinvestment and, since 1979, overpricing to contain government borrowing which has dominated public policy with regard to the nationalised industries since 1976.

The correct microeconomic policies are extremely complex but one of the best-known principles can be summarised briefly. Prices of publicly and privately produced goods and services should have similar price-to-marginal-cost ratios with the qualification that given the

Relative Prices and Resource Allocation

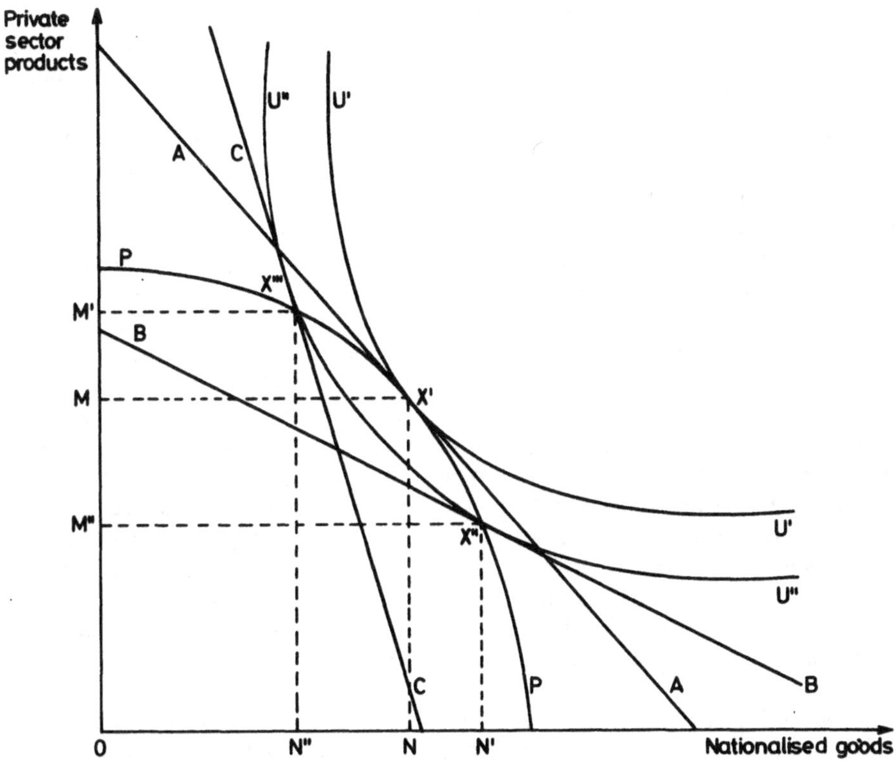

multiplicity of price-marginal-cost ratios in the private sector, it is especially important to achieve similar ratios for close substitutes. In the diagram, PP is the production possibility curve between products produced by the private sector and by nationalised industries and it shows that more can only be produced by the nationalised industries if less is produced by private sector companies. U'U' and U'' U'' are indifference curves which indicate consumers' preferences between these commodities. As is well known, community indifference curves like these can only be drawn if there is a certain homogeneity of tastes within a country, and that assumption must be made here. In the conditions assumed in the diagram, consumers purchase the quantities of privately produced and nationalised commodities which are given by tangency between the budget line and the highest possible indifference curve. If the government has the means to enable an economy to produce at full employment, the economy will produce somewhere on the production possibility curve, and not inside this. If the budget line is AA, consumers will reach the highest possible indifference curve, U'U', at X' and purchase ON of products of nationalised industries and OM of products produced in the private sector. The condition for this text-book optimum is that the slope of the budget line, which is (price of nationalised goods/price of private sector products), should equal the slope of the production possibility curve, which is (marginal cost of nationalised goods/marginal cost of private sector products). If there is a different budget line, for instance BB where the relative price of nationalised industry products is lower than relative marginal costs, or CC where it is higher, consumers will find equilibrium at X'' or X''' on the lower indifference curve U''U''. If relative prices are those shown by BB where relative nationalised industry prices are below relative marginal costs, consumers will find their equilibrium at X'' where they purchase more nationalised industry products, ON' instead of ON, and less privately produced products, OM'' in place of OM, but the combination of ON' and OM'' will place them on a lower indifference curve than the combination of OM and ON that they achieve at X where relative prices are the same as relative marginal costs. Similarly, when relative prices are those shown by the budget line CC, consumers will purchase ON'' of the nationalised goods and OM' of privately produced products at X''', but this will give them less satisfaction than the ON of the one and the OM of the other that they achieve at X.

This basic result that relative prices should reflect relative marginal costs must be modified in a number of ways. First, as has already been indicated, where there are - as is indeed the case in reality - many price/marginal-cost ratios in the private sector against which nationalised industries might match their prices, it is getting the relative prices of substitutes right that matters most. Second, there are all kinds of externalities, positive and negative, which mean that social and private costs and benefits will diverge, and it is the social costs and benefits which should influence actual pricing. There is, however, no justification for disturbing relative prices in order to achieve macroeconomic objectives, because these can always be achieved in a Pareto-superior way without disturbing relative prices.

Thus, if there is a uniform rate of tax which applies to the products of both the nationalised industries and private sector companies such as VAT, this can be raised when governments believe rightly or wrongly that they should raise prices in order to reduce the government's need to borrow, and VAT can be lowered if governments believe that they can slow down inflation by reducing the general price level for a few weeks. A raising or lowering of VAT need not disturb the ratio (price of nationalised goods/price of private sector products), so if this is optimal before an alteration in VAT it should also be optimal afterwards. Finding the optimal ratio is of course an immensely difficult problem, both in theory and in practice, but it is arguably the effort to achieve this that should be the paramount influence over nationalised industry prices and not the authorities' macroeconomic judgements. These can be followed through, for instance, by fixing the appropriate rate of VAT without disturbing the *relative* prices of the products of the nationalised industries which should properly be fixed as a result of microeconomic and not macroeconomic judgement.

For investment, there must be criteria which are independent of macroeconomic exigencies, and the correct mechanism in economic theory for the allocation of capital between the sectors of the economy is the rate of interest tempered by the positive and negative externalities which should influence actual cost benefit calculations. The correct way to reduce investment is to require a higher prospective rate of return from all investment projects; this was the device which Mr. Jenkins used to achieve the reduction in investment that he considered necessary in 1967-1970. Restricting investment through cash limits, the device currently in use in the United Kingdom, can obviously produce extraordinarily inefficient microeconomic results. One possible effect is that there may be virtually no net investment at all, if wages absorb the entire permitted cash limits; in this case, investments with prospective returns much in excess of those of the private sector might not be able to go ahead. Alternatively, within the public sector it is perfectly conceivable that one nationalised industry might be within its cash limit and might then invest to achieve a zero net return in order to absorb its permitted ration of cash while another might have prospective projects which could yield a real return of 20 per cent and be unable to exploit them because it had exhausted its cash allowance. No text-book and no first-year student could devise so absurd a way of allocating investment funds. Why is it, then, that intelligent and sophisticated politicians (and their economic advisers) have adopted this system?

The most plausible explanation is that they have come to the conclusion that the many methods of controlling investment and of monitoring decisions that are Pareto-superior to cash limits are impractical.

It might be thought that this would be the case if it was impossible to obtain dispassionate assessments of the probable returns from investments from the managements of the industries concerned because they saw it as their role to produce overoptimistic forecasts with the objective of obtaining the maximum possible increase in the capital stock of their industries. Britain was at one point spending 3 per cent of its national income on the atomic energy programme which now produces something like 3 per cent of the country's total energy requirements, which is a rather poor rate of exchange [see Maddock, 1975, pp. 314 and 321]. At the time that the decision to go ahead with Concorde was being taken, the aircraft industry was producing forecasts that it would sell 150 mainly for North American routes [The Times, London, 30 September, 1971]. These forecasts were for government consumption: they were not intended to persuade the industry itself to go ahead and produce Concorde with private sector financial resources. British governments have been all too easily taken in by overoptimistic prospectuses for science-based investments. The lack of scrutiny of the calculations of those who sought massive sums calls to mind Professor Flores' Spanish epigram: "The private sector can be defined as the part of the economy which the government controls: the public sector is the part that nobody controls".

A failure to scrutinise the projections of would-be borrowers of public funds effectively was, however, in so far as it occurred, a managerial weakness on the part of the Treasury. Many private companies have divisions with vast and expensive technological ambitions, but they also have accountants independent of these divisions who advise on the investment plans presented. Those companies which are successful necessarily discipline and control the divisions which are overoptimistic in their efforts to obtain massive finance for their own projects. That British governments have often failed to contain over-expensive and ambitious science-based investment projects has been a managerial failure, and it could in principle be corrected through the adoption of methods of financial control and scrutiny of internal accounts and calculations of a kind which are a sine qua non for survival in private industry[1]. If lack of scrutiny of investment projects is the explanation of the appalling investment decisions of the past, then the remedy is more effective scrutiny accompanied by high required real interest rates (as in 1967-1970).

---

[1] See Henderson [1977] for a valuable economic analysis of the errors involved in the British Concorde and nuclear energy decisions, and of the administrative reforms that could avoid their repetition.

There is a further explanation of the belief that there is no alternative to cash limits which is perhaps more plausible. The evidence of Table 1 which indicated that even the huge price rises of the nationalised industries in recent years have failed to raise the net value-added of the public corporations above wage costs is compatible with an appalling productivity performance by several of these industries. That could be indicative of very great X-inefficiencies, productivity levels vastly lower than an effective working of plant and equipment should make possible[1]. This could have several explanations. In periods of rising national unemployment the unions have had clear incentives to sustain employment. They have been strong enough in several nationalised industries to obtain wage increases which were in line with those obtained in the private sector, or indeed which exceeded these and to offer inadequate increases in productivity or reductions in manning ratios as a quid pro quo. British Rail had a current cost operating loss of £707 mill. in 1980/81 before the crediting of government subsidies to keep unprofitable routes open, and an estimated loss before these subsidies of £996 mill. in 1981/82[2]. The unions have managed to insist that there should be two men in the cab of each locomotive, even though the function of the second man used to be to shovel coal. They then often have private arrangements or even rosters where one man stays at home; this emerged after a recent accident in which one driver was killed while the other, who was also being paid, was asleep at home. This is just one example which has recently come to light. There must be innumerable others which the managements of these industries are thoroughly familiar with but which have not been as widely publicised. X-inefficiencies in the nationalised industries of these kinds can only be possible as a result of acquiescence by managements in work practices which many other unions would wish to emulate if they could. Directors who are often appointed in periods of Labour government may be extremely sympathetic to the concept of state control and of non-commercial management and they may sometimes see their goal as the maintenance of good labour relations, and the avoidance of interruptions to services through disputes, rather than the achievement of surpluses over costs.

Objective evidence of X-inefficiencies in the British nationalised industries has been produced in a recent study by Pryke, who had pre-

---

[1] Harvey Leibenstein [1966] pioneered work on the analysis of the causes of X-inefficiency and summarised some of his subsequent work in [1979].

[2] See the Government's Expenditure Plans for the fiscal years from 1982/83 to 1984/85 in HMSO, Cmnd 8494-II [1982, pp. 75 and 77].

viously published a book which made extremely favourable assessments of their efficiency [Pryke, 1971]. In 1982, however, he compared microeconomic efficiency in three activites where private and nationalised companies compete and this led him to form a very different view [Pryke, 1982]. The nationalised British Airways competes with British Caledonian on several routes, the nationalised British Sea-Link ferries compete with Townsend Thoreson in the English Channel, and the nationalised British Gas Corporation and Electricity Boards sell gas and electrical appliances in competition with several private firms. In each case, Pryke found that the real unit costs of the nationalised corporations were between 10 and 20 per cent higher than those of their private sector competitors, despite certain specific advantages which they possessed. He concluded [Pryke, 1982]: "In the areas that have been investigated, and on the basis of the comparisons which I have made, public enterprise has performed relatively poorly in terms of its competitive position, has used labour and capital inefficiently and has been less profitable [p. 70]...What public ownership does is to eliminate the threat of takeover and ultimately of bankruptcy and the need, which all private undertakings have from time to time, to raise money from the market. Public ownership provides a comfortable life and destroys the commercial ethic" [p. 80].

Rightly or wrongly, Ministers in Mrs. Thatcher's government have come to believe that the nationalised industries do not make good use of such capital as they obtain. The Ministers therefore believe that extra money that finds its way to these industries will increase wages, cause overmanning of the work force, or go into capital projects with highly uncertain benefits. By rationing cash to such industries, Ministers believe that they may at least minimise the damage. The trade union leaders in these industries can be assumed to be the true arbiters. They can either use their cash limit to employ a falling labour force at rapidly rising wages, or if they prefer, to keep productivity down and sustain employment for their members, but in this case they have to do without substantial pay increases. The union leadership has a third option of keeping pay per person down and increasing productivity by reducing overmanning which would leave extra resources over for investment. In general, this has not been a popular option and union leaders have preferred to absorb the available cash into payments to their members, differing only as to whether they should take large pay increases and accept redundancies, or the small pay increases that become inevitable (with cash limits) once the continuation of overmanning and low productivity is insisted on.

The Conservative government's resort to cash limits is explicable if this is a true diagnosis of the basic choices in some of the nationalised industries and it can obviously be true of only some. The railways are an obvious candidate, as are the industries from which Pryke's examples are taken. British Steel, where the private sector produces 25 per cent of steel needs with about 10 per cent of those working in the industry, is another. British Telecom is in contrast a well-managed corporation which generates much finance internally and invests heavily. For those industries in which the principal discipline is to be found in cash limits, some alternative approach to economic management is clearly needed. One new initiative whose effectiveness it is too early to assess has been the appointment of new-style managements in the hope that they would reassert their right to establish manning ratios and therefore to have some control over productivity. Sir Michael Edwardes, the Chairman of British Leyland, has persuaded the union rank and file to accept his management rather than that of the unions whom the workers have ignored or over-ruled by voting in a sequence of disputes. In consequence, productivity in British Leyland has been rising rapidly. The financial requirements of the company are still immense, however, and the deficit is still around £500 mill. a year. The next three years will indicate whether the company can go on to generate investable surpluses from its own resources.

It is widely believed in Conservative circles that the institution of nationalisation is itself at the root of the trouble, in that it grants monopoly powers to particular companies, which gives extra power to the trade unions, and at the same time removes the pressures of competition from managements. There might be managements in the private sector who would wish to maintain excellent relations with their trade unions, and who would prefer inefficiency to redundancies, but their companies would head towards bankruptcy if such attitudes then led to actual acquiescence in overmanning on the scale of the nationalised industries. But the trap the Conservatives are in is that those industries which have become chronically inefficient and fallen into the hands of particularly Luddite unions and managerial fellow travellers are precisely those that cannot be de-nationalised or privatised - which would represent an obvious solution to the difficulty. An industry with chronically low productivity and a large external financial requirement clearly cannot be sold on the stock exchange except to a group of shareholders who would buy it in order to sell its assets off at scrap value and close it down. The government has managed to sell off British Aerospace, Cable and Wireless, and to sell some small high-technology firms back to the private sector[1], and it has plans to privatise part of the state's involvements in North Sea oil and gas extraction and distribution and British Airways, but these are precisely those parts of the state's assets which are potentially profitable. What it would desperately wish to be rid of is the Railways, the coal mines, British Steel, and British Leyland, but these are all making large losses. They need to be made potentially profitable before they can be disposed of, and this can only be achieved by new-style managements which Leyland already has, and cash limits to enable them to put pressure on their own unions in favour of necessary productivity improvements.

The other alternative which Mrs. Thatcher's government is pursuing is to increase the pressures of competition upon the nationalised industries themselves. British Airways and British Leyland necessarily face this in any case, but until Mrs. Thatcher's election, the Post Office and the National Bus Company were protected from competition while the British Gas Corporation had the right to buy all North Sea gas. New bus companies can now freely obtain licenses to compete against the National Bus Company. British Telecom is losing its monopoly over telecommunications, and the British Gas Corporation has lost its monopoly of North Sea gas. It would be possible to allow competitors to emerge who could distribute letters more cheaply and quickly than the Post Office, and the introduction of competition may do as much to improve the efficiency of these industries as privatisation.

In assessing the nationalised industries, and government policy with regard to them, two general approaches are possible. First, it can be assumed in line with most text-book accounts that resources are managed as efficiently by publicly controlled as by private companies. The problem is then to ascertain the criteria for optimal investment and pricing so as to achieve the highest practical social welfare - taking externalities fully into account. From the viewpoint of that approach with which parts of this paper have been concerned, British pricing and investment policies have been and are incomprehensible.

The other possibility which cannot be discounted is that the X-inefficiencies of the nationalised industries leave Britain with choices which

---

[1] See HMSO, Cmnd 8494-II [1982, p. 97] for an account of the "Sales of Assets" Mrs. Thatcher's government carried through to yield £999 mill. in 1979/80 and £356 mill. in 1980/81, and the actual assets disposed of.

lie well within the production possibility curve of the figure on page 101. More may then be gained from lessening X-inefficiencies and so moving out to reach the production possibility curve, than from searching for the correct price/marginal cost relationship in order to find the best point on the curve. The excess of wages and salaries over net sales revenues in the public corporations as a whole in 1977-1980 which Table 1 indicates suggests a strong a priori possibility that productivity is inadequate; this is underlined by the fact that wages exceeded net sales revenues by 8 per cent in 1980 when prices had undoubtedly been raised to the point where they should have permitted the emergence of net surpluses. Recession alone ought not to have produced this state of affairs. Pryke's study documents examples where there is no doubt that X-inefficiencies are at the root of the trouble.

The problem of how to remove these is one on which economists are likely to have rather little to contribute. The solution may be greater competition from the private sector, privatisation, or the appointment of new tough managements who may use tight cash limits to compel cooperation from recalcitrant unions. The success of these alternative lines of policy clearly goes far beyond the mere application of correct economic principles.

One question remains. If these vast X-inefficiencies have indeed evolved in the British nationalised industries, and it may be conjectured, almost equally in the nationalised industries of, for instance, Italy, how have they been avoided so far in the nationalised industries of France and West Germany? Which British errors have these countries avoided?

Appendix: The Explanation of the Tables

In an earlier article [Eltis, 1979b], the present author compared the accounts of the British public corporations and British private sector companies on both a financial and a marketed output basis[1]. This data, which forms the basis for several of the lines of Tables 1, 2 and 3, was estimated from CSO [1978]. In the present article the various series are updated from 1977 to 1980, and the years 1976, 1977, 1978, 1979 and 1980 have been estimated from CSO [1981]. Table 3 requires series for the proportion of marketed output which is consumed and invested by government and from government-financed incomes. This was estimated on a factor cost basis by Bacon and Eltis [1979], and the series in their article which ran from 1955 to 1975 has been updated here for the years 1976-1980 from CSO [1981]. The relationship between the lines in the tables of this article and those in the two earlier publications [Eltis, 1979b; Bacon, Eltis, 1979], in which their derivation is fully explained, is as follows[2]:

(1) is ((3)' ÷ (2)') x 100.

(2) is ((4)' ÷ (2)') x 100.

(3) is 100 - (1) - (2).

(4) is ((6)' ÷ (2)') x 100.

(5) is 100 - (1) - (2) - (4).

(6) is ((7)' ÷ (2)') x 100.

(7) is ((8)' ÷ (2)') x 100.

(8) is (5) - (6) - (7). It is also ((9)' ÷ (2)') where (9)' is shown to come extremely close to (10)', the official financial deficit of the public corporations.

---

[1] Mr. Christopher Johnson, the economic adviser to Lloyds Bank and editor of the Review, made a number of extremely helpful suggestions about the correct interpretation and presentation of the data.

[2] In this explanation lines from tables in Eltis [1979b] will be indicated by a prime sign and those from tables in Bacon, Eltis [1979] by a double prime sign.

(9) is income from employment in industrial and commercial companies and institutions [CSO, 1981, Table 1.10] divided by line (16)' times 100 to convert to a percentage.

(10) is dividends and interest paid by companies and financial institutions [CSO, 1981, Table 5.1] with interest paid by building societies and banks omitted (since the interest they receive is omitted from line (16)'), and dividends after 1973 are corrected for the changeover to the imputation system of taxation. This total for interest and dividends is divided by line (16)' and multiplied by 100 to convert to a percentage.

(11) is 100 - (9) - (10).

(12) is ((20)' ÷ (16)').

(13) is 100 - (9) - (10) - (12).

(14) is line (22)'.

(15) is line (23)' .

(16) is estimated similarly to lines (22)' and (23)', viz., the net output of the personal sector is derived by adding its factor incomes [CSO, 1981, Table 1.10] and the rates it pays [ibid., Table 4.8], and subtracting its capital consumption [ibid., Table 11.9]. It is assumed that the same fraction of this income is consumed as that of non-transfer personal incomes in general, and the marketed surplus of the personal sector will be its net output less its consumption and less its total net investment [ibid., Tables 11.10 and 12.4]. The rate of surplus is this surplus divided by the estimate of net output, then multiplied by 100 to convert to a percentage.

(17) is the weighted average of (14), (15) and (16), weighting being by the net marketed outputs of the three sectors.

(18) is ((42)'' + (43)'') x 100.

(19) is (17) - (18).

(20) is line (40)'' times 100 to convert to a percentage.

References

Bacon, Robert, Walter Eltis, Britain's Economic Problem: Too Few Producers. 2nd Ed., London 1978.

--, --, "The Measurement of the Growth of the Non-Market Sector and its Influence: a Reply to Hadjimatheou and Skouras". The Economic Journal, Vol. 89, 1979, pp. 402-415.

Beenstock, Michael, Alan Budd, Peter Warburton, "Monetary Policy, Expectations and Real Exchange Rate Dynamics". In: Walter Eltis, Peter J.N. Sinclair (Eds.), The Money Supply and the Exchange Rate. Oxford Economic Papers Supplement, Oxford 1981, pp. 85-119.

Black, John, "A Savings and Investment Approach to Devaluation". The Economic Journal, Vol. 69, 1959, pp. 267-274.

Central Statistical Office (CSO), National Income and Expenditure. London, various issues.

Eltis, Walter [1979a], "How Rapid Public Sector Growth Can Undermine the Growth of the National Product". In: Wilfred Beckerman (Ed.), Slow Growth in Britain: Causes and Consequences. British Association for the Advancement of Science, Section F (Economics) 1978 Meeting, Oxford 1979, pp. 118-139.

-- [1979b], "The True Deficits of the Public Corporations". Lloyds Bank Review, 1979, No. 131, pp. 1-20.

Harrod, Roy F., Policy Against Inflation. London 1958.

Henderson, Patrick D., "Two British Errors: Their Probable Size and Some Possible Lessons". Oxford Economic Papers, Vol. 29, 1977, pp. 159-205.

Her Majesty's Stationery Office (HMSO), Command Paper (Cmnd) No. 8494-II. London, March 1982.

Johnston, John, "A Macro-Model of Inflation". The Economic Journal, Vol. 85, 1975, pp. 288-308.

Leibenstein, Harvey, "Allocative Efficiency versus X-efficiency". The American Economic Review, Vol. 56, 1966, pp. 392-415.

--, "A Branch of Economics is Missing: Micro-Micro Theory". The Journal of Economic Literature, Vol. 17, 1979, pp. 477-502.

Maddock, Sir Ieuan, "Science, Technology and Industry". In: Proceedings of the Royal Society of London, (Series A), Vol. 345. London 1975, pp. 295-326.

National Economic Development Council (NEDC), Energy Task Force, Reports of the Energy Task Force. NECD (81) 15, London, February 1981; NEDC (81) 59, London, November 1981.

National Economic Development Office (NEDO), Conditions Favourable to Faster Growth. London 1963.

--, The Growth of the Economy. London 1964.

Pryke, Richard W.S., Public Enterprise in Practice: The British Experience of Nationalization over 2 Decades. London 1971.

--, "The Comparative Performance of Public and Private Enterprise". Fiscal Studies, Vol. 3, 1982, pp. 68-81.

Comment

Wolfram Engels

I. Introduction: The Problem Stated

Let us call a "public enterprise" an organization which produces goods or services and sells them in the market and in which the means of production are owned by the government. The definition excludes pure public goods because they can not be sold in the market and it excludes those goods and services which could be sold in the market but which are factually financed through the budget or non-market-mechanisms. This is the case in West Germany with schools, universities and hospitals among others. The question thus is whether the state should be the owner and organizer of the means of production for private goods which are to be sold in the market.

We have different organizational alternatives which have to be valued by the respective welfare function. Assuming a market economy, the state can pursue its goal to increase welfare by setting up a legal framework including the regulation and supervision of private enterprises, by taxing or subsidizing certain activities of private enterprises, or by producing private goods by public enterprises.

The first part of this paper deals with the budgetary consequences of public enterprises. The second part deals with the welfare consequences, and the third part states the conditions under which the public production of private goods may be advisable. Proposals are made to improve the tax system, the public accounting procedures and the organization of public enterprises, to first improve the performance of these enterprises and second hold down the political forces aiming at a further enlargement of the public enterprise sector.

II. Public Enterprises and the Budget

Whatever the purpose of having public enterprises is, the ownership will have budgetary consequences. The state may have to bear losses or receive profits from its enterprises. Public enterprises may need investment capital, which means accumulation of public wealth. In recent years and in more and more countries of the world the public sector enterprises have developed into budgetary problems. That was first noticed in Italy and Great Britain, as was clearly shown in Eltis' paper. It has not yet been noticed in France and West Germany - mainly because of lack of statistics. But the most spectacular cases were Chile and Turkey.

The public enterprise sector in West Germany today is bigger than in most other western countries. More than 20 per cent of manufacturing, 60 per cent of banking, 60 per cent of forestry, large parts of the insurance business, of the housing companies and of real estate is in the hands of the government [Engels et al., 1974]. The federal government alone is involved in about 900 business enterprises, not counting the big public companies, such as the Deutsche Bundespost, Deutsche Bundesbahn, Deutsche Bundesbank. 25 years ago the state (federal, state and local) had an income from economic activity of about 4 billion deutsche mark. This had changed to a loss of about 11 billion deutsche mark by 1980. But this loss is not to be confounded with the deficit. Thus the Deutsche Bundesbahn has a loss of about 4, 5 billion deutsche mark, but a deficit of about 14 billion deutsche mark. In fact the picture is much more friendly on an income level (profits and losses) than on the account level (deficits and surpluses).

Like private enterprises, public enterprises have to finance their investments through retained profits or through outside capital. A number of the public enterprises are profitable - the savings banks, the Bundesbank, the Lufthansa, Volkswagen, Veba, etc. But the profits are needed for investment financing. There is no money for the public treasury left. On the other hand, other enterprises produce losses. In all those cases, not only do the losses have to be covered by budgetary means, but also the state has to finance investments. There is in West Germany no official estimate of the budget burden[1]. The total loss of 11 billion deutsche mark from economic activity of the government is a balance of losses produced by some of the enterprises and profits produced by others. If we suppose that the total sum of losses is 25 billion deutsche mark, then the balance of 11 billion deutsche mark requires profits by other enterprises of 14 billion deutsche mark. If we calculate that all losses have to be covered by the budget but that on the other hand profits do not contribute to the budget, then the net cash burden would be about 25 billion deutsche mark. To calculate the total cash burden we have to increase this sum by the amount for investment financing of loss-producing enterprises. If that is 10 billion deutsche mark, a very rough estimate comes out with a cash burden of 35 billion deutsche mark.

That is not all. Many of the public enterprises are or have been tax-exempt (Bundesbank, Kreditanstalt für Wiederaufbau, Deutsche Pfandbriefanstalt, etc.) or have to pay lower taxes (savings banks, public housing companies, Bundesbahn, Bundespost, etc.). A further part of the public economic activity is not even counted as business. That is the case in many of the activities of the local governments with busses, handicraft and repair shops, garbage collection, printing shops, laundries, parks departments, slaughter houses, building and window-cleaning departments, etc. The Bundespost has to pay a tax of 6 2/3 per cent of total sales. In actuality, this tax duty has normally been changed into a credit to the Bundespost which later has been converted into equity capital. The transportation tax which the Bundesbahn legally has to pay is a mere fiction. The tax receipts forgone are very difficult to estimate. But the total sum should be somewhere between 5 and 10 billion deutsche mark.

---

[1] The estimate given here is updated from my previous estimates [Engels, 1979; 1981a; 1981b; 1981c].

If we want to calculate the total financial burden which the public enterprise sector poses, we have to make up a hypothetical calculation. The governments could sell all their property in enterprises and the proceeds could be used to repay public debts. Let us suppose that in this case the respective companies would be subject to general tax law. The total value of all public enterprises, excluding marketable assets which do not have the form of business firms, should be between 300 and 400 billion deutsche mark. Calculated at an interest rate of 9 per cent, the privatization would save between 27 and 36 billion deutsche mark in interest payments. That altogether leaves us with an estimate of plausible figures between 40 billion deutsche mark at minimum and 80 billion deutsche mark at maximum for the net burden of the public enterprise sector to the budget (losses, investment financing, tax exemptions, interests forgone counted together). Just for comparison: the total proceeds from the income tax (including wage tax) were 145 billion for the same year (1980).

It has been argued that only the profitable public enterprises could be sold in the market. That is not correct. For any enterprise there would be a price with the lowest boundary of zero. But even the Deutsche Bundesbahn would have a positive market value. It has also been argued that the privatization of profitable public firms would be no relief for the budget. That is also not true. The Deutsche Bundesbank did not contribute to the budget between 1970 and 1980, but made an excess payment of 10 billion deutsche mark in 1980 to the budget. Thus for the timespan between 1971 and 1981 the net contribution was about 1 billion deutsche mark per year. If we would sell the Bundesbank in the marketplace it would have a value between 70 and 80 billion deutsche mark cautiously estimated (that is about the value of the hidden reserves alone). If we count a "normal" profit from banking activities and the issue of banknotes of 4 billion deutsche mark then, at normal tax rates, the Bundesbank would have to pay about 2.4 billion in taxes. Interests forgone of about 6.3 billion plus taxes of 2.4 billion yield a cash receipt to the budget of 8.7 billion deutsche mark per year. Thus in any case - whether loss-producing enterprise or profitable enterprise - the privatization would relieve the budget. The figures are very rough estimates. At any rate the evidence is sufficient to show that even in West Germany, the financial burden is very substantial and increasing from year to year.

III. The Welfare Contribution of Public Enterprises

The contribution of public enterprises to total wealth can be much different from their contribution to the budget. The budgetary burden may be caused by underpricing (selling below cost), by inefficiency or by the accumulation of public wealth. Only in the case of inefficiency can the budget burden represent the burden to total welfare. In the case of underpricing of goods or services and of accumulation of public wealth it may be quite different.

Underpricing and Redistribution. One of the justifications of government business activity is the "social" argument: Goods or services are to be provided at a lower price than the market could. There are, however, alternative methods of redistribution which are more efficient. Subsidies in kind are inferior to subsidies in money and unconditioned subsidies are more valuable than conditioned subsidies [see Aaron, Furstenberg, 1971; Muth, 1973]. The liberal, who holds the opinion that all men are equal and that people can judge their own interests better than the government, can not accept that the state pushes prices below or above their market equilibrium values in order to encourage or suppress consumption. The paternalist, whether socialist or conservative, always likes to impose his own value judgements on other people.

The second justification for over- or underpricing of public business enterprises is the situation where the market price of a good or service would be below or above its pareto-optimal value. That is the case with monopolies or if external effects occur. The organizational alternative to public production in this situation would be either the taxation or subsidizing of a private production in the case of external effects, or regulation and supervision in the case of private monopolies. Public production is the worst solution. We do not know of any rule which maintains the manager's interest in high internal efficiency and low prices at the same time[1]. In reality the most probable outcome of such a public enterprise will be high prices, low internal efficiency and low profits or even losses. The losses are justified by the management with their duty to provide the respective good or service at a low price and the fact that the price is low is "proven" with regard to the costs. The telephone service of the Deutsche Bundespost for instance is poor compared to that of AT & T in the U.S., but it charges more than double the price. If on the other hand managers are paid partly according to profits or if the government is interested in profits of the respective enterprises, then the managers will be cost-conscious on the one hand but on the other hand the consumer will be ruthlessly exploited. The worst of all possible solutions is the case of postal services in West Germany. The Deutsche Bundespost charges at the time the highest prices for letters and packages in the world and at the same time produces heavy losses. In any case the government supervision of a private monopoly is the superior solution, for the government is then a countervailing power. Where government production occurs there is virtually no control over the enterprise.

Efficiency and Organization. The main discussion point in the last ten years in West Germany as well as in other countries has been the question of internal efficiency (X-efficiency) of publicly owned firms. The proponents of a denationalization of public enterprises argued that as a rule the internal efficiency of public enterprises is lower than that of private enterprises. Some of the empirical investigations show that private enterprises

[1] The problem has been discussed in the older German literature on Gemeinwirtschaftliche Unternehmen (public-interest-oriented enterprises). For the more recent discussion see e.g. Vogelsang, Finsinger [1979] and Laffont, Mashen [1981].

compare favorably with public enterprises, whereas no case is known where a public enterprise has a superior performance to a private one [Blankart, 1978]. On the other hand, there are quite a number of highly efficient public firms, such as Volkswagen, Lufthansa and the savings banks (Sparkassen) in West Germany, or the nationalized banks and the Regie Renault in France. The dominant opinion in West Germany at the time seems to be that efficiency is not so much a question of ownership as it is one of internal organization and environment. The argument is that public enterprises which have to compete in the market and which pay their managers salaries similar to those paid by private enterprises should as a rule have a productivity similar to that of private enterprises. In the case of big private corporations the ownership has become less and less important.

Intuitively appealing as the argument is, it overlooks two factors. First, it neglects the fact that politicians are motivated differently than private owners and that the power of the government exceeds by far any private power. A private firm which has no profit or produces losses will be closed down, or will at least not get new equity capital. If the losses are big enough the firm fails and disappears from the market. Private owners select the management according to its assumed ability to make and keep the firm profitable. Governments act differently. Political parties attract able people by offering them a political career. The most profitable jobs in a political career are the jobs in the management of public enterprises. The political man is selected according to his assumed political abilities, which may or may not coincide with managerial abilities.

Second, the government or politicians are not personally interested in the profits of public enterprises. If such an enterprise produces losses it is not closed down and if it fails it does not disappear from the market. Since the employees of public enterprises know that the government will save their jobs even at the cost of high losses, their behavior will be different from that of the employees of private firms. It is more probable that they will demand higher wages than are compatible with the competitiveness of the firm and that the management is prepared to grant such higher wages. Ultimately the equity financing of public corporations is not controlled by the market, i.e. it is not selected according to expected profitability (productivity).

Neither of these arguments rules out the possibility that public enterprises are profitable and efficient. But the arguments combined make it at least probable that in an empirical investigation we should observe that, on the average, public corporations are less profitable than private corporations. In the case of West Germany, the national accounting shows that public corporations as a whole do have substantial losses; these are even greater if we exclude the state monopolies such as telecommunication and the issue of banknotes.

From a theoretical point of view we should expect that internal organization and environment (market or monopoly) do count. A public enterprise should be less efficient if it is organized in the form of a public agency than if it is organized in the form of a private company. A public enterprise should be expected to be more efficient if it has to compete in the market than if it has a monopoly (the same is true for a private firm). Ownership would be irrelevant only if the motivations of politicians and managers of public enterprises were the same as the motivations of owners and managers of private firms and if their power were equal.

Accumulation of Public Wealth. If a deficit in the budget is not due to underpricing and is not due to internal inefficiency of publicly owned corporations then it must be due to the accumulation of public wealth. If the government would not only publish the budget but also - like private firms - balance sheets and profit and loss accounts, then a large part of the cash deficit would correspond to an increase in public wealth: The government taxes the citizen in order to build up its net asset position and increases ceteris paribus the capital accumulation of the country. The alternative would be private wealth formation. Again, from a welfare point of view the latter alternative is to be preferred.

The problem is known from the theory of public goods. According to the Wicksell rule, an optimal supply with public goods is achieved when the cost of the public good is charged to the public proportional to utility. If this is done a ballot taken on the question whether to procure the good or not should have an unanimous result: either to buy the good or not to buy it. That rule implies that investment goods are financed out of credit, where the maturity of the credit corresponds to the life of the respective good. Only the interest payments and the repayments of the debts should be financed out of taxes. Other methods of financing investments would have distributive effects, which means that the cost would not be charged to the users but to other people (that means not proportional to utility). If the state had always financed itself according to the Wicksell rule there would be no equity. The value of the assets of the state would match its liability.

Thus, the question is: How big are the welfare losses when the state, instead of private citizens, accumulates wealth? If we suppose that public enterprises are as efficient as private ones and if we assume an infinite life of all taxpayers, then the initial tax burden for the procurement of the public enterprise is set off by later reductions in the tax burdens from the revenues (including saved interest payments) of the public enterprise. Thus under these artificial conditions it does not matter whether the state is the owner of the enterprises or private people are.

The assumptions do not correspond to reality. First of all, we have to take into account welfare losses from intermediation. That means that a direct property, i.e. a property which the owner himself can manage, is as a rule more valuable than an indirect property. That is the outcome of the "theory of the agent" [Jensen, Meckling, 1976; Ross, 1973]. As soon as the interests of the agent are not perfectly identical with the interests of the owner we get intermediation losses. The optimal degree of intermediation is determined on the one hand by economies of scale and the possibility of diversification and intermediation losses on the other. Intermediation losses in turn depend very much on the pay package of the intermediaries, i.e. in the case of the state, on the pay package of politicians and managers of public enterprises. Now it is apparent that these intermediation losses should be extremely high in the case of the state.

Second, expectations are not certain. A private person who owns some shares in private companies can sell the shares, if he needs the money or simply if he has better investment opportunities. The private wealth thus increases the security of the owner. State-owned enterprises are completely illiquid to the citizens. The welfare of the citizens combined is thus lower in the case where the state owns enterprises than if the same enterprise were in the hands of private citizens. But it would at least not be implausible that the value of public enterprises is only half of what it would be if they were privately owned.

Public Enterprises, Welfare and the Budget. Public payments are justified if they add more to welfare than the nominal payment. How much more that has to be depends on the administration cost and the efficiency of the tax system. If a tax system is not completely neutral the sacrifices of the citizens are always greater than the tax receipts. The tax receipts in turn have to be administered. Between the sacrifices of the citizens and public expenditures there is a slack. If this slack is e.g. 30 per cent, then public expenditure is justified; if this expenditure reaches values of more than 30 per cent above the sum paid out, then it is not justified.

Our first conclusion was that public enterprises nearly always are a burden to the budget, whether they are profitable or not, if we compare the holding of such enterprises to their privatization.

The question is whether the budgetary burden corresponds to a welfare contribution. The budgetary burden must be due to the pricing policy of the public enterprise, to internal inefficiency, or to the accumulation of public wealth.

There is no further possibility of explaining the cash burden. In none of these cases does the cash expense correspond to an adequate contribution to welfare. In the case of underpricing with distributional intentions the distributional effects could be achieved more cheaply. In the case of monopolies there are better organizational arrangements to achieve the desired goal. If the cash burden is due to internal inefficiency of public enterprises then the cash expenditures correspond to an equal welfare loss. In the case of accumulation of public wealth this public wealth is less valuable i.e. contributes less to the welfare of the people as a whole than an equal amount of private accumulation of wealth. The welfare loss might, because of the "slack", be larger than the deficit. It might be much smaller, if publicly owned firms are efficient, if they are not used as instruments for redistribution policies and if the public managers keep the intermediation losses small. But it is hard even theoretically to construct a case where the public holding of an enterprise does contribute positively to welfare.

IV. Conclusion: Policy towards Public Enterprises

Let us put the question of public enterprises into historical perspective. At the time of Frederick the Great of Prussia, public agriculture and manufacture contributed substantially to the financing of the state. The present-day public sector industry goes back to the 18th century. Post and railways were state enterprises with the purpose of producing revenues that could be used for the financing of public goods. Throughout the 19th century most local governments were financed by economic activity. The largest banking sector in Germany, comprised of the savings banks, was founded in the second half of the 19th century with the intention first, of offering savings opportunities to low-income earners and second, of earning money for the local government. Central banks of issue were not established with the intention of getting the monetary system in good order; rather, their founding was due to a desire to acquire a powerful instrument of war financing.

From the point of view of Frederick the Great of Prussia the ideal state looked very much like a capitalized foundation. His ideal was that the state should have a large enough fortune and enough enterprises to be financed by the revenues of economic activities. This ideal would have been a non-tax state. Frederick the Great devoted a large proportion of his time to the management and control of his manufacture shops, domains and crown land. His managerial achievements deserve even more admiration than his military talent [Hubatsch, 1973].

From an economic point of view this may at the time have been a rational solution. The king of Prussia was a profit maximizer, because he needed money to make Prussia powerful. In most cases profitability of public enterprises could only be achieved through high efficiency. There were very few monopolies. Most of the monopolies, which later came into the hands of the state, were added in the 19th century. The king of Prussia was motivated completely differently than a modern democratic politician.

The economy of those days was stationary and net investment was near zero. That means that all profit could be disposed of and used for the financing of public goods. The alternative to financing the state was taxation. But in those days the technique of taxation was not highly developed. The possibilities of the citizens to shelter their income and wealth from taxation were much greater than they are today. That means that the economic costs of taxation - including the cost of misallocation and misdirection of activities - were much bigger than they are today. From a welfare point of view the private ownership of public wealth would have been preferable in those days as in our own time. The public ownership in those days meant intermediation losses as well. The intermediation losses had to be weighed against the cost of taxation. It is very probable that the balance was in favor of public enterprises: The state enterprises were highly efficient and saved the citizens taxes whilst taxation was extremely difficult.

The conditions have very much changed. Our economies are non-stationary and net investment grossly equals profit. That means that even in the case of profitable public enterprises they can no longer contribute to the budget because they need the profit to finance investment. Moreover, public enterprises are on the average less profitable and we have good theoretical reasons to believe that this low profitability is due to low efficiency. That altogether means that in our time we do not have to weigh intermediation losses against taxes saved, but have to add intermediation losses and increased taxation because of the existence of public enterprises. Public enterprises which may have been reasonable under an autocratic state and a stationary economy are completely misplaced in a democratic state and a growing economy. Thus the best solution would be to sell all public enterprises to private citizens. We do not know of any exception. Even in the case of natural monopolies the state supervision of private enterprises is superior to state ownership. Some monetary theorists might argue that it is not possible for private banks to issue banknotes. But this private issue of banknotes has not only functioned over centuries, it is still functioning today: Switzerland, the soundest economy of our time in monetary matters, still has its notes issued by a private bank - Schweizerische Nationalbank - under state supervision.

From a political point of view, however, it seems hopeless to demand full denationalization of all public enterprises. Therefore one has to look for a second- or third-best solution. The worst of all solutions is to have a public economic activity incorporated into the budget and to have it organized like a public agency. The nearer we come to a market form the better the solution becomes. A state economic activity in the form of a private corporation with mixed public and private ownership seems to be the second-best solution. This form has been chosen in West Germany in the case of Volkswagen, Lufthansa, Veba and many public utilities such as Rheinisch-Westfälische Elektrizitätswerke (RWE), Hamburger Elektrizitätswerke (HEW), etc. What may be politically achieved are mandatory legal forms for state business activity.

Another reason why the state business sector is still growing is that a lot of state business activities are taxed lower than private competitors or not at all. Thus it may be rational for a local government to have its own garbage collection because this may be cheaper than having garbage collected by a private firm. But the price difference is only due to taxes saved and that means that they are cheaper because the federal and the state governments receive less taxes. Thus the second proposal would be to tax all government economic activity according to general tax laws.

Moreover, we do not have an accounting system which makes the financial consequences of running public enterprises known to the parliament. If the members of local parliaments knew that selling the municipal savings bank to private citizens would relieve the local budget by say 10 million deutsche mark a year, they would be much more prepared to sell than under the present conditions where they do not know the consequences. Thus the third proposal would be to reform the public accounting system in such a way as to show the financial consequences of parliamentary decisions. The story of the discussion in France preceeding the nationalization of some more banks and industrial complexes casts some light on the state of public accounting. The general conviction was that the state should compensate the owners and that the profits from each enterprise would enable the state to pay the interest on the corresponding public debt. But neither the banks, which were nationalized after the war, nor the successful Regie Renault made any contribution to the budget whilst their private competitors did [Schmid, 1982, p. 26]. The French nationalizations were promoted not only by ideology but by ignorance as well.

References

Aaron, Henry J., George M. von Furstenberg, "The Inefficiency of Transfers in Kind: The Case of Housing Assistance". Western Economic Journal, Vol. 9, No. 2, 1971, pp. 184-191.

Blankart, Charles B., "Bureaucratic Problems of Public Choice: Why Do Public Goods Still Remain Public? Constance 1978.

Engels, Wolfram, "Reform der Staatswirtschaft" - eine Problemübersicht". In: Hubertus Zuber (Ed.), Schlankheitskur für den Staat. Stuttgart 1979, pp. 35-70.

-- [1981a], "Die organisierte Verschwendung I (Warum die Staatsbürokratie so wenig leistet und wie sie reformiert werden könnte)". Die Zeit, Hamburg, 13 March, 1981, pp. 9-12.

-- [1981b], "Die organisierte Verschwendung II (Warum der Staat zuviel Geld verbraucht)". Die Zeit, Hamburg, 20 March, 1981, pp. 25-27.

-- [1981c], Wieviel Steuern braucht der Staat? Die neue Staatswirtschaftslehre. Schriftenreihe der Industrie- und Handelskammer Lübeck, 15, Lübeck 1981.

--, Herbert Sablotny, Dieter Zickler, Das Volksvermögen. Seine Verteilungs- und wohlstandspolitische Bedeutung. Frankfurt 1974.

Hubatsch, Walther, Friedrich der Große und die preußische Verwaltung. Cologne 1981.

Jensen, Michael C., William H. Meckling, Theory of the Firm: Managerial Behavior, Agency Costs and Ownership Structure. Journal of Financial Economics, Vol. 3, No. 4, 1976, pp. 305-360.

Laffont, Jean-Jacques, E. Mashen, The Theory of Incentives: An Overview. University of Cambridge, Economics Discussion Paper, Cambridge 1981.

Muth, Richard F., Public Housing: An Economic Evaluation. American Enterprise Institute, Evaluative Studies No. 5, Washington 1973.

Ross, Stephen A., "The Economic Theory of Agency: The Principal's Problem". The American Economic Review, Vol. 63, No. 2, Papers and Proceedings, 1973, pp. 134-139.

Schmid, Klaus-Peter, "Renault - ein teurer Mythos?". Die Zeit, Hamburg, 26 February 1982, p. 26.

Vogelsang, Ingo, Jörg Finsinger, "A Regulatory Adjustment Process for Optimal Pricing by Multiproduct Monopoly Firms". The Bell Journal of Economics, Vol. 10, No. 1, 1979, pp. 157-171.

Mark Blaug

Declining Subsidies to Higher Education: An Economic Analysis

I. Introduction

As a result of the baby boom of the 1950s, most industrialised countries are now facing falling enrolments in primary schools, which is soon to be followed by falling enrolments in secondary schools. At the same time, and years before the decline in enrolments will have reached the tertiary levels of the educational system, almost all industrialised countries have started to cut back on higher education spending. Indeed, there is now a general consensus throughout the Western World that the 1980s will be a decade in which the continual expansion of higher education, which characterised the 1960s and 1970s, will be more or less brought to a halt, if not actually reversed.

Lower financial budgets will force higher education institutions to tap alternative public and private sources of funding, to find new ways of raising fees and to explore new systems of student aid. There will be increased pressures to make colleges and universities more accountable to social and economic needs, meaning that the age-old cry for vocational rather than academic higher education will be heard even more frequently than before. In addition, the current trends towards enrolling more adult students will generate pressures to lower admission standards and to alter traditional modes of study. A contracting system soon discovers that job security for academic staff reduces financial flexibility. No wonder then that tenure rules have already come under fire and may be drastically revised in the years to come. Likewise, contraction will almost certainly involve a new balance between teaching and research, accompanied by the call for problem-oriented rather than basic research. These strains in the system have made themselves felt just about everywhere in Europe and America. Possible exceptions are France and Norway, which have recently announced plans for expanding higher education in the near future. But elsewhere in Canada, the United States, Japan, the United Kingdom, and the continent of Europe, the trend towards cutting back on public expenditure on higher education and towards restricting the autonomy of higher education institutions over courses, staffing, and student numbers appears to be inexorable.

Can economics say anything about this current trend and, in particular, can we show on strictly economic grounds that reductions in the level of spending on higher education are either deplorable or desirable? A brief answer to that question is: very little. Economics has much to say about the form which subsidies to higher education ought to take but almost nothing about the appropriate level of these subsidies: we can no more show that subsidy levels in the 1960s and 1970s were too high than that they are now too low. Those who wish to defend colleges and universities against the New Philistinism will, I am afraid, have to look outside economics for allies.

II. The Efficiency Case for Subsidising Higher Education

The economist's case for subsidising higher education is based on the familiar argument that the production of certain goods and services is subject to "market failures", which inhibit the attainment of Pareto optimality. The list of these market failures usually includes (1) consumer ignorance, (2) technical economies of scale, (3) externalities in production and/or consumption, (4) "public goods", and (5) inherent imperfections in capital and insurance markets. The first two, consumer ignorance and economies of scale, have little relevance to education and certainly do not apply to higher education[1]. If we treat "public goods", that is, non-rival and non-excludable goods, as an extreme version of the case of unrecouped externalities, we are left with two out of the five market failures, namely, externalities and imperfections in capital and insurance markets, both of which appear to be relevant to the production and consumption of higher education.

Let us take first the question of the externalities, spillovers, or "neighbourhood effects" of higher education. An economist would begin by distinguishing real from pecuniary externalities, and marginal from total externalities, concluding that the externalities of higher education, whatever they are, must ultimately take the form of raising the productivity and/or psychic satisfaction of Smith in sole consequence of the higher education of Jones. This is not, however, how the question of externalities of higher education is usually posed. Typically, the real, marginal externalities of higher education are con-

[1] I argue this at length in my "Introduction to the Economics of Education" [1971, pp. 103 ff.].

fused with the much wider question of whether higher education produces "social" benefits over and above the private economic benefits to university graduates. Thus, evidence that higher education changes the attitudes and values of the average graduate, making him or her more inclined to be politically "liberal" - meaning more inclined to vote for politicians who favour government intervention in economic affairs - has nothing whatever to do with the alleged "market failure" of privately financed higher education. No doubt, higher education has all sorts of consequences, some of which are even desirable, but so has going to work at 18 and that is hardly a reason for subsidising wage employment. What we have to show is not that higher education has many unintended social consequences, because so does every other human activity, but that these consequences have economic value and are functionally related to the size of the higher education system. The literature on this question, even when it is written by economists, frequently ignores all such elementary considerations[1].

Having spelled out the nature of the real, marginal externalities of higher education, the next problem is to quantify them, at least ordinally if not cardinally, if only to ensure that the positive externalities outweigh the negative ones. But as the Carnegie Commission on Higher Education [1973, p. 180] in the United States admits: "no precise - or even imprecise - methods exist to assess the individual and societal benefits of higher education as against the private and public costs." The failure on the part of almost all investigators to measure any of the externalities of higher education has produced a new scepticism about their magnitude: in the 1960s the standard view was that the externalities were large in relation to the private benefits of higher education but the new consensus, at least for advanced countries, is that they may well be negligibly small [Friedman, Friedman, 1980, pp. 178 f.]. For one thing, the so-called "screening hypothesis", if true, implies that higher education generates negative external effects in the sense that every successful graduate blocks someone else from a preferred position in the queue for high-paying jobs; in other words, higher education is merely what Fred Hirsch [1977, pp. 41 ff.] has called a "positional good". The "screening hypothesis" is clearly not the whole story [Layard, Psacharopoulos, 1974], but it may be part of the story, reminding us that the externalities of higher education

[1] See Davis [1970]; Hartman [1973]; Mundel [1973]; and, the most notorious example of all, Bowen [1977, especially Ch. 14]. For more careful expositions of the nature of the externalities of higher education, see Blaug [1971, pp. 107 ff.] and the references cited there; Windham [1979]; and Friedman, Friedman [1980, pp. 178 ff.].

are by no means necessarily positive. But even if they were, the fact remains that we can ascribe no number to the externalities of higher education and hence cannot say how much to subidise higher education so as to reduce these externalities to zero.

That brings us to imperfections in capital and insurance markets. Because a non-slave society prohibits people from selling rights to their future labour services, individuals cannot offer a lien on their personal services as collateral against a loan to finance a personal investment in schooling. Even if the personal returns on that investment were expected with perfect certainty, there are no wholly effective legal mechanisms for extracting a repayment of that loan. In addition, however, the variance in private returns to post-compulsory education (education beyond the level required by law) is so large relative to the mean return that the inability to repay a study loan in some individual cases would be almost as large a problem as the unwillingness to repay it. It follows that a private capital market will require a large risk-premium in addition to the market rate of interest, such that student loans will only be available at, say, two to three times the average private rate of return to higher education; at such interest rates, the demand for student loans will be exceedingly small. The problem is one of launching a student loan scheme at a scale large enough to pool risks and so reduce the risk premium. It is in this sense, and only in this sense, that private capital markets for study loans are "imperfect". A student loans scheme, artificially created as a matter of deliberate public policy, may nevertheless be able to employ the funds of the commercial banking system to finance the scheme if the government guarantees all repayments. It is this guarantee which then constitutes the subsidy to higher education. If, in addition, it is argued that student loans must be available at rates below the market rate of interest, there is an additional element of subsidy to higher education in the form of a payment by the government to commercial banks to bridge the gap in the two rates. Notice, however, that the latter subsidy has nothing whatever to do with the inherent imperfections of capital markets but must rather derive from the prior judgement that higher education generates externalities. In either case, however, it is easy to see that economic analysis leads only to a qualitative judgement in favour of public subsidies to higher education but not to any quantitative judgement as to the magnitude of these subsidies.

III. Other Grounds for Subsidising Higher Education

So far, we have only examined what economists like to call "efficiency arguments" for subsidising higher education. In addition, however, there are equity arguments for subsidising higher education resting on the principle of equal educational opportunities, which undoubtedly weigh more heavily with governments and the general public than the efficiency arguments beloved by economists. Since subsidies to promote equity allow wealthy as well as poor students to obtain an inexpensive education, it remains an open question whether higher education subsidies in the United States and elsewhere have actually had the effect of promoting social mobility and greater equality of income distribution. Starting with the work of Lee Hansen and Burt Weisbrod in 1969 on public higher education in California, a long but confusing discussion, largely focussed on the United States but also covering France and one or two Third World countries, has more or less concluded on a note of general agnosticism: the net redistributive effects of higher education subsidies remain uncertain everywhere; at best, one may say that current patterns of subsidies nowhere achieve the dramatic improvements in income distribution that they were intended to achieve[1]. This is not to say, therefore, that a case for subsidising higher education cannot be constructed on equity grounds but merely that the form in which higher education is subsidised - tuition grants to institutions rather than to students, maintenance grants to students rather than loans, tax relief to parents rather than direct aid to students, etc. - matters more for equity than the total level of the subsidy. Once again, we find that economic analysis has little to contribute to the current controversy about the cutbacks in public expenditure on higher education.

This completes our discussion of valid economic arguments for subsidising higher education. But there are yet other invalid arguments which invoke the authority of economists. A principal example of such invalid arguments is the notion that education has been shown to contribute to economic growth and hence that any public policy designed to stimulate growth must include measures to step up participation rates in higher education. Obviously, this contention is a non sequitur:

---

[1] For a review of the literature, see Blaug [1982]. For evidence that the social class composition of the higher education student population has not significantly altered in America and Western Europe since 1965, see Cerych and Jallade [1981].

it may be granted that education contributes to growth but so do many other activities and what must be shown is, not that education contributes to growth, but that more education would contribute more to growth at the margin than more health, more housing, more roads, etc.

All discussions of the question whether education contributes to economic growth sooner or later come back to Edward Denison's book on "The Sources of Economic Growth in the United States" [1962], followed by his study of "Why Growth Rates Differ" [1967]. Much doubt has been thrown on Denison's framework, involving as it does the implicit estimate of an aggregate production function of the Cobb-Douglas type coupled with the arbitrary assumption of neutral technical progress[1]. But even if we waive all such objections, it is interesting to note that even Denison himself concludes that intercountry differences in educational levels of the workforce do not help to explain much of the differences in postwar growth rates experienced by industrialised countries [Denison, 1967, pp. 78, 113 f., 199].

Thus, Denison found that the United Kingdom in 1960 was ahead of the rest of Europe and neck-to-neck with the United States in terms of the number of years of schooling embodied in the labour force. If we update Denison's figures to 1978, the United Kingdom with its low growth rate still stands ahead of every country in Europe, falling only slightly below the United States, whereas West Germany with its high growth rate remains well behind both the United Kingdom and the United States [Daly, 1981]. To be sure, such gross comparisons conceal important differences in the distribution of education in the labour force. Thus, the United Kingdom has a lower starting age for education than almost any country in the world, which alone tends to raise the average amount of education in the British labour force to about eleven years. Similarly, the United States has a much larger proportion of the population with less than nine years of schooling and a much larger proportion with 14-15 years of education than either the United Kingdom or West Germany. Moreover, Denison entirely omits part-time education, which differs more radically between countries than full-time education. Indeed, it has been argued that the German system of compelling all those who are not in full-time schooling between the ages of 15 and 18 to attend a vocational school one day a week, including an elaborate network of vocational training schemes for shop floor workers, is at least in part responsible for the higher productivity

[1] For this and other criticisms, see Nelson [1973].

rates of many German industries compared to British ones [Prais, 1981].

Be that as it may, all growth accounting of the Denison variety at best succeeds in showing what education contributes to earnings differentials between people, which leaves open the question whether such earnings differences reflect changes in the productivity of individuals brought about by schooling or the so-called "screening" or filtering function of the educational system, in effect redistributing a given growth capacity among the participants in the process. If education plays an important role in promoting economic growth, as is so often claimed, it has to be said that the models so far examined in the growth-accounting literature fail utterly to explain the mechanism by which this effect is produced.

We come back to the more fundamental objection that growth accounting ignores the costs of resources invested in the educational system and thus tells us nothing about the net returns of spending on education. This suggests yet another argument for subsidising post-compulsory schooling resting on the demonstration that the social rate of return on investment in, say, higher education exceeds the social rate of return on investment in physical capital or other types of social expenditure. This is not an invalid argument. It is merely one which is hopelessly inconclusive. We can calculate both the private and the social rate of return to education but the latter would be better labelled the "public" rate of return since it does not include any measure of the externalities of education. We can similarly measure rates of return to health, housing, transport, etc., but these will involve variables that do not enter the calculations of rates of return to education, and will also exclude quantified estimates of external effects. We thus end up with an array of rates of return which are incommensurable[1]. We seem to be doomed therefore to analysing allocative efficiency in education at a sub-optimal level. We can ask how to allocate a given budget for education among different levels and types of education, not to mention different clients for the educational process, but we cannot seriously answer the grander question about the overall size of the educational budget.

---

[1] In the case of health, we do not even end up with rates of return to national spending on health care: health economics has not posed this ambitious question [see Drummond, 1981].

Even so, it is interesting to note that recent rate-of-return figures for education suggest that the demand for higher education has by now been saturated all over the industrialised world. Earnings differentials by years of education have been drastically compressed in the 1970s, not just in the United States, but also in the United Kingdom, France, and West Germany. In consequence, social rates of return to educational investment have declined to the point where in many countries they now stand below the common 10 per cent yardstick for the opportunity cost of capital [Psacharopoulos, 1980, Table 5, p. 97]. For example, between 1966 and 1978 social rates of return on education in the United Kingdom declined for university degrees from 8 per cent to 4 per cent, for A-level secondary school qualifications from 8-9 per cent to 6-7 per cent, and for HNCs, an intermediate technical qualification, from 10 per cent to 7 per cent [Daly, 1981]. There has always been a good deal of scepticism about the notion that rate-of-return calculations provide suitable criteria for public investment choices in education, and I am not making any such claims for them, but they do serve to provide one sort of rationale for the present trend towards the contraction of higher education.

IV. Trends and Patterns in Higher Education Expenditures

Our argument has so far been almost entirely theoretical. By considering entirely general principles, we have come to the conclusion that economists can neither condemn nor praise the recent downturn in higher education expenditures. In point of fact, we could have arrived at the same answer by a different route. If we examine past trends and patterns in higher education expenditures around Europe over the last 10 or 20 years, it becomes perfectly obvious that there is little or no relationship between a country's economic performance and its commitment to higher education (or, indeed, to all forms of education taken together). Thus, between 1961 and 1975 the United Kingdom actually spent more in absolute terms on higher education than did West Germany and, I need hardly tell you, these two countries stand at either end of the spectrum of European growth rates over the post-war period.

Let us review the general pattern in more detail[1]. For the period

[1] All the figures in this section are derived from UNESCO data analysed by Jallade [1980]. Data for OECD member-states, which is separately

1965-1977, annual growth rates of public expenditure on higher education fall into four groups: (1) high rates of 20 per cent or more (Austria, Italy, Yugoslavia); (2) above-average rates of 15-20 per cent (Belgium, Denmark, Netherlands, Norway, Spain); (3) below-average rates of 10-15 per cent (France, West Germany, Sweden, the United Kingdom, Bulgaria); and (4) low rates of 10 per cent or less (Switzerland and the entire Eastern bloc except Bulgaria). The European average for annual growth rates in higher education expenditure over this period was 16 per cent as against 14 per cent in the United States. All these figures refer to current prices but even at constant prices, expenditure on higher education in Europe grew at almost 10 per cent per annum over the 15 years 1960-1975, which more or less matches the corresponding figure for the United States. Even after 1975, what slowed down was only the rate of increase in higher education expenditure; it continues to grow to this day at about 5 per cent per annum.

We may also compare European countries in terms of that notorious and rather misleading indicator, the proportion of Gross National Product (GNP) allocated to expenditure on higher education. In 1961, no European country spent more than 0.4 per cent of its GNP on higher education. By 1975, seven countries were spending as much as one per cent of GNP on higher education and four others were approaching the one per cent mark. The biggest spender of all in 1975 was the Netherlands, whose 2.2 per cent of GNP was more than twice as much as any other country devoted to higher education. The smallest spenders were Italy, France, and Spain, who consistently kept higher education spending at 0.4 - 0.6 per cent of GNP throughout the entire period 1960-1975. Again, the United Kingdom devoted a larger proportion of GNP to higher education (around 1.2 per cent) throughout the entire decade and a half than both West Germany and France. These increased expenditures on higher education all over Europe did not come at the expense of lower levels of education but in fact reflected a growing share of GNP everywhere for the educational sector as a whole.

These overall trends disguise vast differences in real expenditure per higher education student across Europe. There were countries with "expensive" higher education in 1975, such as Denmark, the Netherlands, and Switzerland. There were countries with "cheap" higher edu-

---

collected, is analysed by Psacharopoulos [1981]. The differences between UNESCO and OECD statistics are small and refer rather to what is collected and to the number of countries from which data is collected.

cation in 1975, such as Bulgaria, France, Italy, Poland, Spain, and Yugoslavia. In between these two extremes were countries like Austria, Belgium, West Germany, Norway, Sweden, Czechoslovakia, Hungary and the United Kingdom. If we contrast 1965 with 1975, there has been little change in real expenditure per student in most countries; but several, such as Austria, Belgium, the Netherlands, Norway, Denmark, Sweden, and Switzerland, have actually managed significantly to increase and in some cases to double the real resources devoted to each higher education student.

The vast differences in instructional costs per student unit in different countries begin to suggest why there is no correlation between growth rates in educational expenditure and levels or growth rates of economic performance. Within very wide limits, there is in fact no such thing as an objectively determined cost of higher education: higher education institutions raise all the money they can from public and private sources and spend all the money that they raise; unit costs are determined, not so much by standards of quality and certainly not by standards of efficiency, but by changes in revenue. No doubt, tuition costs are necessarily higher in very small and very large institutions (under 1,000 and over 50,000 students) but within these wide limits, costs per student depend more on total revenue available than on the imperatives of teaching and research[1]. Thus, if we compare the Netherlands with Italy, it is difficult to find any objective reason in terms of "manpower requirements" to account for the vast differences in the two systems of higher education. Dutch professorial salaries, measured in U.S. $ of constant purchasing power, are four times those of Italian professors; student-staff ratios in the Netherlands are 10:1 as against 24:1 in Italy; hence, it costs almost ten times as much to educate a Dutch student than an Italian student. Would anyone argue, however, that Dutch professors produce work that is ten times as good as that of Italian professors, or that the Dutch economy is more sophisticated than the Italian one and therefore warrants the much more expensive higher education system? The fact of the matter is that the relationship between higher education spending and economic activity is so loose that it can accommodate almost any size and standard of higher education which politicians decree.

Public expenditure on higher education depends not only on the costs of instruction but also on the volume of direct aid to students. This element in the total higher education bill seems to vary even more be-

[1] This is what Bowen [1980, Ch. 1] calls the "revenue theory of cost".

tween countries than the level of grants to educational institutions to cover the costs of tuition. Some countries, like the United Kingdom and Sweden, provide student aid to almost all higher education students whereas others, like France or the Netherlands, subsidise only one third or less of all students. There are also significant differences in the methods of aiding students, from the reliance on student loans in Sweden, to the exclusive reliance on maintenance grants in the United Kingdom, to the French emphasis on subsidised food, housing, travel, and health care, coupled with generous tax relief to parents [Blaug, Woodhall, 1978]. Whatever we may say about the instructional costs of higher education, levels of public spending on student aid can encourage or discourage the private demand for higher education but cannot directly affect levels of economic development or rates of growth of GNP per head. Here then is yet another reason why we should not expect to find any well-determined relationship between total subsidies to higher education and any measure of economic activity.

V. Educational Expenditures for 16- to 19-Year-Olds

We have concentrated so far on higher education but I wish now to take note of a pronounced tendency in all industrialised countries towards increased spending on the training of out-of-school youngsters aged 16 to 19, which appears to have accompanied the reductions in higher education spending ever since 1975. I know of no documented study of this international trend but it is firmly established in the United Kingdom and seems to be a European-wide reaction to the phenomenon of unusually high rates of youth unemployment which everywhere accompanied the appearance of slumpflation in the early 1970s. Indeed, if we add all such schemes to those that directly subsidise the employment of young people, we reach figures for government expenditure on the employment and training of 16- to 19-year-olds that in some countries equal the level of expenditure on universities [Lindley, 1981, pp. 11 f.].

The motive for these programmes is sometimes taken to be simply that of removing as many people as possible from the unemployment rolls so as to put the best face on deflationary policies. But that is perhaps an unduly cynical interpretation. Governments themselves defend training and work experience programmes for youngsters as repairing the deficiencies of formal schooling. In other words, their theory of why there is so much youth unemployment is that secondary schools have failed to inculcate both the requisite cognitive knowledge and the personality traits that render a school leaver employable. Thus, many youth training programmes include training, not just in the three R's and in low-level technical skills, but also in techniques of interviewing, filling out questionnaires, etc. The difficulty with this theory is that it fails utterly to account for the emergence of heavy youth unemployment all over the industrialised world in the last half of the 1970s except by the implausible supposition that the quality of secondary education suddenly deteriorated badly after 1975 or thereabouts.

There is nothing new about the fact that in a recession the rates of joblessness for young people exceed those for adults. What is new about youth unemployment in recent years is that the gap which always opens up between the two unemployment rates in a recession has never been as large as it is today. Even when we standardise the figures for demographic changes, and for changes in labour force activity rates, the size of the gap seems without historical precedent: in almost all capitalist countries today, unemployment for people under the age of 21 constitutes 40 and sometimes 50 per cent of total unemployment [Sorrentino, 1981; Grimond, 1979]. The causes of this problem remain somewhat mysterious: it is as if employers all over the capitalist world became strangely reluctant after about 1972 or 1973 to hire young people for regular, full-time jobs at any price; in some countries, like France, West Germany, Sweden, Italy, and the United Kingdom, this reluctance manifested itself as early as the late 1960s. One can go some way towards explaining it by taking account of the world-wide shift in the pattern of demand from the industrial sector to the service industries but this phenomenon still leaves unexplained a considerable proportion of youth unemployment. A more significant factor may be the gradual strengthening of job security provisions for adult workers in most industrialised countries. Traditional management prerogatives in dismissing labour have been substantially curtailed everywhere, and increasingly so in the 1970s - consider, for example, the successive impacts in the United Kingdom of the Redundancy Payment Act of 1965, the Industrial Relations Act of 1972, and the Employment Protection Act of 1975 - and this has encouraged the substitution of older, experienced workers for younger, inexperienced workers in order to minimise rates of labour turnover. At the same time, a narrowing of wage differentials between youth and adult workers, frequently as a result of union pressure, has tended to price inexperienced youngsters out of the market. These speculations about the causes of youth unemployment in recent years remain to be confirmed. In the meantime, training, work-experience job creation and subsidised job programmes for the age group 16-19 continue to expand under the impetus of untested if not implausible hypotheses about the collapse of formal schooling coupled with half-baked ideas about alleged skill shortages in the next boom or equally half-baked views about the long-term training requirements of an economy which private industry is somehow incapable of providing. I dare say that the economics of education will in the years to come invade this virgin territory, concentrating its efforts not on the problems of the formal educational system, but on those of nonformal education and training.

VI. The Field of Research

I turn now, however briefly, to questions of research and particularly research performed in the higher education sector, which in most countries comprises one-sixth to one-third of the national R & D effort measured in money terms. I do so with some hesitation since I am not persuaded that economists have contributed much to our understanding of appropriate modes of conducting academic research or for that matter the determination of the desirable level of funding for higher education research.

In the United States, Canada, and most of Europe, the real resources devoted to research are bound up in fixed proportions with the instructional costs of higher education, such that an expansion of student numbers and the addition of academic staff inevitably represents an equiproportionate increase in the resources devoted to research, and vice versa for a contraction of student numbers. Outside the Latin countries, universities are subsidised so as to permit academic staff to devote something like half of their time to research; this 1:1 ratio between instruction and research time is arbitrarily regarded as optimal for each and every member of staff. In addition to this channel of support, there is a second channel of research councils, that is, semi-autonomous bodies which provide additional finance for both pure and applied research carried on in colleges and universities. The funds flowing through this channel do not vary systematically across countries in proportion to the size of higher education systems; moreover, there are few systematic international patterns in the allocation of these funds among specific disciplines or fields of research [Blume, 1980].

The level of direct support for higher education research through research councils represents a decision which is subject to an unusually high level of uncertainty: frequently, the outcome of the research can only be judged after a decade or more, and, moreover, there is little to guide the choice between one researcher and the next other than personal track-records established in the past. Since most research councils are largely made up of senior academics with impressive research achievements, there is an inevitable tendency to favour well-tried approaches building on previous work and to discourage innovatory research. Such tendencies are perhaps stronger in the Anglophone countries who generally prefer the "responsive" model of research councils in which the individual researcher takes the initiative in applying for project funds. France and Italy instead prefer the dirigiste model in which the council itself stipulates the priority projects which it wishes to finance, sometimes going so far as to operate its own laboratories and research units. Obviously, the dirigiste model does not automatically favour innovatory research: it all depends on who actually mans the councils in question and on the influence of relevant ministries on the research agenda of the councils. It is worth noting that both the United Kingdom and West Germany, which at one time were firmly within the "responsive" camp, have recently moved sharply towards the dirigiste model. Clearly, governments everywhere are trying to get a firmer grip on university research in the effort to steer it into applied rather than basic research.

As general university income has declined since 1975, or rather grown at a sharply reduced rate, so have the imputed costs of the time spent on research by academic staff. In addition, however, there has been an absolute decline of external finance for higher education research in almost all OECD countries since 1973, with the exception of Denmark, Norway, the Netherlands, and France; but even in these countries, external research funds have grown less rapidly since 1973 than before [Ferne, 1980; OECD, 1981, Graphs A.10, p. 24 and A.38, p. 84].

It is easy to describe the patterns and trends but it is difficult to say much about them which is not either banal or self-interested pleading. I believe, as you probably all do, that teaching and research are generally complements, not substitutes, and therefore reject the Soviet pattern of financing academic research in specialised research institutes, leaving universities to devote themselves exclusively to teaching. Yet I also believe that academics are not equally endowed with capacities in both teaching and research. This suggests that there would be great advantages in subsidising higher education institutions as if they were largely, although not exclusively, teaching factories; individual university teachers who wished to specialise in research would then have to apply to research councils for funds, not just to purchase equipment and to hire research assistants, but also to replace a fraction of their own teaching time. Rejecting the assumption that teaching and research must always be combined in fixed proportions, we would thus maximise the benefits of the principle of comparative advantage in different activities. If economics suggests anything about the way we conduct higher education, it creates the strong presumption that this would result in a more efficient university system. Needless to say, I know of no country that has ever seriously considered this proposal.

There remains the question of the desirable total level of outside finance for higher education research. Research contributes to the total stock of human knowledge and human knowledge is a "public good" par excellence. Now we know that consumers have no incentives to reveal their demand for public goods and the problem of non-revelation of demand for research findings points firmly in the direction of public support for research activities. Nevertheless, the social benefits of academic research are painfully difficult to assess and with all the monitoring and post-mortems in the world will remain impossible to predict with any degree of accuracy. In the light of these considerations, any level of research support, other than zero, is arbitrary. It is a feeble conclusion but I do not think that economic analysis justifies any firmer pronouncement.

My conclusions have been almost wholly negative and destructive. But that is because we have posed a super-optimality problem - the total level of subsidy to higher education and higher education research - and economics happens to be weak in answering such questions. Its strength lies rather in examining suboptimal problems - should higher education be geared to young people or to adults? ; should higher education be full-time or part-time? ; should we aid institutions or students? ; etc. For example, we noted earlier that there is little evidence that current patterns of higher education subsidies in industrialised countries are effective equalisers of lifetime chances. This is not because the level of subsidies has been too low but because its pattern has been ill-conceived to achieve the objective of greater equality in the lifetime distribution of income. Instead of directing subsidies exclusively towards low-income students, say, by full-cost fees, subsidised grants scaled to parental income, and loans repayable as a proportion of future student income, tuition costs have been largely or wholly subsidised indiscriminately to everyone and even maintenance costs have been partly subsidised on a non-selective basis. And yet, from the viewpoint of equity, there is a simply overwhelming case for "privatising" post-compulsory and particularly higher education, that is, shifting the entire costs from general taxpayers to students and their families, exceptions being made only when the poverty of the individual families has been clearly established. If there is to be any general subsidy to post-compulsory schooling, it should be confined to the completion of secondary education, ideally taking the form of an "entitlement" to two or three years of post-compulsory schooling to be "cashable" at any future date in the working life of an individual.

The case for the "privatisation" of post-compulsory education is easy to make on equity grounds. However, there are also good efficiency arguments for moving in the same direction. The present system of subsidising the whole of the tuition costs of higher education out of tax receipts, which is now universal in Europe but of course not in America or Japan, deprives institutions of higher education of any financial incentives to maximise educational outcomes per unit of student costs, while at the same time reducing the incentives of students to work at their maximum capacity. It has resulted in considerable overinvestment in producer-oriented higher education, lacking any halting mechanism other than the political will to resist the Malthusian pressure of growing numbers.

References

Blaug, Mark, Introduction to the Economics of Education. London 1971.

--, "The Distributional Effects of Higher Education Subsidies". Economics of Education Review, Vol. 2, No. 3, 1982, pp. 123-148.

--, Maureen Woodhall, "Patterns of Subsidies to Higher Education in Europe". Higher Education, Vol. 7, Nov. 1978, pp. 331-361.

Blume, Stuart S., "The Finance of University Research in Western Europe". European Journal of Education, Vol. 15, No. 4, 1980, pp. 72-101.

Bowen, Howard R., with Peter Dlecak, Jacqueline Powers Doud, Gordon K. Douglass, Investment in Learning: The Individual and Social Value of American Higher Education. The Carnegie Council Series, San Francisco 1977.

--, The Costs of Higher Education. San Francisco 1980.

Carnegie Commission on Higher Education, Higher Education: Who Pays? Who Benefits? Who should Pay? A Report and Recommendations. New York 1973.

Cerych, Ladislav, Jean-Pierre Jallade, Student Flows and Expenditure in Higher Education, 1965-1979. Institute of Education, Paris 1981.

Daly, Ann, "The Contribution of Education to Economic Growth in Britain: A Note on the Evidence". National Institute of Economic and Social Research, Paris 1981, unpubl.

Davis, J. Ronnie, "The Social and Economic Externalities of Education". In: Roe L. Johns, Irving J. Goffman, Kern F. Alexander, Dewey H. Stollar (Eds.), Economic Factors Affecting the Financing of Education. National Educational Finance Project, Gainesville 1970, pp. 59-82.

Denison, Edward F., The Sources of Economic Growth in the United States and the Alternatives before Us. New York 1962.

--, assisted by Jean-Pierre Poullier, Why Growth Rates Differ: Postwar Experience in Nine Western Countries. The Brookings Institution, Washington 1967.

Drummond, Martin F., "Welfare Economics and Cost Benefits Analysis in Health Care". Scottish Journal of Political Economy, Vol. 28, No. 2, 1981, pp. 125-145.

Ferné, Georges, "Is University Research on the Decline?". European Journal of Education, Vol. 15, No. 4, 1980, pp. 102-121.

Friedman, Milton, Rose Friedman, Free to Choose: A Personal Statement. London 1980.

Grimmond, John (Ed.), Youth Unemployment and the Bridge from School to Work. Anglo-German Foundation for the Study of Industrial Society, London 1979.

Hartman. Robert W., "The Rationale for Federal Support for Higher Education". In: Lewis C. Solmon, Paul J. Taubman (Eds.), Does College Matter? New York 1973, pp. 271-292.

Hirsch, Fred, Social Limits to Growth. London 1977.

Jallade, Jean-Pierre, "Expenditure on Higher Education in Europe: Past Trends and Future Prospects". European Journal of Education, Vol. 14, No. 1, 1980, pp. 35-48.

Layard, Richard, George Psacharopoulos, "The Screening Hypothesis and the Returns to Education". Journal of Political Economy, Vol. 82, 1974, pp. 985-998.

Lindley, Robert, "Education, Training, and the Labour Market in Britain". European Journal of Education, Vol. 16, No. 1, 1981, pp. 11-21.

Mundel, David S., "Whose Education Should Society Support?". In: Lewis C. Solmon, Paul J. Taubman (Eds.), Does College Matter? New York 1973, pp. 293-316.

Nelson, Richard R., "Recent Exercises in Growth Accounting: New Understanding or Dead End?". The American Economic Review, Vol. 63, 1973, pp. 462-468.

Organisation for Economic Co-operation and Development (OECD), Science and Technology Indicators I. Trends in Science and Technology in the OECD Area during the 1970s. First Draft of Part A: Resources Devoted to R & D. OECD, Paris 1981.

Prais, Sigbert J., "Vocational Qualifications of the Labour Force in Britain and Germany". National Institute Economic Review, Vol. 98, No. 4, 1981, pp. 47-59.

Psacharopoulos, George, Returns to Education: An Updated International Comparison. World Bank Staff Working Paper No. 402, Washington 1980.

Psacharopoulos, George, Higher Education Expenditure in OECD Countries. Organisation for Economic Co-operation and Development (OECD), Paris 1981.

Sorrentino, Constance, "Youth Unemployment: An International Perspective". Monthly Labor Review, Vol. 104, No. 7, 1981, pp. 3-15.

Windham, Douglas M., "Economic Analysis and the Public Support of Higher Education". In: Douglas M. Windham (Ed.), Economic Dimensions of Education. Washington 1979, pp. 117-140.

Herbert G. Grubel

Reassessing the Cost of Social Insurance Programs

The central theme of my paper is that the cost of social insurance programs in most industrial countries of the West has risen dramatically during the last 20 years because they have induced changes in behavior that have led to increased need for benefits and reduced output and productivity. As a result, it has been necessary to raise taxes which in turn has stimulated the development of the underground economy and a shrinking of the tax base. Consequently, Western mixed economies are suffering from a vicious circle in which the growing cost of social insurance programs requires increasing tax revenues which have to be raised through higher tax rates from a base that shrinks continuously through the effects of the insurance programs and the tax-induced growth of the underground economy.

In line with the objectives of this symposium, the operation of this vicious circle requires a reassessment of the government's role in the provision of social insurance. I intend to provide such a reassessment by presenting in Section I some data on the growth of insurance expenditures in Canada, which may serve as an illustrative example of the kinds of developments which have taken place in other mixed economies. In the following section I shall develop the concept of moral hazard and discuss through the example of unemployment insurance and aid for single parents what adjustments in behavior result in increased need for benefits. In Section III other costs of the social insurance programs are presented and I shall argue that they may be greater than the pure money costs of increased demand for benefits, consisting of such effects as reduced incentives for work, risk-taking and the formation of real and human capital. The paper closes with some ideas on possible changes in government policies.

The analysis of this paper contains little that is basically new or that early critics of the welfare state such as Hayek [1944] had not predicted. However, I believe that the empirical evidence to be presented is powerful support for arguments that previously had relied mainly on general and theoretical propositions about the nature of man and free societies.

I. The Growth of Social Insurance Programs and Expenditures

Social insurance programs in all Western countries are complex systems that have grown in recent decades at different levels of government and that address wide varieties of need. It takes a great deal of specialized knowledge to understand and analyze these national programs. For this reason, the following analysis will focus on conditions in Canada, with which I am familiar.

Figure 1 presents government expenditure by categories consolidated at all three levels, federal, provincial and local. The statistics show a continuous growth of social welfare expenditures from 4.3 percent of Gross National Product (GNP) in 1965 to 10.0 percent in 1977. It should be noted that during this period total government expenditures rose from 29.4 to 43.0 percent of GNP. The growth in social welfare expenditures therefore accounted for 42 percent of this total growth in government outlays.

Figure 1 - Canadian Government Expenditures[a], 1965-1977 (Percent of GNP)

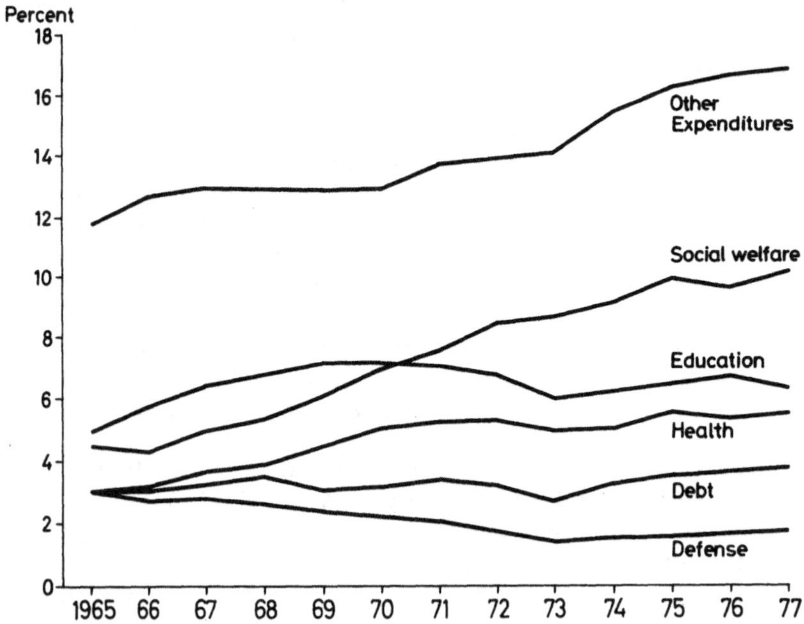

[a]Consolidated Federal, Provincial, and Local.

Source: Canada Yearbook [various issues, Tables 22.1 and 23.1].

Figure 1 also shows that during this period defense expenditures fell by one half while education spending rose a miserly 1. 5 percentage points or 25 percent on the 1965 base. Health expenditures also rose 2.5 percentage points or 83 percent on the 1965 base. The largest category of government expenditures is a catchall "other". It also rose sharply, but started from a much higher base. It contains many government services which might be categorized as providing social welfare, such as the expenditures of the departments of housing, agricultural and Indian affairs. The adjustment of published welfare expenditure figures to reflect such other spending is a most difficult and contentious task and will not be undertaken here.

The Nature of the Growth

Further information on Canada's social insurance expenditures useful for later analysis may be summarized as follows. In 1959 there were 20 different expenditure programs comprising pensions, unemployment benefits, general locally administered welfare, central government assistance to Indians, outlays for health and many others. In 1969 these 20 programs had grown to 33 and in 1979 to 43. Buried in the program titles are several "other", suggesting that a complete list would be even longer and complex. It should also be noted that during the 20 years under observation only four programs have disappeared through consolidation.

The absolute dollar values of expenditures on these welfare programs show a growth rate of 1, 271 percent over 20 years: $2. 8 billion in 1959 grew to $35. 6 billion in 1979. However, these figures are difficult to evaluate in the light of the concurrent growth in population and price levels; the accompanying table adjusts for these factors. As can be seen, Canada's welfare expenditures per capita rose from $145 in 1957 to $539 in 1979 in constant 1971 dollars, resulting in an average annual compounded rate of growth equal to 6. 1 percent. The last column of the table shows that welfare expenditures during this period rose from 6. 9 to 12. 0 percent of personal income.

Guilder [1981] estimated that in 1979 in the United States a welfare family of four received an *average* of close to $18, 000 in government benefits and subsidies. This must be compared with the earnings of $9, 000 accruing to someone working full time at the minimum wage. I could not find similar calculations for Canada since there appear to be no data on the number of recipients of benefits. However, a simple calculation may be useful to attempt getting an idea about Canada's per capita and family welfare expenditures.

Welfare Expenditures in Canada, 1957-1979

	Per capita expenditures[a]		Expenditures in percent of personal income
	absolute value	annual increase	
1957	145	8.3	6.9
1962	174	0.5	7.9
1972	342	21.0	10.1
1977	502	4.4	11.3
1979	539	5.2	12.0
Average		6.1	

[a]In constant 1971 Canadian dollars.

Source: Canada Yearbook [1980-81, Table 8.19].

Thus, consider that in 1979 in Canada there were $36 billion on social security expenditures in total. Subtracting the costs of health ($13 billion), family allowances ($2 billion) and Unemployment Insurance Commission (UIC) unemployment benefits ($4 billion), we find an expenditure of $17 billion for retirement and welfare. Assuming that all 2 million Canadians over 65 are beneficiaries of the retirement programs, there are 20 million additional Canadians of all ages. If 10 percent of the latter receive benefits, the $17 billion are spent on 4 million individuals, or about $4,200 per recipient. A family of four would therefore receive about $17,000 a year. This figure is surprisingly close to the one quoted by Guilder for the United States, but should be treated with great caution given the rough nature of the preceding calculations. Nevertheless, these data suggest that per capita and family transfer payments have reached lofty heights in Canada as well as in the United States.

As a final piece of empirical information on Canada's social insurance expenditures I present Figure 2, which shows the level of welfare expenditures in 1965 at $2.4 billion. The upward sloping lines from that point indicate the levels of expenditures that would have been necessary to maintain the real services per needy person at their 1965 levels, assuming that need is proportional to the general population, the share of the aged in the population and general inflation. Figure 2 shows that an expenditure of $7.7 billion in 1977 would have permitted the delivery of unchanged 1965 real services per needy person.

Figure 2 - Growth in Social Welfare Expenditures in Canada Attributed to Different Factors[a], 1965-1977

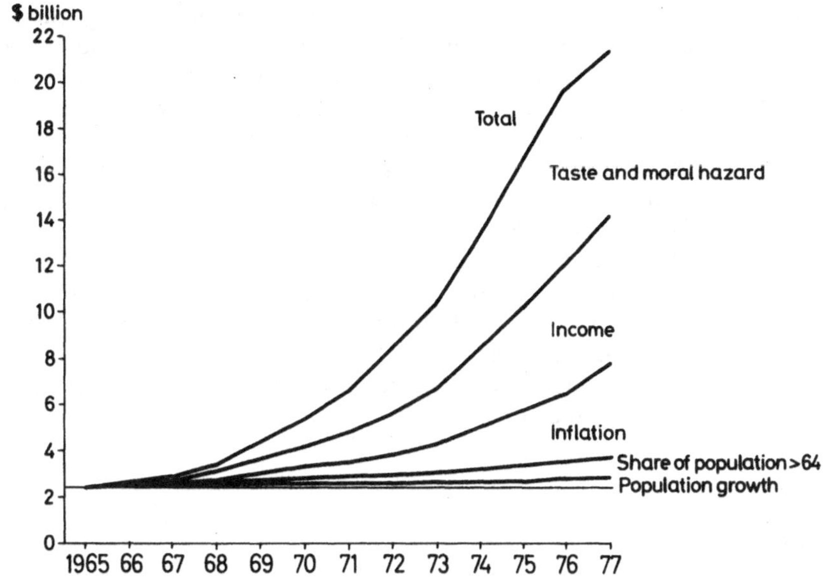

[a] $WE_{p,i} = (WE_{65} \cdot P_i)/(P_{65})$, where WE is welfare expenditure, P indicates adjustment for population growth, the subscript 65 refers to value in 1965 and i indicates the year. Further adjustments are made by multiplying $WE_{p,i}$ by A_i/A_{65}, where A is the share of the population above 64; and so on for each variable. The final value adjusted for population, age, inflation (I) and income per capita levels (Y) is: $WE^{*} = (WE_{65} \cdot P_i \cdot A_i \cdot I_i \cdot Y_i)/(P_{65} \cdot A_{65} \cdot I_{65} \cdot Y_{65})$.

Source: Calculated from time series in Canada Yearbook [1980-81].

However, during the period real income per person in Canada rose substantially. Arguments can be made in support of the view that there is no need to increase benefits proportionately since public charity is supposed only to provide a minimal safety net for the needy. By the same token, arguments can be made that the higher incomes permit a more generous treatment of the needy and benefits should grow more rapidly than income. Figure 2 reflects the view, which may well appeal to most people's sense of fairness, that the needy should receive a constant proportion of average incomes. As can be seen, under these conditions, 1977 expenditures should have been $14 billion. In fact, Canada spent in that year $21 billion, or 50 percent more.

In Figure 2 I have identified this last cause of increased expenditure as being attributable to taste or moral hazard or both of them. If it is due to society's desire to share increasing proportions of its growing income and wealth with the needy, then the data merely reflect this fact and in a sense there is no problem requiring any changes in policy. I cannot present analytical or empirical evidence to support or refute this proposition, which implies that society's income elasticity of demand for welfare is greater than one (in fact during this period it has been two since the assigned growth due to real income and taste are $7 billion each). Therefore, I can only advance as a hypothesis that during this period all or at least a substantial part of the growth in expenditures has been due to moral hazard behavior and therefore does not fill needs which the social insurance programs were originally designed to meet. Instead, they are required to fill needs which the programs have themselves created. If this hypothesis is correct, then there exists a case for policies designed to control moral hazard and through such measures to lower the level or rate of growth of welfare expenditures.

II. Moral Hazard

The term moral hazard has been developed by the insurance industry to describe the phenomenon that whenever a class of risk is insured, the incidence of the hazard is increased. Figure 3 may serve to make the concept more precise. Along the vertical axis we measure the percentage of the total cost of affliction by a hazard which is borne by the victim. In the absence of insurance, victims bear 100 percent of the cost. Insurance lowers it by amounts that are determined by the provisions of the insurance contract. Some costs of hazards, such as pain, inconvenience and social disapproval, are always borne by the afflicted so that in fact even the most generous contracts fail to reduce costs to zero.

Along the horizontal axis of Figure 3 we measure the number of hazard victims per 100 people. The function KL reflects the degree of moral hazard characteristic of a particular risk. As an illustration consider that in the absence of all unemployment insurance over the full business cycle the unemployment rate averages OM percent. After the introduction of universal unemployment insurance covering all but 40 percent of the total cost of being unemployed, the average rate of unemployment rises to ON percent.

Figure 3 - Moral Hazard

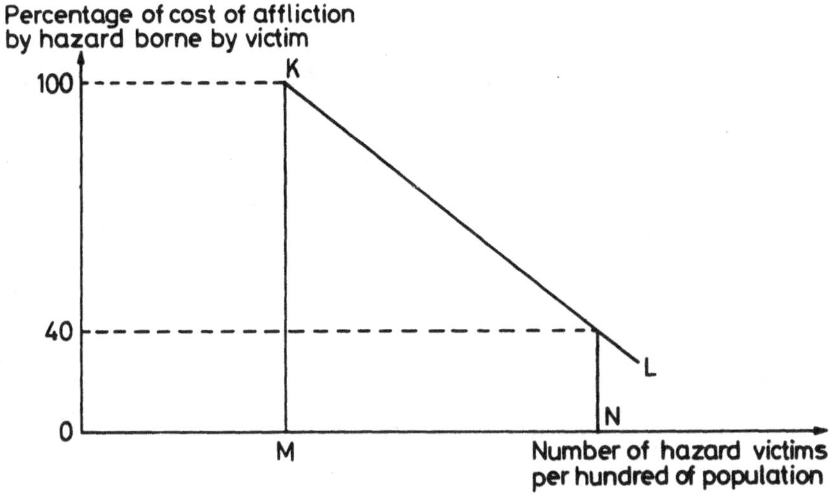

The elasticity of the KL curve which corresponds to the strength of moral hazard is different for each type of hazard, depending on the tastes of the insured and the technical possibilities for taking advantage of benefits. The determinants of the elasticity are discussed further below. The function KL is shifted by institutional changes affecting the general incidence of the hazard. For example, minimum wage legislation which leaves some low productivity workers unemployable shifts the curve to the right.

1. Causes of Moral Hazard

The term moral hazard creates a false impression about the cause of the phenomenon. It is not based on any changes in morality but instead is the outcome of economically rational behavior. This important point needs to be made with the help of a numerical example.

Let us consider a worker who can earn \$7 per hour or \$280 in a 40-hour week, taking home a net income of \$200 after payment of taxes and work-related expenses. For such a person the cost of *not* working is \$5 per hour or \$200 a week. Now consider that the government introduces nontaxable unemployment benefits at 50 percent of gross income. As a result the worker receives a \$140 income per week. In effect, the insurance scheme has lowered the cost of *not* working to \$60 per week or \$1.50 per hour. For many people not working is a "good", at least for part of the working year. More of this good is consumed the lower its price is and it should therefore not come as a surprise that when the availability of unemployment benefits lowers the cost of not working, on average there will be more people taking advantage of the opportunity.

The preceding argument made in terms of unemployment insurance benefits can be made for all kinds of other social security benefits. Blind persons, single parents, the handicapped, sick, victims of accidents and many other hazards find that the availability of insurance benefits lowers the cost of not working. The extent to which any objectively measurable impairment leads to the inability to work is greater the lower are the costs of not working due to the availability of the benefits.

One important determinant of the inducement effect of any given level of monetary benefits is the perceived cost of being afflicted by the hazard. In our Western societies not working was traditionally considered to be a sign of failure and carried the cost of social ostracism and stigma. In recent decades not working has lost much of this non-monetary cost and in some circles it is considered to be a matter of a "right" to draw on insurance benefits. "Fiddling", as the English call it, is becoming more and more a socially acceptable norm of behavior. In terms of Figure 3, such changes in public attitudes lower the effective level of coinsurance for any given monetary benefit.

While the preceding analysis discussed the way in which the availability of insurance benefits increases demand for them by people with a given set of objectively measurable handicaps, the availability of benefits also increases the incidence of the handicaps themselves because they lower the return on self-protection measures. For example, there are more single parents since the availability of benefits makes it less costly for unmarried women to become pregnant, forego abortions and put up children for adoption, while married mothers suffer less from divorce and marriage is discouraged. Unemployment insurance indirectly subsidizes seasonal and cyclical industries at the expense of the rest. It encourages employers to lay off workers more readily during periods of low business activity since they know that their employees can subsist on benefits and wait for recall rather than find work elsewhere. As a final example, consider the fact that the availability of public pensions has caused people to save less during their working age so that the availability of the pension benefits in fact has increased the need for them.

In sum, the causes of moral hazard behavior are public reaction to the lowered cost of being afflicted by insured risks, the lowered returns on preventing the risk from occurring and the change in public attitudes towards being in need of government benefits[1].

2. The Control of Moral Hazard

The private insurance industry has developed efficient methods for the control of moral hazard. It uses risk classes with different premiums to maintain incentives for the insured to protect themselves against the risks. For example, in the United States, automobile insurance premiums rise after a person has had an accident. Fire insurance premiums are lower for buildings with sprinkler systems than for those without. Risk classes are also used to attribute costs efficiently. Teenage drivers with higher accident propensities pay higher insurance premiums than the rest. As a result, there are fewer teenage drivers and accidents among the population of insured drivers.

A second method for the control of moral hazard used by the private insurance industry is coinsurance. For example, the first $100 of any automobile accident claim has to be borne by the insured. This practice reduces the level of small claims that are expensive in the aggregate while retaining the essential benefits of protection against catastrophic losses. Finally, private insurance reduces moral hazard behavior by the use of exclusion clauses and investigation procedures. For example, fire insurance is void in case of arson by the insured and life insurance benefits are not paid after suicide. Teams of investigators enforce compliance.

---

[1] It should be noted here that for the present purposes of analysis of the costs of public insurance programs it matters little what people do while they are not working and receive public benefits. Some time is spent on leisure activities, some spent on participating in the underground economy or in do-it-yourself work. Some time may be spent looking for better jobs or in training. From the perspective of overall welfare that includes the value of leisure and of non-market production, the cost of insurance-distorted behavior is much less than is measured by welfare payments and forgone market output. But such broad measures of welfare are not commonly used to evaluate the performance of market economies and they neglect the costs of the shrinking output and tax base and the distortions caused by the need for higher taxes on the rest of the population, which will be discussed below.

It can be shown that private industry measures to control moral hazard are efficient in that competitive forces encourage their use until marginal costs and benefits are equal. Premiums are set to reflect the costs of moral hazard control and competition assures that consumers can purchase what they consider to be the optimal package of benefits, moral hazard control features and premiums [see Grubel, 1971].

Public insurance has retained some of the private industry's moral hazard control measures. For example, unemployed workers face the coinsurance cost of not receiving benefits for a certain period after initial employment. In addition, the duration of benefits is limited and they have to produce evidence of job search. There are some basic rules determining eligibility of physically handicapped, single parents, etc. The problem with all of these rules is that they involve judgments that are difficult to make objectively. How can one know with any degree of certainty whether a person's unemployment is planned or forced by circumstances? There are cases where the evidence is quite unambiguous but there are many others where it is not. However, we do know that bureaucrats who have to make these judgments usually face the wrong incentives in the difficult task of evaluating individual circumstances. Being harsh on claimants brings appeals and political intervention, while being lenient has no costs. Certainly there are none of the penalties faced by lenient enforcements of moral hazard controls in competitive private insurance markets. For these reasons, we would expect public insurance to be subject to more moral hazard effects than private industry providing insurance against the same risks.

However, public insurance also has been designed deliberately without some of the private insurance control methods because such controls were conceived to be inequitable. For example, teenage drivers typically have low incomes and therefore it is unjust that they should pay the highest premiums. To redress this injustice, the compulsory, universal government automobile insurance company of British Columbia equalized insurance premiums for teenage and other drivers a few years ago. There are now more teenage drivers and higher accident rates than ever before. As another example, consider that unemployment insurance premia based on frequency of unemployment would burden most those who are the poorest with the most unstable employment opportunities. Consequently, uniform premia are used for all employees with the result that the incentives to seek jobs with stable work are reduced. As a final example, consider the case of coinsurance in public health programs. The payment of a nominal fee for a doctor's visit required by most private health insurance schemes has been waived in Canada, the United Kingdom and many other countries because the sickly and poor can least afford to pay it. The moral hazard effect has been so great that demand for medical services in these countries has had to be rationed by queuing.

Finally we should note that outright criminal fraud is rampant in many public social insurance programs. Convictions for the counterfeiting of food stamps and their illegal trade and use regularly are reported in the U.S. press and surely are only the tip of the iceberg. The receipt of multiple pension and unemployment insurance checks, the skimming of medical lab fees and many other practices have been exposed. These and many other types of fraud are facilitated by the very large scale of the government programs, which make virtually impossible the enforcement of the kinds of controls usually employed by smaller private insurance companies. Yet, such fraud raises public insurance costs and represents a form of induced moral hazard behavior responsible for the slope of the function in Figure 3.

3. Measuring Moral Hazard

The foregoing discussion of the nature of moral hazard in social insurance schemes is qualitative only. The arguments about the direction of the incentive effects of social insurance schemes basically are not new and are accepted as valid by most people. The central and crucial issue for the reassessment of policies in this field is the magnitude of the moral hazard effects. Just as in the case of private insurance the existence of moral hazard does not make the industry inefficient, so no argument about the need for changes in social insurance can be based solely on the proof of the existence of the phenomenon. As Okun [1975] put it, a leak in the bucket delivering relief for the poor does not justify abandonment of the relief effort. What is needed is an assessment of the size of the leak.

Unfortunately, systematic measurement of moral hazard has been made very difficult by the absence of suitable data and, perhaps more important, until recently in academic and government circles the need for such studies had not been realized. However, since the middle 1970s several efforts have been made to measure the elasticity of the moral hazard function in Figure 3. One of the first attempts to do so was done for the Canadian and U.S. unemployment insurance programs

[Grubel et al., 1975; Grubel, Maki, 1976][1]. These studies showed that increases in benefits relative to wages of about 20 percent may have induced additional unemployment equal to 1 to 2.5 percentage points in the official unemployment rates. In a careful survey of similar U.S. academic work done in the late 1970s, Danziger et al. [1981, p. 998] concluded that for four major U.S. social insurance programs "...because of supply restrictions by transfer recipients, total work effort in the economy was 3.3 percent less than it would have been. Adding the reductions due to other programs ... gives a total reduction of 4.8 percent".

While the empirical study of moral hazard is in its infancy, already existing results suggest quite strongly that the phenomenon is quantitatively important. The bucket has leaks large enough to justify a careful scrutiny of its use.

III. Other Costs of Social Insurance Programs

There is no doubt that Canada's social insurance programs have contributed to the dramatic rise in that country's tax burden noted by Pipes and Walker [1982, Table 8]. During the period 1961-1980 taxes rose 500 percent and real incomes only 350 percent. The preceding analysis suggests that this increased burden was due in large part to the rise in benefits per person and to the induced increase in the number of recipients and in the average duration of need. The latter two causes of increased social insurance expenditures have an additional effect important for the analysis of the overall costs of social insurance programs in that they result in a shrinking of the tax base and the need for higher average and marginal tax rates on the remaining productive persons.

The incentive effects of high tax rates in a world with substantial social insurance programs have only recently been given the theoretical attention they deserve. As Lindbeck [forthcoming] points out, when taxes are used to provide services taxpayers previously purchased

---

[1] Studies of unemployment compensation programs in other countries modelled after the Grubel-Maki study came up with analogous results. See the proceedings of a conference on this subject sponsored by the Fraser Institute [Grubel, Walker, 1978].

privately, then the traditional ambiguity between the dominance of income and substitution effects disappears and substitution effects dominate clearly. For example, when the government imposes taxes to finance a pension scheme, taxpayers face no income effect since the tax payments replace the previous contributions to private retirement schemes. However, the taxes reduce the returns from work and generate a pure substitution effect.

The social insurance programs themselves facilitate institutionally the ability of people to take advantage of the lower cost of not working as noted above. Because of the problems associated with deciding genuine and induced need for sick leave, unemployment insurance benefits and support of the handicapped, it is quite easy to substitute leisure for work, the return on which has been lowered by high tax rates.

The preceding analysis suggests that in empirical studies of the effect of social insurance programs on work effort the independent variable should be the benefit level relative to income *after* taxes. To the extent that existing studies have taken the tax variable into account, results already reflect the tax-induced substitution effect.

However, high taxes have additional effects not measured in these studies but known to have become increasingly important in recent years. Lindbeck [1980] notes that Swedish engineering schools lack students while university programs leading to lower-income and consumption-oriented careers are overcrowded. Canadian firms report a growing reluctance of executives to trade higher pay for the cost of moving to new locations. The growth of the underground economy in many countries is believed to have accelerated in recent years. The main motive for this growth has been the rise in tax burdens [Grubel, 1982], although participation in the underground economy may in turn be facilitated by the availability and generosity of social insurance programs. While the welfare implications of substitution of employment into underground activities are different from those generated by substitution into leisure, the synergistic link between welfare programs, the incentive effects of high tax rates, shrinking tax bases and the underground economy suggest that the total effects of social insurance on effort and welfare are larger than that implied by the analysis of moral hazard alone.

Changes in the Nature of Society

Social insurance programs and high tax burdens caused by them change the nature of society subtly and slowly, but over the longer run fundamentally in a number of ways.

- Attitudes towards work, education and savings are changed because the traditional penalties of failure and rewards for success are much reduced. Employers' complaints about the poorer work habits and absenteeism, especially of the young, are probably correct on average. We already noted above the decreased interest in engineering studies in Sweden. Average savings in the United States and many other countries have decreased as insurance takes the place of private assets for use during medical emergencies and retirement.
- There are growing social and political tensions between those with the traditional values and high incomes, paying high taxes, and the young generation with the new values, for whom the benefits and chosen behavior patterns are a matter of right.
- Aid to people with marginal ability to work such as single parents, pensioners and the handicapped creates a sense of frustration and dependence. It is difficult to find the energy and resourcefulness to learn skills, work-habits and take on the discomfort of work when the effective pay rate is lowered so much by the availability of welfare benefits and taxes on income.
- Single parent support programs increase the number of children who are raised without a father or mother in the home. Many of the crime problems of New York's Harlem are attributed to the effects which this welfare program has had on the black families living there.
- The traditional multi-generation family relationships are broken up as welfare programs reduce intergenerational dependence. This may be welcomed for some of the benefits it brings, but one of the costs must be the reduced influence of grandparents and the increased influence of television on the formation of character and values of young people.
- The welfare programs have led to a vast proliferation of laws and regulations that invite "fiddling". As a result, general standards of honesty have been eroded. "Everyone is doing it" and "I have paid my taxes" are the easy rationalizations used.
- The administration and enforcement of laws concerning the operation of the social insurance programs have led to an expansion of

the coercive power of the state and judiciary. Efforts to control moral hazard behavior and the avoidance and evasion of taxes have reinforced those tendencies. It is not just libertarians who regret these developments. Many people fear the tax auditor, and many single parents and sick persons have been spied upon by authorities attempting to establish whether they fake illness, work surreptitiously or have common law spouses.

- The state paying for the consequences of poor diet, accidents or lost investments has taken on the task of assuring that people are protected from these hazards. The vast body of economic regulation has been motivated at least in part by these considerations. Most economists accept the view that this regulation is inefficient and lowers overall standards of living[1]. In addition, it interferes with freedom of choice and changes the very nature of our pluralistic society.

What the nature of society should be is not a question which can be answered objectively and people hold many different and defensible views. For these reasons the preceding list of social changes induced by public insurance programs and accompanying taxes produces no concerns in the minds of many people. For others they are simply an acceptable cost of creating a more humane society that takes good care of its needy. For still others, however, the developments signal an alarming move away from the pluralistic model of democracy with decentralized markets and individual freedoms which has served Western societies during the last three centuries and has resulted in the highest living standards and economic and social mobility in the history of mankind. They also see the changes as a move towards the organization of society that has worked so poorly in recent decades in the Soviet Union and other socialist countries. Seen from these perspectives, the changes in the nature of society induced by public insurance programs represent a serious cost that is at least as important as the more obvious monetary and direct incentive effects. In a rational reassessment of social insurance programs, all three types of cost should be considered.

---

[1] For a balanced view on this issue, see Economic Council of Canada [1981].

IV. Summary and Policy Conclusions

The analysis of this paper provided price-theoretic explanations of the rapid growth in social insurance expenditures observed in Canada and, by implication, in other countries during the last two decades. The main conclusion of the analysis is that social insurance programs of necessity stimulate changes in behavior that increase their costs in the form of needed taxation, reduced effort and risk taking, the growth of the underground economy and changes in the nature of society. Empirical evidence on the magnitude of those effects that can now be distilled from the experience of the last 20 years suggests that these costs are much higher than many people would have expected when "need" was assumed to remain unaffected by the programs themselves. I believe that the evidence on current and expected costs implies the need for a fundamental reassessment of the nature and scope of social insurance programs in Western societies.

The analysis of the causes of excess costs of social insurance programs suggests a feasible alternative in the form of private insurance and charity. As was seen, under these arrangements for looking after society's needy, moral hazard behavior is controlled by efficient and equitable methods while the costs associated with high tax burdens are eliminated. Perhaps, to satisfy a possibly high income elasticity of demand for security the government can create special tax incentives to support the activities of private charities.

In my view, unfortunately the replacement of public by private insurance schemes is politically not very likely for two main reasons. First, the existence of the excess cost of social insurance programs discussed in this paper is not widely understood; in my personal experience I found that there exists a great reluctance by many intellectuals and opinion makers to even discuss it. The humanitarian benefits of social insurance programs are so obvious and great that many people consider the programs to be sacred cows the maintenance cost of which is irrelevant. Second, the existing programs have created powerful vested interests, as has been experienced by politicians and publicists who dared to suggest changes in social insurance schemes.

The existence of these reasons for strong political opposition to the substitution of private insurance and charity for public programs does not mean, of course, that advocacy of the economically first best system should stop. In fact, the present paper should be interpreted as an attempt to influence political reality through the rational analysis of the total costs and benefits of alternative systems evaluated in the light of historic experience guided by fundamental price theoretic principles.

However, the analysis of this paper also suggests second-best policies for dealing with the problems of social insurance programs. First, the lowering of benefits relative to wages would do much to reduce moral hazard while permitting continued achievement of the objective of having an economic safety net for the needy. At the same time, more of the private controls of moral hazard can be introduced with the clear understanding that social insurance programs must not be perverted to serve other objectives than the ones for which they were designed. Second, simultaneous private insurance and charity should be encouraged through the removal of restricting policies and taxes to compete with public programs. The result should be an optimum mix of private and public schemes for care of the needy.

The choices are clear, but this does not make them easy. It remains to be seen whether politicians in Western countries have the courage to make these choices or whether they will take the easy way out and disregard the growing costs of the welfare state.

References

Canada Yearbook, various issues.

Danziger, Sheldon H., Robert Haveman, Robert Plotnick, "How Income Transfers Affect Work, Savings and the Income Distribution". The Journal of Economic Literature, Vol. 19, 1981, pp. 957-1028.

Economic Council of Canada, Reforming Regulation 1981. Ottawa 1981.

Grubel, Herbert G., "Risk, Uncertainty and Moral Hazard". Journal of Risk and Insurance, Vol. 38, No. 1, 1971, pp. 99-106.

--, "The Underground Economy as Rational Adjustment to Government Policies". Simon Fraser University, Discussion Papers, 80-03-2, Vancouver 1982.

--, Dennis Maki, "The Effects of Unemployment Benefits on U.S. Employment Rates". Weltwirtschaftliches Archiv, Vol. 112, 1976, pp. 274-299.

Grubel, Herbert G., Michael A. Walker (Eds.), Unemployment Insurance: Global Evidence of its Effects on Unemployment. The Fraser Institute, Vancouver 1978.

--, Dennis Maki, Shelley Sax, "Real and Insurance-Induced Unemployment in Canada". The Canadian Journal of Economics, Vol. 8, 1975, pp. 174-191.

Guilder, George, Wealth and Poverty. New York 1981.

von Hayek, Friedrich A., The Road to Serfdom. Chicago 1944.

Lindbeck, Assar, "Work Disincentives in the Welfare State". University of Stockholm, Institute for International Economic Studies, Discussion Paper No. 164, Stockholm 1980.

--, "Tax Effects versus Budget Effects on Labour Supply". Economic Inquiry, forthcoming.

Okun, Arthur M., Equality and Efficiency: The Big Tradeoff. The Brookings Institution, Washington 1975.

Pipes, Sally, Michael A. Walker, Tax Facts 3: The Canadian Consumer Tax Index and You. The Fraser Institute, Vancouver 1982.

Comment

Hermann Albeck

In commenting on Grubel's paper I shall concentrate my remarks on unemployment insurance in West Germany, thus complementing Grubel's statements which highlight the situation in Canada and the United States.

I. The need for reform

1. Current discussion is frequently based upon the severe budgetary problems of the Federal Government, especially of the Federal Employment Office which administers unemployment insurance. Sometimes the current deficits are pointed to as a problem showing the necessity of reform; however, the present deficit reflects cyclical short-run as well as medium- and long-run developments.

In the textbooks, unemployment insurance is regarded as a very efficient automatic stabilizer: stabilization is achieved by balancing the budget in the medium run, i.e. over cyclical movements of unemployment. In discussing the financial problems of the unemployment insurance scheme, one should make a distinction between the cyclical and the structural (medium- and long-term) component of the deficit. Corrections need only be made with respect to the structural component.

2. The structural problem is partially due to basic incentive problems. The existence of social security institutions implies that they will also be made use of in cases other than those for which they had originally been created. This problem is generally known as moral hazard: Social security enters cost-benefit considerations of individuals as a given factor and alters their behavior - creating a demand for social security benefits (a type of Say's law).

a. The influence that this incentive exerts on behavior depends largely on the institutional design of the system which provides security in times of unemployment. Important factors are eligibility criteria, level of benefits and length of the entitlement period.

In West Germany, the system of unemployment insurance is organized in the following way:

- Unemployed persons who are available for placement and have completed the necessary qualifying period are entitled to regular unemployment benefits; they must be registered at the local employment office and must have applied for regular unemployment benefits (according to § 100, I of the "Arbeitsförderungsgesetz (AFG)").

  Availability (for placement) is defined as ability and capability to pursue a suitable employment. It also includes the ability of the persons unemployed to contact the local employment office daily and to be reached by the office at any time.

  Until the end of 1981, the qualifying period was considered to be completed if, within the last three years (limit period) prior to unemployment, an insured employment had been engaged in for a total of 180 calendar days (for changes since then, see the Appendix).

- The regular unemployment benefit amounts to 68 per cent of the former net wage. Additional earnings of the unemployed person are taken into account (so far as the necessary information is available to the employment office). It is important to note that the unemployment insurance scheme pays the contributions to the other branches of the social security system for the unemployed, and at the same level as those persons had previously paid when in employment. Hence the capital value of the unemployed person's claims upon the pension insurance system increases.

- The length of the entitlement period for regular unemployment benefit was (until 1981) about half the number of days within the limit period for which an insured employment had been engaged in, with a general limit of one year. After this entitlement is exhausted, unemployment assistance can be received in case of need; it amounts to 58 per cent of the standardized net wage. This benefit is financed by the Federal Government. It is actually a welfare benefit and must not be assimilated to unemployment insurance.

An international comparison of the respective amounts of unemployment benefits paid shows West Germany in a medium position. This result is derived by taking as an indicator a "net replacement rate", which is defined as net unemployment benefit divided by actual net earnings (not including transfer payments). (See the Table.)

Net Replacement Rates[a] for Various Industrialized Countries, 1981

Country	Unemployment insurance scheme	Unemployment assistance
West Germany	65	55
France[b]	69 (85)	22
United Kingdom	39	-
Japan[c]	50 (71)	-
Sweden[d]	84	37
United States[c]		
California	27 (42)	-
Illinois	46 (60)	-
Pennsylvania	48 (64)	-

[a]Net unemployment benefits as a percentage of actual net earnings ("net replacement rates"). - [b]The number in parentheses indicates a special type of benefit ("allocation spéciale"). - [c]The number in parentheses indicates the benefit without subtraction of social security contributions (to be paid by the unemployed). - [d]Highest benefit class.

Source: Albeck, Blum [forthcoming].

b. Various types of behavioral incentives can be distinguished. Until now, investigations of such incentives have been made predominantly as an analysis of disincentives to work. The formal aspect of this analysis is well known, but some empirical attempts have also been made to measure these effects [e.g. Grubel et al., 1975]. It should be borne in mind that the usual static model of microeconomic theory neglects the influence of expectations about future employment prospects on the choice between working and not working. In practice, however, an employee will see his prospects as a function of his previous "employment biography"; in this sense, periods of unemployment will have a negative effect on his prospects.

It may be useful in this context to give a brief analysis of the actual behavior usually designated as misuse of the unemployment insurance scheme, which includes the following. Female employees register as unemployed without having any real interest in finding a job, since they intend in the future to stay at home and raise children. Employees take their time before starting on a new employment or a training course. Unemployed persons who are offered a job by the employment office purposely create the impression of unwillingness to work during an interview with a prospective employer; thus they are either not hired at all or are dismissed after a brief period of employment.

The part played by behavior incentives in the case of management and unions has not been analyzed to the same extent, although their effects are at least as important. Numerous examples can be given of employers making their employment policy partly dependent upon the system of unemployment insurance actually in operation. In West Germany, the following very often happens. Employees are dismissed at the age of 59 because they will be paid an "early retirement benefit" from the funds of the pension insurance system if they have been unemployed for at least 52 weeks during the period of one and a half years preceding their 60th year of age (they must also have a minimum entitlement period of 180 months in the pension insurance scheme). The employees generally accept their dismissal, because they are eligible to receive a regular unemployment benefit in the meantime, and are also paid the difference between that benefit and their former net earnings by the employer. This is a fast and cheap way to make jobs vacant. Behavior incentives may be important in the unions as well. Guaranteeing a high security of income in case of unemployment can seriously diminish the attention paid by unions to the possible consequences of wage bargaining activity for employment. This is true for both the structure and the level of real wages. It must be admitted, however, that it may be difficult to diagnose the effects of wage bargaining by unions in the individual case.

The different types of behavior outlined above bring about changes in the level and structure of registered unemployment, and increase the expenditures that have to be made for the unemployed. By how much is difficult to determine in detail; it will be assumed here that the importance of behavioral incentives in the system operating in West Germany has been overestimated, at least as far as employees are concerned. Thus some doubts may remain about the extent to which reform is necessary, but definitely not about the direction in which the corrections will have to be made.

II. Reforming Unemployment Insurance - Some Reflections on Various Methods

There are different methods of coping with the problem of disincentives. In the following, attention shall be concentrated on three types of reform or - to be less ambitious - three types of corrective measures. The borderlines between the first two types are somewhat blurred.

1. The first type is characterized by measures to strengthen administrative control and will be effected within the systems as they exist at present. Since the formal organization of the present scheme is left unchanged, this policy seems to be the easiest to put into practice.

It was applied to the system in West Germany in 1982 (see the Appendix). The most important measures taken were:

- More rigorous eligibility criteria for those receiving unemployment benefits.
- Refusal of regular unemployment benefits to employees receiving special payments from their former employer; employers having dismissed older employees have to reimburse to the labor office the benefits it has paid to the employee dismissed.
- Extension of disqualification periods.
- A widening of the term "suitable employment".
- Measures ensuring that unemployment benefits together with wage tax refunds cannot amount to more than net earnings from employment.

On the whole there was no linear curtailment of benefits, since the only effect of doing this would have been to ease the deficit problem; the measures taken reflect the efforts to limit payments only to those who actually are in need.

In general, administrative measures suffer from the problem that they must be exercised by bureaucrats who are to some extent incapable of performing the difficult task of evaluating individual circumstances and are perhaps unwilling to do so. In the case of West Germany some impediments to such deficiencies in administrative behavior may exist because of the particular organizational features of the employment services (decentralized self-administration by employers' and employees' organizations); yet the general problem remains. It has to be combatted by strengthening the interest of individuals and social groups in avoiding unemployment.

2. The second type of reform changes the organizational framework by introducing (more) private insurance elements. Different versions can be conceived of:

- The individual employee's stimulus to moral-hazard behavior is reduced if he himself partially bears the costs of his unemployment. This is the familiar principle of co-insurance used by private insurers. There are various forms in which this can be organized in practice - for instance, the payment of regular unemployment benefits only after a certain minimum period of unemployment (and correspondingly the payment of a lower general contribution rate). Another method would be to calculate different insurance premia according to different frequency distributions of risk: the higher the risk of being unemployed, the higher the premium. The distributive consequences are a high level of contributions by the poor, and a low level by the rich. As far as the incentive problem is concerned, the drawback of this method is that there is a lack of efficiency because of a lack in direct participation.
- The employers' willingness to offer employment can also be influenced by means of the introduction of insurance elements. "Experience rating" is a common practice in the United States; it is a kind of "no-claim bonus" granted to employers according to the consistency of their employment over some period of time. The basic principle is conceived as follows: The labor administration keeps records of the individual firm's contributions and its dismissals, including the benefit costs occurring; the contributions are based upon wages paid. The higher and more consistent the employment level of an employer, and the lower the number of persons he dismisses, the more favorable will his record balance be; a favorable record balance ("credit balance") will yield him a bonus in the form of lower contribution rates. There is a multitude of such "rating systems" in the various states.

3. The third type differs not only in degree from the former two. Its main characteristic consists in the fact that, if unemployment differs from a normal or desired level, either employers or trade unions or both become liable to participation in the financing of the scheme. If unemployment is abnormally high, additional contributions have to be paid; if unemployment is abnormally low, surpluses can be collected from the scheme.

- The concept of compulsory additional contributions by the unions has been elaborated by Risch [1980]. The basic idea is that - with economic policy creating the appropriate conditions for a stable value of money - the level of employment depends upon real wages. If the unions push real wages up to a level which is not compatible with full employment, thus causing deficits in the unemployment insurance scheme, these deficits should be borne by those who were responsible for them. This corresponds to the general principle that external costs are to be prevented or reduced by internalizing them.

- In analogy to compulsory additional contributions by the unions, it would be possible to make employers as well pay an additional compulsory contribution, for both groups participate in collective bargaining and have to sign the agreements. Wallich and Weintraub [1971] have suggested a penalty tax on employers agreeing to pay wages at "too high" a level. This is the same reasoning that characterizes the proposal outlined directly above but extends it in a symmetrical fashion. Employers paying below-average wages will be paid a bonus to the extent that surpluses occur in the unemployment insurance scheme.

The organizational measures which would be needed to give effect to a change of this type reflect the width of the underlying policy concept: Unemployment insurance should be reformed in such a way as to make the pursuit of basic targets of stabilization policy more effective. However, there also are certain problems connected with proposals of this third type. Only two of them can be mentioned here. The first is the definition of a "normal" level of employment. It implies direct financial consequences for unions and employers respectively, and will therefore be highly controversial. Second, there is the problem of diagnosis. The proper functioning of the system requires the determination of the rate of wage increase which corresponds to the "normal" level of employment. This applies to both the level and the structure of wages. The difficulties arising are well known from attempts at constructing and operating incomes policy (for instance the concept of "Kostenniveauneutrale Lohnpolitik", developed by the Council of Economic Experts in West Germany). The third type of proposal is particularly appealing because the parties to collective wage bargaining themselves determine the wages corresponding to the "normal" employment level. The task of the incentive system is to enforce this "tâtonnement". This system, however, makes the collective bargaining parties responsible for any deviation from the "normal" level of employment. They will only accept this responsibility, if at all, if the deviations are solely due to the behavior of wages - but in reality such deviations clearly may occur for other reasons. Hence the diagnosis problem will remain.

Appendix

The following corrective measures in unemployment insurance were introduced in West Germany in 1982:

(1) ALG ("Arbeitslosengeld", regular unemployment benefit): Until 1982 a minimum of 180 calendar days of employment subject to contribution was required within the last three years prior to unemployment; starting 1982, the minimum is 360 calendar days. ALH ("Arbeitslosenhilfe", unemployment assistance): Until 1982 a minimum of 70 calendar days or 10 weeks of remunerated employment within the last year prior to unemployment was required; starting 1982 the minimum is 150 calendar days (not applicable to the unemployment assistance that is received after exhaustion of entitlement to the regular unemployment benefit).

(2) Employees receiving payments from their former employer for leaving their job, or receiving an indemnity payment after having left their job without respecting the regular term of notice, will be refused the regular unemployment benefit; employers dismissing older employees who have been employed by the firm for ten years or more must reimburse the Employment Office for the regular unemployment benefit (as well as the social security contributions) paid to the employee dismissed for the period after the completion of the 59th year of age.

(3) Disqualification periods are extended if the job has been left without any important reason or a suitable employment has been rejected; the disqualification period is extended from 4 to 8 weeks; if the compulsory registration at the Employment Office is not performed regularly, further disqualifications may be imposed.

(4) Full-time employment requiring a daily total of two and a half hours travel to and from work is considered suitable; if a job cannot be found for an unemployed person which corresponds to his actual qualifications in the first four months, employment at the next lower level of qualification is regarded as suitable. After another four months of fruitless placement activity, employment on the next lower qualification level becomes suitable (there is a total of five qualification levels from university and technical college graduates down to the unskilled).

(5) The different types of unemployment benefits are taken into account for the annual employee tax declaration, ensuring that unemployment benefits together with wage tax refunds do not amount to more than net earnings from employment.

(6) The regular unemployment benefit for unemployed persons who had been employed by their spouse or close relatives will be calculated with reference to the standard wage paid for a comparable activity at any employer's firm.

(7) The unemployed have to be willing to participate in a vocational training course, or in courses to improve their placement possibilities, and in vocational rehabilitation activities. A lower benefit is paid in the case of vocational training.

References

Albeck, Hermann, Julius Blum, Ökonomische Auswirkungen unterschiedlich hoher Leistungen an Arbeitslose in ausgewählten Industrieländern. Cologne, forthcoming.

Grubel, Herbert G., Dennis Maki, Shelley Sax, "Real and Insurance-Induced Unemployment in Canada". The Canadian Journal of Economics, Vol. 8, 1975, pp. 174-191.

Risch, Bodo, Arbeitslosenversicherung, Gewerkschaften und Beschäftigungsgrad. Die Weltwirtschaft, 1980, H. 2, pp. 49-57.

Wallich, Henry C., Sidney Weintraub, "A Tax-Based Incomes Policy". Journal of Economic Issues, Vol. 5, No. 2, 1971, pp. 1-19.

Roland Vaubel

Reforming Social Security for Old Age

The decline of the birth rate and the deceleration of economic growth in most industrialized countries have focussed attention on the need to reform our social security systems for old age. In West Germany, for example, the ratio of contributors to retirees is projected to decrease by almost half within the next fifty years, declining to 1.12 in 2030, if the present birth rate continues. If the current benefit formula were maintained, the social security tax rate would have to increase from 18 per cent in 1982 to 32 per cent in 2030. If the current tax rate were maintained, the ratio of social security pensions to current after-tax wages would have to be almost halved. Qualitatively similar results have been obtained for most other industrialized countries[1].

The question of social security reform cannot be addressed without reference to a conception of the optimal social security system. Such a conception will be developed in Section I. Section II contrasts present-day social security systems with the ideal of the optimal system. Section III analyzes the economic and political problems of transition to the optimal system. The final section summarizes the policy implications of the analysis: it sketches a blueprint for reform.

I. The Case for Mandatory Insurance for Old Age

The case for some form of social security for old age has been based on mainly three arguments.

According to the first, mandatory social security is required to prevent those who could save for old age during their working life from relying on public assistance when they have to retire. Social security is designed to prevent public assistance from generating moral hazard;

[1] For the German case see Jüttemeier, Petersen [1982]. The prospects for France, the United Kingdom, Italy, Japan, Sweden, Switzerland and the United States are also analyzed in Rosa [1982].

for just as, say, unemployment insurance reduces the incentive to seek employment, public assistance reduces the incentive to provide for one's old age. The temptation to rely on public assistance in old age is, of course, stronger, the less public assistance falls short of (or the more it exceeds) the old-age income that would have been chosen in the absence of public assistance. Whether moral hazard is a serious problem thus depends crucially on the size of the minimum income which society guarantees for humanitarian reasons.

Moral hazard can be eliminated by forcing everybody to save for an old-age income equal to the social minimum. Since the time of death is uncertain, it may be impossible to predict whether a given amount of savings is sufficient to generate an old-age income equal to, or larger than, the social minimum. Hence, the argument goes, insurance for old age (i.e., insurance against the risk of an unexpectedly long life) must be made compulsory; there must be forced saving in the form of annuities.

The argument from moral hazard is theoretically impeccable as far as it goes. It probably has more appeal with conservative than with socialist economists. This explains why it was the dominant economic argument used by Bismarck's followers in the 1880s[1]. The practical relevance of the argument is open to doubt: Friedman [1962, pp. 188ff.] and Browning [1979, pp. 188 f.], for example, object that, in the absence of mandatory social security, only a negligible proportion of the old would be in need of public assistance. Since many of the old could continue to work or would be supported by their spouse or their children, Browning estimates that only about 1.5 per cent of the old would be on the dole. He suggests that the payment of public assistance to these people would probably be cheaper than a program requiring everyone to save specified amounts.

However this may be, the argument from moral hazard cannot justify an obligation to insure with a government agency or any other specific insurance company. The government, if it requires a specific type of

---

[1] The main motive, however, was political: the establishment of social security seemed to be an expedient way of stealing the socialists' thunder. This was stated by Wilhelm I with Germanic frankness in his imperial message to the Reichstag on November 17, 1881: "The detrimental social tensions should not only be dealt with by repressing [sic] social democratic excesses but also by positively furthering the welfare of the workers" (translation by the author).

insurance coverage, must, it is true, also be willing to supply such an insurance policy[1]. However, the citizen must be free to decide whether he accepts this offer or whether he prefers to purchase the mandatory insurance from a private insurance company. Moreover, the argument from moral hazard does not justify a mandatory system of graduated (for example, flat-rate) insurance contributions and benefits. Lifetime contributions and monthly benefits would have to be the same for everybody over a given period. Contributions would have to be calculated in such a way that their accumulated value at the official age of retirement would equal the discounted value of otherwise available public assistance up to the life expectancy age for those who have reached the official retirement age. The insurance would thus be actuarially fair.

The second argument for mandatory social security goes beyond the first because it purports to show that insurance for old age must be provided by government only and that it must be subsidized from general tax revenue. In its most general form, this argument states that insurance for old age is a natural monopoly, i.e., that it cannot be competitively supplied by private producers under laisser-faire and that it should be supplied by government rather than by a private monopolist. Since insurances benefit from the law of large numbers and possibly from other, non-stochastic economies of scale, their production may be subject to decreasing marginal costs. If marginal costs decline over the whole range of the market size, competition - if left to itself - destroys itself, and a private monopoly arises. In these circumstances, according to a widespread view, a government monopoly which sells at marginal cost and has its deficit covered by general tax revenue (ideally from a lump-sum tax) is superior to a private monopoly (unless perfect price discrimination is feasible), and it is also preferable to private competition enforced through merger control and market share limits.

The natural-monopoly argument can also be based on the argument from adverse selection. If, for some reason, it is impossible to detect the "bad risks" among those who apply for insurance, they will be the first to insure, thus making for a (more) downward sloping marginal cost curve (and a more downward sloping demand curve). Hence, adverse selection is a possible cause of a natural-monopoly situation.

[1] The comments by the discussant have led me to abandon this view.

Moreover, since it implies imperfect monitoring, it makes price discrimination by a private monopolist more difficult[1].

The argument from adverse selection has little relevance for the problem of old-age insurance. Very few of those who live longer than the average ("the bad risks") can predict this in advance. To the extent that it can be predicted, a private insurance will usually be in a position to predict it as well. Unlike a social security system, a private insurance has also a sufficient incentive to monitor. Finally, if the argument from moral hazard and thus the case for mandatory old-age insurance is accepted, the argument from adverse selection is redundant, as far as insurance for the social minimum is concerned: to the extent that everybody is required to insure for the social minimum, the private insurance industry cannot suffer from adverse selection because there cannot be selection at all[2].

Even if insurance for old age were a natural monopoly, it would not follow that a government monopoly is superior to a private monopoly, whether regulated, auctioned or even unregulated with free entry or that it is preferable to enforced competition[3]:

---

[1] It should be emphasized that adverse selection does not prevent the private insurance industry from supplying an insurance which, given the imperfections of information, it would be efficient for government to supply. If the demand curve cuts the downward sloping marginal cost curve from above, a private monopoly is viable (though not ideally efficient) at output levels left of the intersection. If the demand curve cuts the downward sloping marginal cost curve from below, a private monopoly is viable (though not ideally efficient) at output levels right of the intersection.

[2] Pauly [1974] has argued that mandatory public insurance for the income desired by the "good risks" may be necessary to find out who are the bad risks: all those, who demand additional insurance (from the public insurance or from private insurances) are likely to be bad risks. The difficulty with this argument is that the demand for additional insurance may also reflect higher risk aversion or a lower rate of time preference. Moreover, to achieve Pauly's aim it is not necessary for government to establish mandatory social security for old age; it would be sufficient for government to collect and provide information about each person's total purchases of old-age insurance. The external effects emanating from adverse selection do not indicate a need for social security but, if at all, only for differential taxation of good and bad risks.

[3] For a very illuminating graphic analysis of the welfare implications of the various alternatives see Rowley, Peacock [1975, pp. 176 ff.].

- A government monopoly is likely to suffer from severe X-inefficiency so that its marginal cost curve is higher.
- The deficit of the government monopoly cannot be covered with revenue from a lump-sum tax; financing of the deficit will create large distortions elsewhere.
- Historical experience shows that governments are incapable of keeping the insurance actuarially fair.

Moreover, even if a government monopoly were the optimal solution, insurance in excess of the social minimum would have to be optional instead of mandatory.

The natural-monopoly argument cannot be refuted by pure logic. The issue is empirical. There is no empirical evidence that old-age insurance is subject to permanently decreasing marginal costs and that public provision is more efficient than private provision. Nor has the contrary been demonstrated through empirical research. However, if old-age insurance were a natural monopoly, the reason for the government's activity in this field should have been that private competition had given way to a private monopoly. This has not been the case. Nor are private pensions today offered by only one firm. Therefore, the argument from natural monopoly is not convincing. At the very least, it should be tested by admitting private competition: each working citizen should be permitted to opt out of the governmentally administered social security system and to purchase his annuity from a private insurance[1]. In order to make sure that the government's old-age insurance is not kept alive with subsidies, anti-trust law should provide that, if the governmental social security system receives subsidies, the same subsidies should also be offered to private insurances for old age.

The third argument for mandatory social security goes still further than the preceding two and concludes that opting out must not be permitted and that mandatory social security may have to exceed the social minimum. This view defines the aim of social security as intergenerational (and possibly intragenerational) redistribution. Social security is viewed as an "intergenerational contract" by which each working generation collectively transfers part of its income to the old.

[1] This is also Friedman's fallback position [1962, pp. 185 ff.]. His conclusion is shared by Buchanan [1968, p. 391]: "Nothing inherent in this program requires a government monopoly".

The implication is that social security should not be run as an actuarially fair, funded system but on a pay-as-you-go basis. If opting out were permitted, those who receive less than their actuarially fair benefit would leave, and compulsory redistribution through social security would become impossible[1].

The argument from intergenerational redistribution raises the question of why transfers to the old should be compulsory and why they should be given collectively rather than individually. A possible argument is that a collective transfer system might reduce transfer costs; if this is true, it could explain why there seems to be almost unanimous agreement that some minimum standard of living should be guaranteed by the government. However, no such unanimity exists with respect to more far-reaching public redistribution. Those who object to such redistribution need not prefer a smaller volume of transfers; rather, they may suggest that private charity is more likely to concentrate on the deserving among the old than indiscriminate collective handouts in excess of the social minimum. For this reason, even the argument that private giving has positive external effects on all others who like to see poverty relieved, does not justify coercive public income transfers in excess of the social minimum, but merely public subsidization of private transfers to the poor among the old. The case for mandatory social security as an intergenerational transfer mechanism cannot even be based on distributive objectives; for redistribution could be brought about more efficiently (i.e., without a governmental monopoly) through the tax system.

From this I conclude: from an economic point of view, the optimal social security system is an actuarially fair public old-age insurance that is purely optional. If everyone is required to insure for the social minimum in old age, then all must be free to choose a private insurance agency.

---

[1] Feldstein and Pellechio [1979] have shown that, at least in the United States, social security wealth net of future social security taxes is negative for all who are less than 35 years of age and receive an income of at least $6,000 per annum. The same can be expressed in terms of rates of return: almost all who enter the system now face a rate of return that is not only below the market rate of return but even negative in real terms. The contributions by Kaplan, O'Neill and Browning in Campbell [1979], for example, offer various comparisons of rates of return for the United States.

II. The Case against Present-Day Systems of Social Security

The optimal social security system has never existed in any of the industrialized countries. Even Bismarck's social security scheme involved intergenerational and some intragenerational redistribution; although it was essentially a funded system, it was subsidized from general revenue to pay for the pensions of the initial generation of beneficiaries who had not contributed during all of their working life. Nowadays, only the Japanese social security system still has a large capital fund. All other industrialized countries have either turned to outright general revenue financing (Canada, Denmark and, to a very large extent, all other Scandinavian countries) or to an (almost) pure pay-as-you-go system (France, Netherlands, the United States); both elements are combined in Belgium, Italy, the United Kingdom, Switzerland and West Germany. Only in the British system are citizens permitted to contract out of the earnings-related component of social security pensions in favor of private occupational pension schemes[1].

What are the main effects of the present-day systems of social security?

1. Present-day systems of social security do not only *redistribute* among generations but also within generations:

- In most countries, the benefit schedule is not proportional to the earnings schedule, if only because there are upper and lower bounds on benefits, but wider bounds or none at all on social security tax; as a result, there are intragenerational transfers from high-income earners to low-income earners.
- To the extent that pensions are financed with general tax revenue from a progressive tax system, similar transfers result from general-revenue financing.
- Politicians tend to redistribute revenue between different social security programs.
- Social security discriminates in favor of women at the expense of men to the extent that women have a longer life expectancy and are entitled to earlier retirement.

---

[1] Occupational pension arrangements are frequently objected to on the ground that they reduce labor mobility. However, this disadvantage may be more than offset by the increased incentive to provide on-the-job training and the reduced need for monitoring.

- In most countries, the social security system discriminates in favor of married couples because the surviving spouse receives more than half the pension (irrespective of the number of children).

- In some countries, the social security system discriminates in favor of married men as compared to housewives because a widower receives a larger pension than a widow[1].

- In most countries, the social security system discriminates in favor of those who retire earlier, and/or against those who retire after the official retirement age.

- Since earnings-related benefits do not depend on the accumulated value of contributions but on some unweighted or arbitrarily weighted average of past annual earnings or on an average of highest or most recent annual earnings, social security tends to discriminate in favor of those whose life-time earnings profile is steepest.

2. The redistributive effects of social security tend to reduce the supply of labor:

- Present social security schemes tend to encourage earlier retirement. Although, as a result, some may work more before retirement, the total effect on lifetime labor supply is likely to be negative: the intertemporal substitutability of the "irksomeness" of labor can hardly be assumed to be perfect.

- To the extent that social security tax is a burden, say, because it offers a lower rate of return than other investments or exceeds desired savings for old age, there is a negative substitution effect on the work effort of those who are losing. It is often pointed out that the losers will also be subject to an income effect which increases their work effort. What tends to be ignored, however, is that the winners experience income and substitution effects, too, and that both these effects induce them to work less.

3. The most controversial issue is the effect of social security on private capital formation:

- Pay-as-you-go financing is likely to reduce the saving/income ratio below what it would be in a privately funded system. Social security claims for old age are part of individual wealth. As they increase, other forms of saving for old-age consumption and precautionary

[1] This is the case in West Germany where a widower continues to receive his full pension while the surviving housewive receives only 60 per cent.

purposes are likely to be reduced (if social security wealth is a perfect substitute for private wealth, possibly even on a 1:1 basis). The increasing social security claims, however, are not backed by any social security savings. They are backed by nothing but the hope that the next generation will be prepared to continue the chain-letter game.

Barro [1978] has emphasized that there is likely to be compensating behavior. Pay-as-you-go social security will not reduce the saving/income ratio to the extent that

(i) each generation gives correspondingly more to the following generation in other ways, say, through bequests, and

(ii) the following generation gives correspondingly less to its parents in other ways, say, by reducing their assistance.

However, as Feldstein [1978] has pointed out, offsetting can hardly be assumed to be complete:

(i) a parent who believes that his children will be richer than he himself may consider the optimal bequest under perfect foresight to be negative anyhow;

(ii) present social security transfers are much larger than what private old-age assistance used to be.

As is so often the case, the econometric evidence is consistent with both views[1]. Almost all studies obtain a positive regression coefficient for social security wealth in the consumption function, but the statistical significance of the coefficient depends crucially on the specification of the other explanatory variables in the consumption function as well as on the period of observation. As so often, we find ourselves in the uncomfortable situation of having to choose between competing hypotheses on the basis of the realism of their assumptions.

While Barro assumes that pay-as-you-go social security is exogenously imposed by the government and that information and compensating behavior are costless, Feldstein and his followers believe that the system is desired as a redistributive measure by a large section of the population and that, largely for this reason, compensating changes in private transfer are not a full offset. Barro's view that compensation is perfect implies that the detrimental effects of

---

[1] For recent surveys of the econometric work see Darby [1979] and Feldstein [1981].

pay-as-you-go social security are smaller than its critics claim. However, it also implies that social security does not achieve any intergenerational redistribution and therefore loses the rationale put forward by its adherents. On Barro's view, social security is redundant at best.

- To the extent that present social security schemes lead to earlier retirement, there is also likely to be compensating saving behavior before retirement: during their working lives people save a larger portion of their income than they would otherwise have done. However, as one would expect, the econometric evidence indicates that the positive induced-retirement effect on the saving-income ratio tends to be much smaller than the negative asset-substitution effect.
- Even if the saving-income ratio were not affected by social security, the amount of savings would fall as lifetime labor supply and income fall.
- If pay-as-you-go social security is not compared with a comprehensive funded system but with a world where saving for old age is voluntary and where private or public provision of the social minimum creates moral hazard, the loss of savings is less drastic. However, since most people save for their old age even when they are not forced to do so and although moral hazard exists, pay-as-you-go financing results in less saving than complete laisser-faire. It is an irony of history that social security, which originally was to make sure that everybody saves for his old age, has degenerated into a system which makes sure that, as far as public pensions are concerned, nobody saves for his old age.

4. Even more serious than the negative effects on the supply of labor and capital could be the *government's interference* with individual decision-making which social security entails. Present-day social security systems force many of the young to cut their consumption at a time when their income is lower and their responsibilities are greater than when they are old; since non-transferable social security claims are an imperfect collateral for borrowing, the intertemporal distribution of individual lifetime consumption is distorted. The retirement earnings test induces the individual to retire earlier than he might otherwise have desired. The young are forced to pay pensions to old people who have a higher income than they themselves. And the living generations make decisions at the expense of the unborn generations, as if the latter could be bound in this way.

> "We put those payroll contributions there so as to give the contributors a legal, moral, and political right to collect their pensions... With those taxes in there, no damn politician can ever scrap my social security program" [F.D. Roosevelt, quoted in: Leuchtenburg, 1963, p. 133].

III. The Political Economy of Social Security Reform

Many of those who agree that the establishment of present-day social security systems for old age was a mistake, nevertheless believe that, once a pay-as-you-go system has been started, it should not, or at least cannot, be stopped in a democratic society. I shall argue in this section that this conclusion does not follow. We thus turn from the static comparison of different social security systems to the dynamics of social security reform.

It may be that the damaging effects of present-day social security systems are not yet sufficiently realized by the general public to mobilize a majority against their continuation. To change this situation, as Browning [1979, p. 205] has pointed out, it would be desirable

- to send each taxpayer an annual statement reporting his social security wealth net of future contributions and the real rate of return on social security tax payments that has been observed in the past and is likely to accrue in the future[1];
- to have the employer portion of the social security tax borne explicitly by the employee;
- to reduce or eliminate the taxation of income from capital.

It would already be a great improvement if inflation were prevented from augmenting the real burden of taxation on income from private savings.

Nevertheless, Browning predicts that "there will be no major changes in the social security system at least until the next century. Prospects for meaningful reform now are not very great, and they will be even poorer in the future. Since the population will probably become much

[1] In countries where pensions are financed from general revenue, this part of the tax burden would have to be deducted as well.

older in the first half of the twenty-first century, political pressures at that time will generally favor a substantially larger system" [1979, pp. 206 f.].

To counter these tendencies which he expects, he suggests two possible reforms of the political decision-making process:
"First, the level of social security taxes (and, hence, benefits in an unfunded system) could be decided by majority vote in an annual referendum in which only those below a certain age - say, forty or fifty - are permitted to vote. Alternatively, a voting procedure in which three-fourths of the entire voting population must approve of the level of taxes for the policy to be enacted could be used" [1979, p. 206]. Since such changes are unlikely, it is important to emphasize that they are not necessary to achieve the aim.

First of all, it is not at all obvious that the chances for a meaningful reform are deteriorating. The decline in the birth rate, it is true, will tend to raise the average age of the population. However, since the decline in the birth rate also reduces the ratio of social security taxpayers to retirees (unless this is offset by increased immigration), the ratio of benefits to taxes deteriorates for each taxpayer so that the marginal age of those for whom net social security wealth is negative must rise[1]. Second, the reduction in the ratio of social security taxpayers to retirees does not only reduce the rate of return which the individual taxpayer would earn if the system were continued, it also increases the risk that the next working generation will stop the chain-letter game; this reduces the expected value of pension claims and increases their expected variance [see also Buchanan, 1968, p. 389]. Finally, the decline in the growth of real per capita income is likely to reduce the attractiveness of a pay-as-you-go system to the decisive voter of the centre.

It is an open question whether these developments will lead a majority of voters to abolish the social security system, if no compensation is paid for past contributions. The political chances are probably better for the proposal to permit opting out; for the case for individual freedom of choice is easier to understand than technical arguments about reductions in the supply of labor and capital and distortions of

[1] Feldstein and Pelechio [1979, p. 101] even believe that "the changing demographic structure... will increase the fraction of the population with negative net social security wealth and could thereby weaken the political support of the program". They estimate that at present one third of all U.S. voters face negative net social security wealth.

lifetime consumption patterns. Nevertheless, since in most countries freedom to opt out in favor of private old-age insurance is likely to entail the gradual extinction of social security, it is just as unlikely to be in the interest of a majority of voters as outright abolition, unless at least some of those who have contributed in the past receive compensation.

Buchanan [1968; 1979; 1981] and Friedman [1976; 1980, pp. 123 f.] have suggested that all claims on the social security system that have been accumulated in the past should be honored but that no new claims should be generated. Those who had acquired claims in the past should be compensated with a special issue of transferable government bonds that would bear a market rate of interest.

The proposal raises two major questions:

(i) How are social security claims to be valued?

(ii) Who is to pay for the servicing of this debt?

As for the first question, there are two obvious possibilities. One is to compute the accumulated value of past social security tax payments using past market interest rates. Alternatively, as Buchanan [1981] suggests, the compensation could be calculated as the discounted present value of the social security wealth to which the individual's past social security tax payments would have entitled him at his official retirement age. The value of the bonds could then be linked to the price index or wage index, whichever happens to be used to adjust benefits in the present system[1]. While the first method may be simpler, the second has the advantage of not disappointing contributors' expectations[2].

To suggest bond financing of compensation payments is to imply that the burden of compensating past contributors should not only be borne by the current working population. Indeed, Buchanan [1981] recommends the issue of indexed perpetuities so that the financial burden

[1] In Denmark, Ireland, Italy, Sweden and the United States, benefits are linked to a price index. In Canada, Finland, France, West Germany and the Netherlands, wage-indexing is practiced. The two types of indexing are combined in Belgium, Norway, Switzerland and the United Kingdom.

[2] Note that most other proposals for social security reform (e.g., changes in the indexation formula, increases in the retirement age, introduction of a means test, etc.) involve disappointment of contributors' expectations.

could be borne more or less equally by the current and all future working generations[1]. He believes that this would be a Pareto-improvement. However, if the current working generation has to pay additional taxes to service the perpetuities, it may not be in their interest to terminate, or to admit termination of, the pay-as-you-go system. Termination would only make the young better off, and what they would be willing to pay for the abolition of the system might be less than the net interest payments on compensation bonds for which they would be taxed during their working life.

What this means is that the dismantling of social security is not necessarily a Pareto-improvement unless the doomsday generation is taken into account as well. For it is the last generation which is the main loser in the chain-letter game. If the termination of the pay-as-you-go system is also to be a Pareto-improvement for the current generation, part of the debt service may have to be financed by issuing further debt. If it is to be a Pareto-improvement for all living and future generations, all generations except the last may have to finance part of the debt service by issuing further debt.

To say that this is a Pareto-efficient solution is not to say that it is likely to be preferred by the majority of voters. To rally a majority in a democracy it is necessary for the young merely to bribe a sufficient number of middle-aged voters by offering them compensation for the social security benefits which they expect to receive on the basis of their past contributions. The compensation could be financed from the gains to the young and/or by taxing the minority. The young may not even have a bad conscience about this majoritarian approach. No generation, they might argue, can morally oblige any following generation without the latter's consent. Any generation which starts or continues a chain-letter game by transferring income to the old, must be aware of the risk that the following generation may not want to participate in the cost of that transfer. There cannot be a moral obligation to continue a chain-letter game which has been started and continued by others and which may not be continued by the next generation. Even if every single working person were willing to support his parents in case of need, he might legitimately vote to discontinue the collective pay-as-you-go system of intergenerational transfers.

[1] Like Feldstein and unlike Barro, Buchanan thus assumes that changes in private intergenerational transfers do not fully offset changes in public intergenerational transfers. This assumption also underlies the following analysis.

Our analysis has shown that the dismantling of the pay-as-you-go system need not be politically infeasible in a democracy, and that it can even be achieved in a Pareto-efficient way if the total cost of net social security transfers in the past is passed on to the doomsday generation through cumulative debt financing. The extent to which the current and/or future generations should participate in the cost of past net transfers cannot, of course, be determined by the economist qua economist, for that question is purely distributive. It would seem, however, that, since general government expenditure does not tend to be primarily financed through debt issues, most members of the living generations do care about the welfare of the following generations. They do not want to maximize the financial burden to be borne by their offspring, let alone that borne by the doomsday generation. This leads me to conjecture that a majority would prefer the cost of past mistakes to be distributed more or less evenly over living and all future generations. The issue of interest-bearing perpetuities to compensate for past contributions would achieve this aim, if the interest burden is financed from tax revenue. Since those who are now retired have participated in the mistake of continuing the pay-as-you-go system, they are not likely to be exempted from this increase in general taxation. For all others, the total burden of taxation would diminish because the increase in general taxation would be much less than the revenue that had been collected from social security tax.

Buchanan's (and Friedman's) proposal for (at least partial) debt financing should be contrasted with Feldstein's [1975] suggestion that social security taxes should be raised so as to permit a gradual return to a fully funded system. The disadvantage of debt financing is that during the period of transition in which there are still original recipients of compensation bonds who sell them to finance consumption, the increase in the absorption of private savings is likely to exceed the increase in the supply of private savings for old age because the latter is likely to be smaller than the social security tax payments would have been. This outcome is particularly probable because those who leave the governmental system expect private saving for old age to be less risky and/or more remunerative (negative income effect on saving) and because we assumed that the obligation to insure for old age would be confined to the social minimum. Feldstein's scheme, in contrast, would raise the savings rate immediately. On the other hand, whereas Buchanan and Friedman want to dismantle mandatory social security for old age, Feldstein merely wants to stop the pay-as-you-go system. Historical experience, however, provides no support for the view that a fully-funded mandatory public insurance for old age is politically feasible (let alone, efficient and desirable). The existence of a large capital fund seems to be too great a temptation for politicians; it is depleted at the time of crisis or for some apparently worthy cause. Probably, in the long run, only a private system of insurance for old age can be a funded one.

A variant of the Buchanan-Friedman proposal has been implemented with the Chilean social security reform of May 1981. Although insurance for old age is mandatory (at least 10 per cent of the wage has to be used for this purpose), Chileans have a choice among eleven private insurance companies. Claims on the governmentally administered social security system that have been acquired in the past, can be transferred to the private pension funds. Old and new claims can also be transferred among the private pension funds. Those who have been contributing to the government's social security system at the time of the reform could continue to contribute to that system. Those who enter the labor market after the reform must join one of the private pension funds. The government guarantees a minimum pension in case a private pension fund fails; moreover, private pensions that fall short of the minimum pension because past income was too low, are supplemented out of government revenue.

IV. Policy Conclusions: A Blueprint for Reform

1. Nobody must be compelled to insure for more than the social minimum in old age. The social minimum is equal to the level of public assistance ("the dole").

2. Everybody must be permitted to insure with a private pension fund rather than the government's social security system.

3. Claims on the government's social security system that have been acquired in the past must be honored. They should be redeemed by issuing transferable perpetuities that bear a market rate of interest and whose principal is linked to the price or wage index that has been used to adjust benefits in the government's social security system.

4. Private pension funds must be permitted to sell indexed annuities and to buy indexed debt from their borrowers.

5. The taxation of income from capital must be reduced and especially be reformed in such a way that it is not affected by the rate of inflation.

6. To avoid disincentives to work, the start and the size of pension payments must be made independent of old-age earnings.

7. The social security system should become an actuarially fair insurance, and it will do so, or disappear, if proposals 2.-5. are implemented.

References

Barro, Robert J., The Impact of Social Security on Private Savings: Evidence from the U.S. Time Series, American Enterprise Institute Studies, 199, Washington 1978.

Browning, Edgar K., "The Politics of Social Security Reform". In: Colin D. Campbell (Ed.), op. cit., pp. 187-207.

Buchanan, James M., "Social Insurance in a Growing Economy: A Proposal for Radical Reform". National Tax Journal, Vol. 21, 1968, pp. 386-395.

--, "Comments on Browning's Paper". In: Colin D. Campbell (Ed.), op. cit., pp. 208-212.

--, Dismantling the Welfare State. September 1981, unpubl. manuscript.

Campbell, Colin D. (Ed.), Financing Social Security. American Enterprise Institute, Washington 1979.

Darby, Michael R., The Effects of Social Security on Income and the Capital Stock. American Enterprise Institute Studies, 227, Washington 1979.

Feldstein, Martin S., "Toward a Reform of Social Security", The Public Interest, 1975, No. 40, pp. 75-95.

--, "Reply". In: Robert J. Barro, op. cit., pp. 37-47.

Feldstein, Martin S., "The Effect of Social Security on Saving". In: David A. Currie, A. Robert Nobay, David A. Peel (Eds.), Macroeconomic Analysis: Essays in Macroeconomics and Econometrics. Association of University Teachers of Economics, London 1981, pp. 1-23.

--, Anthony J. Pellechio, "Social Security Wealth: The Impact of Alternative Inflation Adjustments". In: Colin D. Campbell (Ed.), op. cit., pp. 91-117.

Friedman, Milton, with the assistance of Rose D. Friedman, Capitalism and Freedom. Chicago 1962.

--, Second Lecture. U.S. Congress, Report of the Consultant Panel on Social Security to the Congressional Research Service. Prepared for the use of the Committee on Finance of the U.S. Senate and the Committee on Ways and Means of the U.S. House of Representatives, 94th Congress, 2nd session, August 1976.

--, Rose Friedman, Free to Choose: A Personal Statement. London 1980.

Jüttemeier, Karl Heinz, Hans-Georg Petersen, "West Germany". In: Jean-Jacques Rosa (Ed.), op. cit., pp. 181-205.

Leuchtenberg, William E., Franklin D. Roosevelt and the New Deal. New York 1963.

Pauly, Mark V., "Overinsurance and Public Provision of Insurance: The Roles of Moral Hazard and Adverse Selection". The Quarterly Journal of Economics, Vol. 88, 1974, pp. 44-62.

Rosa, Jean Jacques (Ed.), The World Crisis in Social Security. Paris 1982.

Rowley, Charles K., Alan T. Peacock, Welfare Economics: A Liberal Restatement. London 1975.

Comment

Hubertus Müller-Groeling

Having been allotted the task of commenting on Vaubel's paper, I would be glad if I could disagree more with him. To my regret, I found myself admiring his lucid exposition and in fundamental agreement with his central tenets. I will therefore have to be content to add a few marginal points and to disagree with others[1].

After a short introductory remark, I shall touch on four issues: the relation of present to future generations, insurance and discrimination, the problem of mandatory minimum insurance, and the political economy of reform.

In my view - and I believe Vaubel would agree with this - the strongest argument also in the economist's case against present-day systems of government old-age insurance still is freedom of choice (and its consequences for economic welfare): it is difficult to see why governments take away the decision about the use of an important part of income from the individual, especially since a very large part of the redistribution - at least in the German social security system - is *intertemporal*, not interpersonal. What, then, does the government have to do with the individual's job of distributing income and consumption over his lifetime? Of course, a general tendency toward myopic behaviour could be a reason for intervention, but we would need rather severe cases of this as a sufficient reason, especially if we eschew the danger of people relying on public assistance in their old age by requiring a minimum insurance.

---

[1] Since Vaubel in his remarks on the political economy of reform places importance on differences in interest due to age, I may be permitted to mention that the few differences of opinion that remain, which I shall try to exploit, may be due to the fact that I belong to an older age cohort than he does.

I. Present and Future Generations

Thus in my argument against the present insurance system I tend to take the individualistic point of view (as Vaubel does), but I have less sympathy with his arguments in favour of the young and of the unborn generations (p.182). To be sure, intertemporal redistribution may distort individual lifetime consumption, and it is quite possible that it will force the young to cut their consumption more than many would think appropriate in view of their needs and responsibilities, or more than they would have done themselves in their (myopic?) plans. But Vaubel's assertion that "the young are forced to pay pensions to old people who have a higher income" is one-sided: they also pay for the pensions of old people who have a very low income (not to mention the fact that the old people, when young, also paid their social security contribution). More importantly, when Vaubel objects that "living generations make decisions at the expense of the unborn generations", I would like to stress the point that the living generation has to make many decisions for the unborn generations, many of them at their expense but hopefully, even more to their benefit.

One of the most important decisions in the latter category - a very expensive one for the older generation at that - is the decision to have children (even this, by the way, may be food for endless child-parent discussions whether it is a decision in favour of the younger generation or at their expense). The very decision of the older generation to reduce the number of the younger (and thereby in part avoid the economic costs of and the income loss caused by child-raising) is at the core of the present and the expected financial difficulties of the German old-age insurance system[1].

I will abstain from delving deeper into this intriguing problem of intergenerational equity; it should, however, be pointed out that it is fashionable today to speak of the obligations the older generations pass on to the younger and the unborn, but that it tends to be forgotten that they inherit much of the fruits of the work of former generations, al-

---

[1] This should not be construed to imply a criticism of the reduction of the number of children per family, which definitely is (and should remain) a private decision; if critical implications are to be drawn, they should be directed against the insurance system and its designers.

most all much less well to do than they are or can hope to be[1]!

In short, one has to take the whole picture into account before talking about the injustice of passing obligations on to the following generation without its consent, quite apart from the technical problems in getting this consent from the yet unborn. Admittedly, there is much room for value judgements in questions of equity, let alone intergenerational equity, but there is also room for rational discussion.

II. Insurance, Redistribution and Discrimination

In his case against present-day systems of old-age insurance, Vaubel states that they not only redistribute among generations, but also within generations (p.179), and he gives a number of examples. Quite apart from my contention that the bulk of redistribution, at least in the German social security system, is only intertemporal, and therefore, as a government activity, to a large degree redundant from an individualistic point of view, it would be good to remember that redistribution is the very essence of insurance. Even if it were actuarially fair (ex ante), there would be and there is intended to be redistribution ex post even in the very homogeneous group. In the case of old-age insurance, the redistribution is effected between those whose lives are shorter than the normal life expectancy of the group of insured and those who live longer, quite apart from any equity considerations[2].

---

[1] When talking about shifting obligations, one should perhaps also remember that one of the main reasons given for abandoning the funded system of old-age insurance for a pay-as-you-go system in West Germany was that - in real terms - the old would have to live more or less off the product of the period, together with the young that produced it, although the size of the product depends crucially on savings and investment, and therefore on the influence the method of funding the old-age insurance system has on capital formation.

[2] So there is a strong redistribution element in insurance just as well as there is an insurance element in redistribution, and perhaps this should not be underrated when speaking of the political economy of social security reform. Ideally, insurance is a perfect example for a redistribution agreement concluded behind the Rawlsian veil of ignorance. Whenever this veil is less than perfect, there is good reason to form different groups of insured persons and to differentiate premiums, thus restoring the veil of ignorance.

No wonder social security discriminates in favour of women on account of their longer life expectancy (p. 179)[1].

Speaking of discrimination, I would like to mention in passing that, from a purely insurance point of view - and the views of the German constitutional court notwithstanding - the German social insurance system does not discriminate against housewives and in favour of married men "because a widower receives a larger pension than a widow", since the widow as a housewife never paid insurance premiums. In my opinion there are two forms of discrimination in this context (both against males!)[2]:

First, unmarried men are discriminated against, because married men are automatically insuring their wives, and this without extra payment, to receive pensions in case of widowhood (although the widow then receives only 60 per cent of what her husband received and would have gone on receiving had he become a widower).

Second, married men are discriminated against, because married women, when they become widows, automatically go on receiving their husbands' pensions (although, again, only 60 per cent), whereas widowers at present benefit only in rare circumstances from the old-age insurance of their former wives: Only when the wife has contributed the greater part of the living costs of the family will the widower receive 60 per cent of his deceased wife's pension[3].

III. Optimal and Mandatory Minimum Insurance

Discussing the case of public insurance in his search for an optimal social security system, Vaubel concedes that if there were no mandatory minimum old-age insurance, there would be the danger of moral

[1] Of course, insurance could (and I believe should) group women together and charge a higher contribution. (I will return to the problem of grouping in old-age insurance.)

[2] This is not to deny that women are discriminated against because they are often not sufficiently insured or not insured at all for their old age. But this is not an insurance question.

[3] This case is deemed to be a discrimination by the German constitutional court and is the main reason why the court has ruled that the old-age insurance system has to be changed by 1984.

hazard. People would be inclined not to insure (save) for old age and to rely on public assistance, although this moral hazard would be less, the smaller public assistance is. But he then cites Browning, who estimates that only a small fraction (1.5 per cent) of the old would have to be paid public assistance and that this would probably be cheaper than a program of mandatory minimum insurance.

I would think such an experiment in moral hazard quite risky, since I think the estimate of 1.5 per cent of the old falling back on public assistance quite unrealistic. The question is not whether they could still work in old age to support themselves; the question would be whether they would be employed, especially in the present situation. Their greatest chance to get odd jobs would be in the shadow economy, but this would not prevent them from applying for public assistance. The second reason given is also unconvincing: To hope that the spouse (who normally will also be old) or the children will support the old person in need without trying first to have him supported by public assistance (and perhaps then supplement these payments) would require a different society, one without moral hazard and one in which the three-generation family is still intact. Before forcing the children by law to support the old, I would prefer to legislate minimum requirements for old-age insurance. And I don't see how such a requirement could be more expensive than public assistance to a realistic number of old people falling back on it for lack of insurance.

But this seems to be only Vaubel's first line of defense, since he then discusses the conditions and properties of a required minimum insurance, stating quite correctly that such a requirement does by no means imply an obligation to insure with a specific insurance company, let alone a government agency.

Where I disagree is with his opinion that the government requiring such an insurance must be willing to supply it (p.175) and with his conclusion that "from an economic point of view, the optimal social security system is an actuarially fair public old-age insurance that is purely optional" (p.178)[1]. Does this mean that we have to have a

[1] I am not driving at the point here that an optimal social security system might have to consist of other insurance requirements like health insurance, or at the much more difficult question of insurance against the risk of invalidity (disability), which still is very difficult to obtain privately in a sufficient form. If Vaubel would be inclined to insist that a social security system is unthinkable without a government insurance, which I

government insurance company monopoly or one competing with private insurers? Why can't we have an all-private competition for the required insurance, just as is the case in mandatory liability insurance for car drivers? This insurance can teach us another lesson: there are differences in premiums according to risk and there is competition between companies in regard to administration and acquisition costs. Why, then, should this be different in old-age insurance and why would lifetime contributions have to be the same, as Vaubel asserts (p.175)? Is it really true that only "very few of those who live longer than average (the bad risks) can predict this in advance"(p. 176)? If there were no survival tables of sufficient quality adjusted for differences in sex, religion, race, education, etc., they would soon be established, and everybody would be glad to find himself in the group with the highest contribution, (although many would be tempted to argue with the insurance that, on account of poor health, their contribution should be much lower than it is). There will hardly be much temptation to start chain smoking just to reduce life insurance fees.

IV. The Political Economy of Social Security Reform

I have not much to say on the political economy of social security reform, although I feel somewhat uneasy with simple calculi of respective advantage applied in this discussion. General fear and uncertainty might be important obstacles on the way to reform.

Until quite recently, in West Germany a reform of old-age insurance away from social and towards private insurance would not have been accepted by the insured. The memories of inflation and currency reform, which reduced pensions from private insurance to a fraction of their former value while social security benefits remained practically uncurtailed, were very strong and still are a sizeable obstacle. Perhaps it will take another generation to overcome them[1].

think he is not - I would object and ask him to be more radical and state that an optimal old-age insurance system is one which is supplied by private insurances competing with each other and in which government requires a minimum old-age insurance.

[1] If there remains an official insurance, as Vaubel suggests, there will be quite a fraction of people who bet on this type of "insurance" against policy risks and legislation, but they will be difficult to separate from those who simply do not have sufficient information about old-age

On the other hand, there is hope for reform, because there is now a growing awareness that the present old-age insurance system is a fair-weather system, and the strong changes in population structure pose a real danger to the finances of the system and to the benefits expected by (and promised to) the individual. This, together with the growing recognition that politicians tend to take a short-term view even in matters of social security, will find people more ready to think about reforms of the kind Vaubel suggests[1]. With the general thrust of Vaubel's blueprint for reform, I have no quarrels whatsoever.

---

insurance or wish neither to collect nor to digest it, and therefore stay in the *official* insurance. Of course, if it is actuarially especially unfair to certain groups and fair or more than fair to others, there will be adverse selection.

[1] There remains, however, the problem of financing the transition, and it is doubtful whether in a time of high and growing government debts, in which fiscal illusion has been destroyed almost completely, Buchanan's elegant solution would be easy to implement.

Edgar O. Olsen

The Role of Government in the Housing Sector

The purpose of this paper is to scrutinize the arguments for government involvement in the housing sector, summarize what is known about the effects of several major government housing programs in the United States, and develop the implications of the preceding for housing policy. Any critique of housing policy will of necessity be highly selective. In the United States alone, there are hundreds of government programs, the majority have never been seriously studied, and evidence on the effects of most of the others is scanty. High-quality studies of housing programs outside of the United States written in English are even rarer[1].

In light of these considerations, I have chosen to limit my discussion to four major programs - rent control, tax subsidies for homeownership, public housing, and housing allowances - that span much of the range of government activity in the housing sector. Rent control is an important type of government regulation of housing in those parts of the United States that have ordinances as well as in many other countries. The special income tax treatment of homeownership is by far the largest program of housing subsidies in the United States. Public housing, which involves the public production of housing services, has been the largest program of housing subsidies to low-income families in this country for almost fifty years. The most important new mechanism for delivering housing subsidies being seriously considered in the United States is a housing allowance plan. Under this program, low-income families would be given a cash grant on the condition that they occupy housing meeting certain standards.

The major types of government activities in U.S. housing markets omitted from this paper are interventions in mortgage markets intended to stabilize and stimulate the construction of new units and attempts to reduce racial segregation in housing. Little is known about the latter, and I am in no position to speak with authority about the former.

---

[1] An economist with good linguistic skills could make an important contribution by selecting and overseeing the translation of the best studies written in other languages.

I. Rent Control

Rent control has been a major type of government regulation of housing throughout the world for many years[1]. In the United States, the primary argument for rent control has been that landlords make excessive profits, and ordinances have typically been adopted when vacancy rates are low and housing prices are rising faster than the prices of other goods. This argument together with the belief that landlords are wealthier than their tenants has convinced many people who do not have an obvious economic interest to support rent control.

The belief that landlords make excessive profits is not supported by any systematic evidence and few economists share this view. They believe that easy entry into the rental housing business precludes a greater than competitive rate of return on the typical investment. After the fact, some investments will yield a higher and others a lower return. For a single investment, net returns will be higher during some time periods than during others. However, excess profits are not typical.

Housing economists have made few attempts to calculate rates of return on rental housing and to compare them with returns on other types of investment, but they have provided indirect evidence in support of their views by deriving and testing other implications of competitive models of housing markets [e.g., Muth, 1969]. Generally speaking, the empirical evidence supports the view that housing markets are competitive. One problem with this type of evidence is that it is extremely difficult to convey to a non-technical audience. Direct evidence would be more persuasive provided that the underlying data can be collected in a way which casts little doubt on its credibility.

Unless the belief in persistent economic profits in rental housing can be dispelled, many arguments used by economists against rent control will fall on deaf ears and indeed some are not valid. Consider, for example, the argument that by limiting net revenues when they would be high and doing nothing about them when they are low, rent control reduces rates of return on investment in rental housing and so results

---

[1] For an insightful analysis of other types of government regulation of housing such as controls on condominium conversions, exclusionary and inclusionary zoning, and building codes, see Muth [unpubl.].

in less housing. If housing service were produced by a profit-maximizing cartel, a price ceiling could lead to more housing even though profits are lower. Therefore, this argument against rent control is based on the assumption that the housing market is competitive which is inconsistent with the widespread belief that excessive profits typify investment in rental housing.

Rent control has probably had important effects on the allocation of resources and distribution of well-being in many places and times. Nevertheless, empirical evidence on the economic effects of this form of government regulation is scanty and crude.

Despite this, economists seem confident of their ability to predict the qualitative effects based on theoretical reasoning[1]. For example, in a recent survey of opinions of economists [Kearl et al., 1979, p. 30], only two percent disagreed with the proposition that a ceiling on rents reduces the quantity and quality of housing.

Unfortunately, the rent control schemes that have been analyzed bear little resemblance to actual ordinances, and so the implications derived may be quite erroneous. Since this is a heretical position, I will develop it at some length.

Many theoretical analyses treat rent control as an instance of price control on a good of invariant quality. At the simplest level this is incorrect because what is controlled is the total revenue from each apartment rather than the price per unit of service. Although many rent control ordinances contain provisions for reducing or increasing the controlled rent when the flow of services is reduced or increased, none guarantee that the ratio of controlled to market rent will remain constant[2]. As a result, rent control could lead owners of controlled housing to upgrade their units. This is easily seen by reference to Figure 1 where TR' shows the relationship between the rent and quantity of housing service provided by a particular dwelling unit in the absence of rent control. The simplest theoretical analyses assume

---

[1] For two of the better theoretical analyses, see Frankena [1975] and Muth [unpubl.].

[2] Furthermore, some ordinances contain provisions for changing the controlled rent even though there has been no change in services with the result that the ratio of controlled to market rent is quite different for different units. For example, the New York City ordinance increases the controlled rent 15 percent each time the apartment is vacated but not more frequently than every two years.

that under rent control the relationship is similar to TR''. Under an actual ordinance, the relationship could be TR'''. Now suppose that MC in the right-hand diagram shows the marginal cost of providing housing service from this unit during a certain period of time and the MR are marginal revenue curves associated with the total revenue curves in the left-hand diagram. In the absence of rent control, OD units would be provided and the simplest model would predict a decline to OC, but the actual outcome would be an increase to OE.

Figure 1

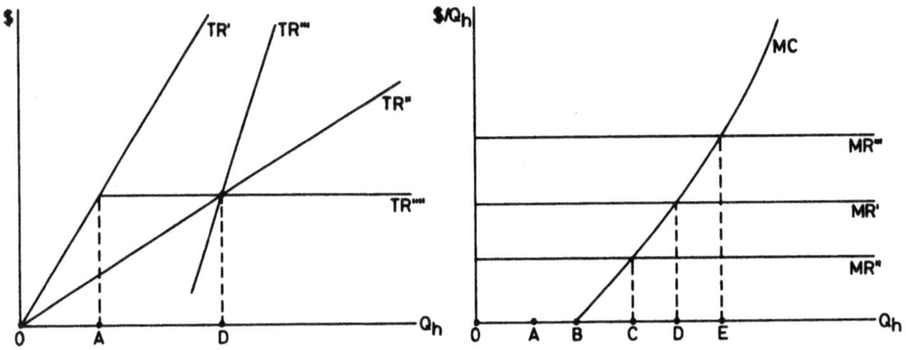

Somewhat more sophisticated theoretical analyses assume that total revenue from an apartment is invariant with respect to the flow of services over the relevant range. In Figure 1, total revenue TR'''' is the same for quantities of housing service greater than OA. For smaller quantities market rent is less than controlled rent and so TR'''' coincides with TR'. Since marginal revenue is zero for quantities greater than OA, the landlord will provide OB units of housing service during the period, that is, the quantity that can be provided with no variable cost. This argument has led to the conclusion that controlled housing will not be maintained as well as uncontrolled housing.

There are two major problems with this analysis. The first has already been mentioned. Many, possibly all, rent control ordinances contain penalties for failing to maintain a unit and rewards for upgrading it. Second, tenants have an incentive to maintain their own apartments, especially when rent control ordinances contain severe limitations on the rights of landlords to evict tenants.

The implication of this consideration can be seen by reference to an indifference curve diagram for an occupant of a controlled apartment. In Figure 2, JF is this person's budget constraint in the absence of rent control and R is his chosen consumption bundle. The immediate effect of rent control is to reduce housing expenditure and hence increase nonhousing expenditure without changing housing consumption. For example, his consumption bundle might change from R to V in Figure 2. Since the owner of the controlled apartment will not maintain it, the quantity of housing services provided by the unit will decline unless the tenant spends money on maintenance. If the tenant does not maintain the unit, then as time passes he will consume less housing service and the same quantity of other goods, for example, move from consumption bundle V to W. However, by spending on maintenance the tenant is able to offset reduced landlord maintenance at the expense of non-housing consumption. The curve WE in Figure 2 reflects this trade-off. Its shape is due to the rising marginal cost of providing additional housing from an existing structure and possibly the tenant's comparative disadvantage in producing housing service. Since the income and substitution effects of rent control on housing consumption are in opposite directions, the result could be better maintained housing as shown in Figure 2.

Figure 2

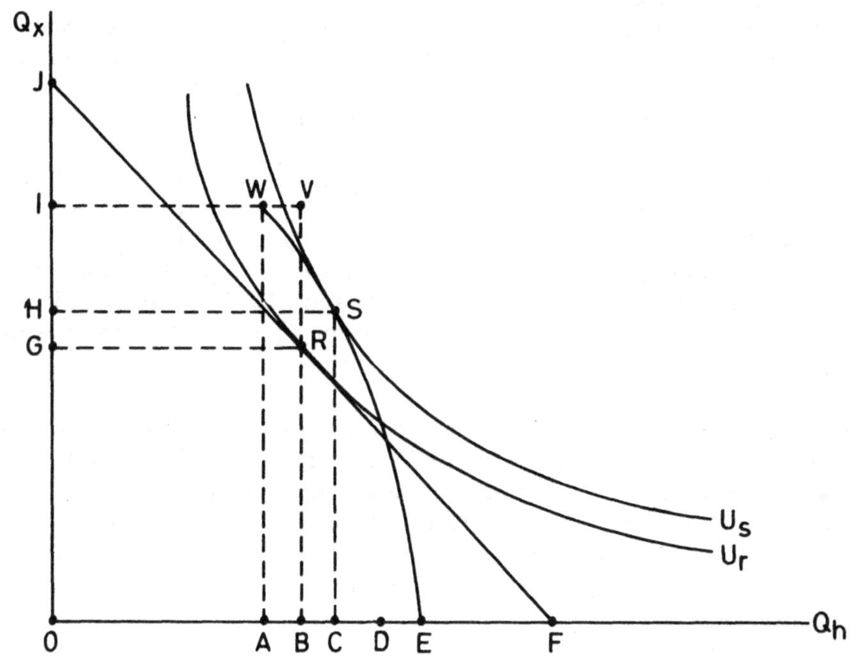

Another issue often confused with the question of whether controlled units provide more or less housing service is whether their occupants live in better or worse housing. To see the difference, let us reinterpret Figure 2. Suppose that the dwelling under consideration has been vacated and that in the absence of rent control this unit would provide OD units of housing service. In the presence of rent control, the unit would provide OA units of housing service unless it is maintained by the tenant. Suppose that this unit is considered by a person with private market alternatives JF and indifference curves U_r and U_s, and suppose that if this person occupied the unit, he would face choices along WE. Clearly, he prefers this controlled unit to any private market alternative, and he may judge that the expected costs exceed the expected benefits of further search among controlled units. In this case, the controlled unit will provide less housing than it would have provided in the absence of rent control, OC rather than OD, but its occupant will consume more housing, OC rather than OB.

Despite the shortcomings of existing theoretical analyses and dearth of empirical evidence, a reasonably strong case can be made against rent control. In assessing the strength of the evidence, it should be recognized that different rent control ordinances have different provisions and these differences can lead to different results. Furthermore, the immediate effects of rent control may be quite different quantitatively from its effects in later years. Since the reliable knowledge about these effects is limited to a few ordinances at several points in time, we cannot be confident that it is universally applicable. With this caveat in mind, let us consider the merits of rent control.

It is often argued that rent control is simply a way of redistributing income from the rich to the poor because landlords are richer than tenants. For this reason rent control is supported by many people who want to help low-income families. Of course, it is not true that every tenant is poorer than his landlord [Johnson, 1951], but even if this were the case, rent control would be a very poor redistributive device.

One important reason is that it distorts consumption patterns substantially. Many occupants of controlled housing live in apartments much less desirable than they would choose if they were given unrestricted cash grants each month equal to the difference between the market rent and the controlled rent of their apartment in lieu of rent control. Other occupants of controlled housing live in much more desirable apartments.

One indication of the distortion in consumption patterns of occupants of controlled housing is the divergence between the benefit to tenants and the cost to landlords. Olsen and York [1982] have estimated that the mean difference between the market and actual rent of controlled apartments in New York City in 1965 was $395. Their estimate of the annual unrestricted cash grant, which - if given to the family in place of rent control - would make the family neither better nor worse off than it was under the ordinance, is $107. If rent control were equivalent to a program of unrestricted cash grants and hence did not distort consumption patterns, there would be no difference between these estimates. In fact, the cost of rent control to landlords was almost four times its value to tenants[1].

Rent control is not only an inefficient redistributive device but also a grossly inequitable one. To summarize, there is undoubtedly a great variance in the cost borne by equally wealthy families, rent control is not limited to low-income families and does not serve all such families, and among families who occupy controlled housing and are similar in many respects there is an enormous variance in benefits. In short, there is nothing approaching equal treatment of equals under rent control.

While there is no detailed evidence on the distribution of the cost of rent control, the following propositions are almost certainly true. The majority of families at each income level do not own rental housing. The cost of rent control is borne overwhelmingly by people who own rental housing at the time that it is adopted. Equally wealthy owners of rental property do not bear the same cost because they hold different proportions of their assets in this form. These propositions lead to two questions that are in my opinion unanswerable. Why should rent control which allegedly serves a public purpose be financed by an implicit tax on such a small proportion of the population, and why should the magnitude of this tax on equally wealthy people depend upon the proportion of their assets held in the form of rental housing?

Table 1 presents the distribution of income in controlled and uncontrolled housing in New York City in 1968. Clearly, rent control is not limited to low-income families and does not serve all such families.

---

[1] A previous study [Olsen, 1972] using data for 1968, somewhat different methods, and a Marshallian rather than Hicksian measure of tenant benefit also found a large difference between tenant benefit and landlord cost.

Table 1 - Distribution of Renter Households in Controlled and Uncontrolled Housing by Income: New York City, 1968

Income of head and related persons[a]	Controlled[b]	Uncontrolled[b]
0- 2,000	12.2	4.1
2,000- 3,999	21.6	9.0
4,000- 5,999	22.5	14.8
6,000- 7,999	17.3	16.9
8,000- 9,999	10.7	15.1
10,000-14,999	10.7	24.6
15,000-24,999	3.8	11.7
25,000 or more	1.0	3.9
Total	100.0	100.0

[a]In U.S.$. - [b]In percent.

Source: Lowry et al. [1971, p. 249].

Even among families who occupy controlled housing and are the same with respect to income, family size, and the age, sex, and race of the head of the household, there is an enormous variation in benefit because the excess of market rent over actual rent is different for different controlled units and because some families experience greater distortions in their consumption patterns than other families. Olsen and York [1982] have estimated that the mean benefit for families with average characteristics was $107 during 1965 and that the standard deviation in benefit is $403.

Existing studies have provided tentative answers to some of the more important questions concerning rent control but they have left many other questions unanswered. For example, to what extent are the apparent gains to occupants of controlled units offset by the necessity to pay bribes to obtain occupancy and by spending on maintenance that would have been provided by the landlord in the absence of rent control? To what extent has rent control resulted in higher prices for rental housing in the uncontrolled sector? To what extent has it affected tenure choice?

Although the evidence is not overwhelming, it leads me to conclude that rent control is a policy with no redeeming social value. It is both inefficient and inequitable. Political jurisdictions that have rent control ordinances are well-advised to terminate them, perhaps gradually by increasing controlled rents more rapidly than market rents and decontrolling vacant apartments. Assistance to needy households should be provided by explicit transfers financed by broadbased taxes.

II. Income Tax Treatment of Homeownership

The individual income tax is the largest source of revenue for the United States government. Under the federal income tax, investment in owner-occupied housing is treated more favorably than most other investments. In order to treat investment in owner-occupied housing similarly to investment in rental housing, owners would declare as income the difference between the market rent of their home and their expenses such as mortgage interest, property taxes, depreciation, and maintenance. Under the federal income tax, owner-occupants do not include the market rent of their home as income but are allowed to deduct mortgage interest and property taxes. As a result, their income is understated by the excess of market rent over non-deductible expenses such as depreciation and maintenance. Alternatively, we could say that income is understated by the sum of net market rent, mortgage interest, and property taxes. These income tax provisions not only make homeownership more attractive relative to renting but also make housing more attractive relative to other goods for homeowners.

The individual income tax provides subsidies to other forms of investment including investment in rental housing by permitting deductions for depreciation in excess of true depreciation, but these subsidies are relatively small. In fiscal year 1981, the income tax provided subsidies to owner-occupants amounting to substantially more than $33 billion compared with about $2 billion to renters [U.S. Pres., 1981, p. 236][1]. (About 65 percent of households in the United States are homeowners.) Since all direct housing subsidies of the federal government amount to less than $7.5 billion and subsidies by subnational governments are certainly smaller, it is clear that the income tax treatment of homeownership is the largest housing program in the United States.

---

[1] The subsidy to owner-occupants is underestimated because it does not include the tax saving due to the failure to include net market rent in taxable income.

Despite the magnitude of the income tax subsidies for homeownership, no coherent justification for them has been developed. There are, of course, many arguments for housing subsidies based on externalities[1]. If you consider these rationales carefully, you would conclude that the subsidy should be largest for the poorest households. Since the poorest households pay no federal income tax and since marginal tax rates rise with income, the income tax treatment of homeownership produces the opposite pattern of subsidies.

This is illustrated in Figure 3 which depicts the budget constraints of two homeowners who have the same amount of leisure. In this diagram, the quantity of housing service is measured along the horizontal axis and expenditure on other goods along the vertical axis. The richer person has earnings OH and in the absence of the income tax would have budget constraint HD. Assume that without the special treatment of homeownership this person would be in the second tax bracket, pay a tax HG, and face a budget constraint GC. The income tax provisions

Figure 3

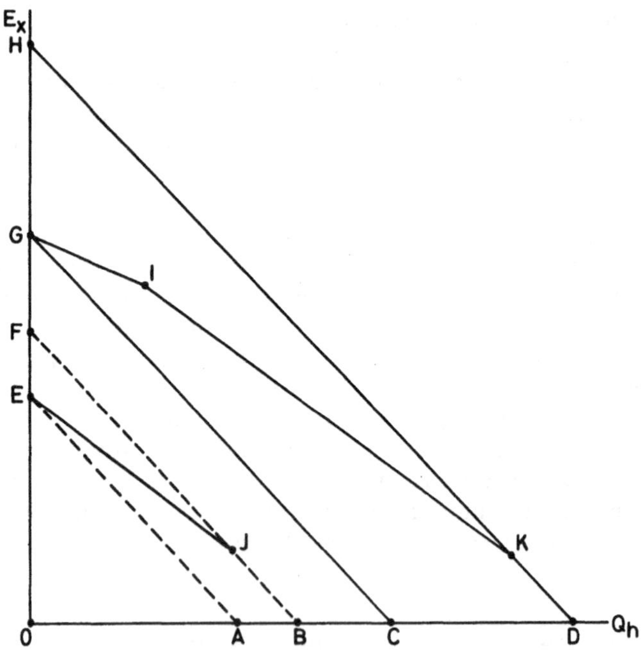

[1] These will be discussed in considering the rationales for housing subsidies to low-income households.

reduce the prices of some, but not all, inputs used to produce housing service for owner-occupants. These reductions are greater for families in higher marginal tax brackets [MacRae, Turner, 1981]. Therefore, the price per unit of housing service is lower the higher the marginal tax bracket. As the richer person increases his consumption of housing service from zero up to some point, his taxable income falls but he remains in the same marginal tax bracket and so faces the same price per unit of housing service. Beyond that point, I in Figure 3, his deductions are large enough so that his taxable income is in the next marginal tax bracket, and if his housing consumption is sufficiently large, he will pay no income tax. Ignoring the distortion in input choices that results from the income tax provisions that favor homeownership, an income tax with these provisions has the same effect as a comprehensive income tax that shifts the person's budget constraint from HD to GC combined with an explicit housing subsidy that shifts the budget constraint from GC to GIKD. The other budget constraints in Figure 3 refer to a poorer person who would be in the first marginal tax bracket in the absence of the special income tax treatment of homeownership. This person has an income OF and without these provisions would pay a tax FE. Since the income tax is progressive, FE/OF is less than HG/OH. As the poorer person increases his housing consumption up to some point, he remains in the first tax bracket and hence moves along the line segment EJ parallel to IK. Beyond J, this person pays no income tax. Since the subsidy provided by the special treatment of homeownership at any quantity of housing service consumed is the vertical distance between the comprehensive tax budget lines GC and EA and the actual budget lines GIKD and EJB, the richer person will receive a larger subsidy than the poorer person at each quantity of housing service and will face a price at least as low.

I dare say that the United States Congress is unlikely to pass an explicit program of housing subsidies with this feature, and I conclude that it is only widespread ignorance of the true nature of this program that has allowed it to persist.

The primary justification for subsidizing homeownership is that it contributes to social stability. Although this rationale is of ancient vintage, no compelling evidence supports it. Furthermore, people who offer this justification have not provided answers to the most obvious questions. For example, does social stability depend more on the ownership of a home than on other forms of property? If social stability depends on the distribution of total property owned, it is inefficient to subsidize the ownership of some, but not all, types of property to account for the externality. Does social stability depend upon the homeownership rate of the wealthiest families? Does it depend not only on how many families have some equity in their home but also on the magnitude of their equity? Even if homeownership makes a greater contribution to social stability than the ownership of other forms of property, plausible answers to these two questions suggest that we should provide cash grants to homeowners that are largest for the poorest families and for families with the greatest equity. In short, a persuasive case for increasing the homeownership rate has not been made, and I doubt that a case can be developed that would justify the present income tax treatment of homeownership.

It has been suggested that the failure to tax the net market rent is justified by the cost of estimating the market rents of owner-occupied housing. Since local governments are able to estimate the sales prices of all dwellings with tolerable accuracy at modest cost each year in connection with the property tax, this justification is not persuasive. Furthermore, neutral treatment of homeownership could be approached by disallowing the deductions for mortgage interest and property taxes.

Not only is there little serious discussion of the rationales for these income tax provisions but also there is a dearth of empirical evidence on their effects. Much of the literature analyzes the distribution of tax savings under the assumption that individual choices concerning tenure and housing consumption would not change if these income tax provisions were eliminated. That is, the literature focuses on very short-run effects.

It is generally agreed that the mean tax saving rises with income among homeowners and all households [Aaron, 1970, p. 793]. There is a substantial variance in tax saving among equally situated households because some are renters, others take the standard deduction, and the magnitude of the itemized deductions is different for different homeowners [White, White, 1965]. However, since these differences stem from differences in taste (similarly situated families face the same budget constraints under the federal income tax), the complaint that these provisions create horizontal inequities is not entirely persuasive. Even a proportional tax on earnings with no loopholes would lead to variations in tax payments among people with identical pretax budget spaces due to differences in tastes concerning different types of jobs and different trade-offs between leisure and other goods.

The tax saving is the difference between the market value of the goods consumed with and without the provisions. This is not a satisfactory measure of the benefit of these provisions to itemizing homeowners because individuals are not indifferent between all consumption bundles with the same market value. A better measure of benefit is the difference between the income necessary to attain the level of well-being with the provisions and that necessary to attain the level of well-being without them at some set of prices. The distribution of this measure of benefit can be quite different from the distribution of tax saving [Olsen, York, 1982]. It is now common practice in housing policy analysis to estimate such a measure of benefit, but this has not been done for the tax subsidies for homeownership.

Rosen [1979] has estimated the welfare cost of this tax subsidy for 1970 at $107 per homeowner. Since there were about 40 million homeowners at that time, the total deadweight loss was substantial. Indeed, it probably exceeded the total expenditure on housing subsidies to low-income households.

Almost all analyses of the effects of removing these subsidies take no account of what is done with the increased tax revenues. In an admirable departure from this tradition, Rosen [1979] has estimated the effects of eliminating the favorable treatment of homeownership and lowering marginal tax rates proportionally so that tax revenue is unaffected. Table 2 reveals that this change has little impact on the mean disposable income of families in different income groups but a noticeable impact on housing consumption and tenure choice. This type of analysis is important in part because this reform is much more likely to be adopted if accompanied by compensating reductions in tax rates.

Despite the important recent studies by Rosen and others, the amount of empirical evidence on the rationales for, and effects of, the income tax treatment of homeownership is appallingly small. For example, little is known about the relationship between the distribution of property ownership in general or homeownership in particular and social stability. The distribution of gains and losses *within income classes* of removing the favorable tax treatment of homeownership and using the increased tax revenues in particular ways has not been estimated, nor has the effect of such changes on output and input prices.

Table 2 - Effects of Removing Favorable Treatment of Homeownership and Lowering Marginal Tax Rate Proportionally so that Tax Revenue is Unchanged

Gross income group[a]	Status quo		New regime		
	disposable income[a]	house value[a]	disposable income[a]	change in house value[a]	change in owners[b]
0- 4,000	2,686	10,991	2,675	-1,235	-2.5
4- 8,000	6,024	14,022	6,018	-2,427	-3.8
8-12,000	9,452	17,856	9,478	-2,850	-4.5
12-16,000	12,715	21,134	12,736	-3,323	-4.7
16-20,000	15,829	26,665	15,795	-3,680	-4.8
20-24,000	19,088	29,893	19,086	-3,880	-5.1
24-28,000	22,248	36,477	22,208	-3,195	-4.8
28,000 or more	30,306	48,031	30,186	-2,380	-4.5

[a]In U.S.$. - [b]Change in the percentage of the income group who are homeowners.

Source: Rosen [1979, p. 20].

Nevertheless, since I doubt that it is possible to make a convincing case for the pattern of subsidies resulting from these income tax provisions, I conclude that they should be eliminated. In order to keep this issue separate from the question of the appropriate size of the government, I think that it would be best to lower tax rates so as to maintain government revenue. Although any practical proposal will undoubtedly make some people worse off, there may not be many big losers and such people have been the unintended beneficiaries of government largess.

III. Housing Subsidies to Low-Income Families

1. A Brief History

For more than forty years, federal housing programs for low-income families have emphasized the construction of new units beginning in the 1930's with the public housing program[1]. Under this program, local housing authorities commissioned the building of projects funded primarily by the federal government. Tenants and local governments paid the cost of operating these projects. With the surge in redistributive programs in the 1960s and the weakening support for public housing, two new programs emphasizing the construction of units were inaugurated. Section 235 subsidized homeownership for the richest of the poor; Section 236 subsidized the rent of low-income families in privately owned units. A few years earlier Congress had authorized the Section 23 program intended to use the existing stock of standard units to house subsidized families. Within a few years the bureaucracy of the U.S. Department of Housing and Urban Development (HUD) had subverted it. By the early 1970s half of its participants lived in units built for the program.

When scandals and high default rates brought Sections 235 and 236 to the attention of the press, President Nixon ordered a halt to additional commitments under all housing programs pending a thorough review of their performance. In response to a negative evaluation of these programs, HUD developed new programs, known collectively as Section 8, that were intended to eventually replace all other housing programs. The new programs all involved the leasing of privately owned housing. Some were newly built for the program, others were substantially rehabilitated as a condition for participation, and still others were existing units meeting program housing standards. The existing component grew most rapidly in the early years. By 1978 there were 580,000 families in Section 8 Existing Units, 70,000 in Section 8 New, and 15,000 in Section 8 Rehab. Since then the new and rehab components have more than tripled in size while the existing component has stayed about the same. Furthermore, a substantial proportion of the budget of the Section 8 Existing program is now used to bail out projects under the older new construction programs that are on the verge of default. Of the more than 3 million families receiving housing assistance from HUD, fewer than a fifth are allowed to choose their housing subject only to constraints on its condition.

HUD administers other, small housing programs, and the programs mentioned above typically have several variants and variants within variants. However, research has shown that the fundamental distinction for housing policy is between programs involving the construction of new units or the major rehabilitation of units selected by bureau-

[1] This section on the history of housing subsidies is taken from Olsen [1982].

crats, on the one hand, and those involving assistance to families who are free to choose any unit meeting housing standards, on the other hand. The effects of programs within each category are basically the same, and the differences between programs in different categories are marked. Therefore, the rest of the paper will focus on the program in each category about which the most is known.

2. Rationales

First, however, we should consider the justifications for housing subsidies to low-income families. Since recipients prefer an unconditional cash grant to a housing subsidy, it is difficult to justify housing subsidies unless taxpayers receive tangible benefits particularly related to the housing of recipients or care about recipients but think that these people undervalue housing. The existence of tangible benefits is frequently asserted. For example, it has been argued that better housing for low-income families leads to better health for its occupants and, since some diseases are contagious, to better health for the middle and upper-income families with whom they come in contact. Available evidence suggests that some such externalities exist but that their magnitudes are small [Weicher, 1979, pp. 489 ff.][1]. If the goal of housing subsidies is to make both recipients and taxpayers better off, it is doubtful that substantial expenditures can be justified on the basis of these externalities alone.

I believe that the major rationale for housing subsidies to low-income families is paternalistic altruism. That is, I believe that many people are concerned about the well-being of these families but think that they undervalue housing. If only one other person was concerned about each person's well-being, then there is every reason to expect that the two people would reach an agreement resulting in an efficient allocation without any government intervention. The case for redistribution through government is that many people are concerned about the

[1] The majority of studies that are considered to be a part of the literature on the social cost of slums do not deal with externalities at all. They estimate, for example, the relationship between a person's housing and his own health. The absence of such a relationship proves the absence of an externality along these lines, but the presence of a relationship does not show that an externality exists. Many of these studies are also of extremely low quality in that they do not account for non-housing determinants of the variable to be explained.

well-being of the same person. This utility interdependence may result in some private transfers. However, after all such transfers, it is quite likely that many parties to this externality will value increased housing for the recipient, but not enough to justify unilateral giving. If all paternalistic altruists think that the objects of their concern undervalue housing, then all allocations preferred by everyone to the allocation in the absence of government action involve better housing than would result from equally costly lump-sum transfers [Olsen, 1981, pp. 159 ff.].

Although a case can be made for housing subsidies to some low-income families, it is difficult to argue for such subsidies to all of these families. There is a great variance in the housing of families having the same income and size and facing the same set of prices. Many low-income families occupy housing meeting the standards that have been used in housing programs.

Consider, for example, evidence from the Experimental Housing Allowance Program (EHAP). The major type of housing allowance tested in the Experiment offered each eligible family a cash grant on the condition that it occupy housing which met certain standards. In deciding which standards to use, a search was made for scientific evidence concerning the effects of specific housing defects on the health, safety, and behavior of occupants. Municipal housing codes in the experimental sites and similar localities were reviewed and compared with the model codes promulgated by various organizations [Lowry et al., 1974, pp. 13 ff.]. Neither existing nor model codes are based on any substantial scientific evidence, and the evidence available does not suggest any obvious choice of standards. The Demand Experiment adopted a modified version of the American Public Health Association-Public Health Service Recommended Housing Maintenance and Occupancy Ordinance [Bakeman et al., 1980]. In the Supply Experiment, the Building Official's Code of America, with minor modifications, was used. It seems reasonable to presume that model housing codes are designed by people who have particularly strong feelings concerning the value of better housing for low-income families. To the extent that such families already occupy housing meeting these standards, the argument for housing subsidies based on taxpayer preferences is undermined.

It has been estimated that about half of the eligible families in the Supply Experiment sites occupied housing meeting its standards and about a fourth of the eligible families in the Demand Experiment sites occupied housing meeting its more stringent standards prior to receiving assistance [HUD, c, p. 107]. Even at the lowest income levels, many households occupied units meeting the standards of the Demand Experiment [Budding, 1980, pp. 31, A-100]. I draw two conclusions from these findings. First, almost all low-income families are able to occupy housing meeting the standards embodied in model housing codes. Some choose not to do so. Second, low-income families are not as poorly housed as is widely believed. If these conclusions are accepted, it seems reasonable to believe that many taxpayers who favor housing subsidies have a distorted perception of the housing conditions of low-income households and of the reasons that families are poorly housed. Therefore, a reconsideration of the desirability of housing subsidies versus unconditional cash grants seems to be in order.

If many taxpayers still feel that they receive tangible benefits especially related to the housing of low-income families or care about these families and think that they undervalue housing, then it remains to consider the merits of alternative means of delivering housing subsidies.

3. Public Housing

Public housing has been the largest program of housing subsidies to low-income families in the United States for forty-five years. Federal involvement in the construction of housing for low-income families began earlier in the Great Depression in an attempt to stimulate employment. However, the inefficacy of public housing as a counter-cyclical program soon became evident, and by 1937 the emphasis was clearly on the provision of good homes and healthful living conditions for low-income families.

For many years, almost all public housing units were newly built for the program. Local housing authorities selected the sites (subject to veto by city councils or comparable local bodies), planned the projects (subject to many federal guidelines), and let the construction contracts. Once completed, the projects were operated by employees of the local housing authorities. Federal taxpayers paid the cost of developing the projects; tenants and local taxpayers paid the operating cost.

The basic criteria for determining eligibility for public housing are income and family size. Each local housing authority establishes an upper income limit for families of each size. The larger the family, the higher the upper income limit. The number of families eligible for public housing has always greatly exceeded the number of public housing units. Perhaps the best estimate [HUD, b, pp. 55-61] is that about 50 percent of all households in the United States were eligible for at least one of HUD's housing programs in 1975, but only 7 percent were served. Waiting lists for public housing are long, and frequently closed. Rationing of the existing stock of public housing units is the perquisite of the local housing authorities, and therefore generalizations are hazardous. However, it appears that units are rationed on a first-come first-serve basis except that families displaced by government action or living in the worst housing, veterans, and the elderly are given some preference.

An important modification in the development of public housing projects was implemented in 1967 when local authorities were authorized to advertise their desire to purchase a project without specifying its location or detailed characteristics. The authority could then accept the bid providing its preferred combination of location, housing characteristics, and price. Since 1970, more than half of all public housing units entered the program through this "turnkey" mechanism.

There are about 1.3 million public housing units in the United States occupied by almost 4 million people. It has been estimated that tenants pay between 25 and 35 percent of the total cost of the services provided by their units [Mayo et al., 1980, Part 2, Ch. 4; HUD, a, pp. 123 ff.]. In 1979, the explicit cost of the public housing program to taxpayers was about $1.7 billion, but not all of the cost borne by taxpayers can be obtained from HUD records. At least 30 percent is in the form of two hidden subsidies. The interest on local housing authority bonds used to finance the purchase of land, site improvement, and construction of projects is exempt from federal income taxation. As a result, housing authorities are able to borrow at below-market interest rates. Furthermore, authorities do not pay full property taxes on their projects and so face a cost of capital lower than private producers.

Economic theory has been useful in providing a framework for empirical analyses of public housing but cannot yield qualitative predictions of the effects of the program due to the way in which it changes the budget space of an eligible family. Once an eligible family reaches the top of the waiting list and a unit of an appropriate size becomes available, the family is offered the unit. Many authorities allow the family to reject a few offers before it is removed from, or put to the bottom of, the list. Since the offers could be identical and since waiting lists are long, it is accurate enough for present purposes to assume that the family faces a simple all-or-nothing choice. The unit offered may be better or worse than the housing currently occupied by the family. The rent paid by the family typically depends upon its characteristics, most notably its income, but not on the characteristics of the unit. Since this rent may be more or less than the family is currently spending on housing, the family may have more or less to spend on other goods if it accepts the offer. Therefore, economic theory yields no qualitative predictions concerning the effect of the program on consumption patterns. Nor can we say that the program distorts consumption patterns because the consumption bundle offered by the program could be the one that the family would have chosen had it been given an equally-costly cash grant. Fortunately, there is some empirical evidence on the effectiveness, equity, and efficiency of the program.

Effectiveness

The scarce evidence available indicates that a substantial majority of the participants in the public housing program occupy housing better than they would choose if they were given cash grants with no strings attached [Kraft, Olsen, 1977, pp. 58 ff.; Olsen, Barton, 1982, pp. 28 f.] [1]. What is not known is whether the families served by the program were the worst-housed families at each income level. Therefore, we cannot say whether the public housing program has had the desired effects on consumption patterns.

Equity

The public housing program is fraught with inequities. Among similar eligible families that are not served by other housing programs and

[1] An important defect of almost all studies of the effects of housing programs is that they fail to make this comparison. Instead consumption patterns in the presence of the program are compared with those in its absence. The limited relevance of this comparison is easy to see. Suppose that the government offered to pay certain families a fixed fraction of their expenditures on all goods except good X and that the price elasticity of demand for non-X is less than 1. Consumption of good X would increase, and the percentage increase in consumption of good X could exceed that for other goods. Nevertheless, this is not a successful program for subsidizing good X because it results in less consumption of this good than would an equally-costly unrestricted cash grant.

willing to participate, a fortunate minority receive large subsidies while the majority receive nothing [Kraft, Olsen, 1977, p. 62; Olsen, Barton, 1982, pp. 30 ff.]. Among similar households that are served, the variance in the subsidy is large primarily because there is a great variance in the desirability of different subsidized units but little variance in the rent paid by tenants. There is also a substantial variance in benefit for this reason and due to differences in taste. Households that have incomes near the upper limits for eligibility and occupy the best subsidized units receive substantial subsidies with the result that their effective incomes are greater than those of the poorest ineligible households [Olsen, Barton, 1982, pp. 33 f.].

Efficiency

All estimates indicate that it costs more to provide housing under the public housing program than to provide equally desirable housing in the private market. The more meticulous estimates of inefficiency [Mayo et al., 1980, Part 2; Olsen, Barton, 1982, p. 25; HUD, a, Ch. 4] range from 10 to 100 percent.

Many explanations of this finding have been suggested. Some involve program features that provide incentives for inefficiency. For example, until 1970 the federal government paid the development costs of public housing projects while tenants and local taxpayers paid the operating costs. It is reasonable to believe that local housing authorities are sensitive to costs borne by local residents but insensitive to costs borne by other taxpayers. If so, local authorities would build housing as maintenance free as possible, even though the extra development cost is much greater than the present value of the savings in maintenance costs. In 1970 the Congress authorized HUD to reimburse housing authorities for the excess of their operating costs over their revenues. This reduced the price of maintenance and rehabilitation faced by housing authorities to zero. Since maintenance and rehabilitation were free to local authorities during the early 1970's, it is reasonable to believe that they did much that was not worth its cost.

Another explanation of the estimated inefficiency involves the state of the housing market at the time that the subsidized units are built. If comparable unsubsidized units are not being built at this time, it is because they cannot compete with existing units. That is, their costs including a competitive rate of return cannot be recouped at existing and expected future rent levels. This indicates that the vacancy rate among units of this overall quality is high, and therefore public construction makes no more sense than private construction.

One explanation of the inefficiency is common to all public production of goods and services. If a businessman finds a way to produce the same output at a lower cost, he gets to keep the difference. If an administrator of a housing program does the same, he does not get to keep the difference. Similar statements can be made about producing a better product at the same cost. The effect of this difference in incentives between private and public providers of housing is obvious.

4. Housing Allowances

The United States does not currently have a national housing allowance program although the existing housing component of the Section 8 Housing Assistance Payments Program is similar in many respects. Nevertheless, we have had considerable experience with housing allowances, and this experience has been the subject of an enormous quantity of research. During the 1970s over 30,000 households in twelve locations across the United States were involved in the Experimental Housing Allowance Program. Full scale programs were operated in two urban areas.

Three types of subsidy were used. The percent-of-rent plan paid each family a certain fraction of its housing expenditure without any restrictions on its housing consumption. The minimum rent plan gave each family a cash grant on the condition that it spend at least X on housing. The two full scale housing allowance programs used a minimum standards plan. Under this plan, low-income families were given cash grants on the condition that they occupy housing meeting certain standards. The amount of the grant was greater for families with lower incomes and more members.

Based on evidence from this experiment, we can be confident that housing allowances could have been used to induce participants in the public housing program to occupy units as satisfactory as their program units at a much lower cost to taxpayers. This could be achieved without forcing them to reduce their spending on other things. Of course, we would not want to have a housing allowance program that had the same effects as the public housing program because it is highly inequitable. The housing allowance programs that have been proposed are much more equitable than one that would simply reproduce the effects of public housing because they offer equally situated households the same grant under the same conditions and provide a subsidy to all eligible families who wish to participate. Since the upper income limit for eligibility for families of each type is the income at which the subsidy is zero, a notch is avoided.

The major objections to an entitlement housing allowance program have been that it would result in significantly higher rents without leading to much better housing and that it would be too costly.

The argument that landlords of allowance recipients would raise rents without upgrading their units is easily dismissed. In the Supply Experiment, recipients who remained in pre-program housing that already satisfied program standards experienced virtually no change in their rents. Even non-movers whose units had to be improved in order for them to participate experienced only small rent increases [Rand, 1978, p. 82].

Few experts on the workings of housing markets believed that the effects of an allowance program on rents would be limited to recipients. Instead, most believed that the rents of similar units would be affected similarly. The rents of the least desirable units would fall and rents of modest units meeting the standards would rise at least in the short-run. Disagreements among experts concerned mainly the magnitude of these short-run price changes[1].

Evidence from the Supply Experiment shows beyond any reasonable doubt that an entitlement housing allowance program similar to the one tested will have no significant effects on rents even in the short run [Barnett, Lowry, 1979; Mills, Sullivan, 1981]. Reasons for the program's small effect on rents are easy to find. Eligible families account for a small fraction of the demand for housing services, and many of these families choose not to participate. So even a large increase in demand by participants will have a small effect on aggregate demand for housing services, and this small increase occurs gradually over time because not all families respond instantly to the offer of a subsidy. Furthermore, it is clear that even over short periods of time suppliers are willing to make many changes in existing units in response to small changes in the profitability of housing with different characteristics.

Those who argue that an entitlement housing allowance program would be too costly fail to appreciate its flexibility. By adjusting the subsidy

[1] See e.g. President's Committee on Urban Housing [1969, pp. 71 f.]; Olsen [1969, pp. 619 ff.]; De Leeuw, Ekanem [1973].

schedule or the standards or both, an entitlement program can be designed to have any cost desired. For example, it could be designed to have a cost less than the current system of housing programs.

Evidence from the Experimental Housing Allowance Program and studies of current housing programs for low-income families support two propositions about housing policy. If we want to help low-income families, think that these families know better than others what is good for themselves, and receive no tangible benefits from their improved housing, then current housing programs should be terminated. The money currently devoted to housing subsidies could be used to expand cash assistance or to provide relief to taxpayers or both. If we want to help low-income families and have a special interest in inducing them to occupy better housing than they would choose in response to equally-costly cash grants, then current housing programs should be replaced with an entitlement housing allowance program. Such a program avoids the inefficiencies of the new construction programs by subsidizing households and not requiring them to occupy newly-built units. It reduces the inequities of these programs substantially by offering equally situated households the same grant under the same conditions and providing a subsidy to all eligible families that wish to participate.

References

Aaron, Henry, "Income Taxes and Housing". The American Economic Review, Vol. 60, 1970, pp. 789-806.

Bakeman, Helen E., Carol Ann Dalto, Charles S. White, Minimum Standards Requirements in the Housing Allowance Demand Experiment. Abt Associates, Cambridge, Mass., 1980.

Barnett, C. Lance, Ira S. Lowry, How Housing Allowances Affect Housing Prices. The Rand Corporation, Publ. No. R-2452-HUD, Santa Monica 1979.

Budding, David W., Housing Deprivation Among Enrollees in the Housing Allowance Demand Experiment. Abt Associates, Cambridge, Mass., 1980.

De Leeuw, Frank, Nkanta F. Ekanem, "Time Lags in the Rental Housing Market". Urban Studies, Vol. 10, 1973, pp. 39-68.

Frankena, Mark, "Alternative Models of Rent Control". Urban Studies, Vol. 12, 1975, pp. 303-308.

Johnson, D. Gale., "Rent Control and the Distribution of Income". The American Economic Review, Vol. 41, 1951, pp. 569-582.

Kearl, J.R., et al., "A Confusion of Economists?" The American Economic Review, Vol. 69, 1979, pp. 28-37.

Kraft, John, Edgar O. Olsen, "The Distribution of Benefits from Public Housing". In: F. Thomas Juster (Ed.), The Distribution of Economic Well-Being. National Bureau of Economic Research, Studies in Income and Wealth, Vol. 41, Cambridge, Mass., 1977, pp. 51-65.

Lowry, Ira S., Joseph S. De Salvo, Barbara M. Woodfill, Rental Housing in New York City. Vol. 2, The Demand for Shelter. The New York City-Rand Institute, Publ. No. R-649-NYC. New York 1971.

--, Barbara M. Woodfill, Tiina Repnau, Program Standards for Site I. The Rand Corporation, Publ. No. WN-8574-HUD, January 1974.

Mac Rae, C. Duncan, Margery Austin Turner, "Estimating Demand for Owner-Occupied Housing Subject to the Income Tax". Journal of Urban Economics, Vol. 10, 1981, pp. 338-356.

Mayo, Stephen K., Shirley Mansfield, David Warner, Richard Zwetchkenbaum, Housing Allowances and Other Rental Housing Assistance Programs - A Comparison Based on the Housing Allowance Demand Experiment. Abt Associates, Cambridge, Mass., 1980.

Mills, Edwin S., Arthur Sullivan, "Market Effects". In: Katharine L. Bradbury, Anthony Downs (Eds.), Do Housing Allowances Work? The Brookings Institution, Washington 1981, pp. 247-283.

Muth, Richard F., Cities and Housing. Chicago 1969.

--, Redistribution of Income through Regulation in Housing. 1982, unpubl.

Olsen, Edgar O., "A Competitive Theory of the Housing Market". The American Economic Review, Vol. 59, 1969, pp. 612-622.

--, "An Econometric Analysis of Rent Control". Journal of Political Economy, Vol. 80, 1972, pp. 1081-1100.

Olsen, Edgar O., "The Simple Analytics of the Externality Argument for Redistribution". In: Maurice B. Ballabon (Ed.), Economic Perspectives: An Annual Survey of Economics, Volume 2, New York 1981, pp. 155-173.

--, "Housing Programs and the Forgotten Taxpayer". The Public Interest, Vol. 66, 1982, pp. 97-109.

--, David M. Barton, The Benefits and Costs of Public Housing in New York City. University of Virginia, Thomas Jefferson Center for Political Economy, Discussion Paper No. 123, Charlottesville, February 1982.

--, Kathy York, "The Effect of Different Measures of Benefit on Estimates of the Distributive Consequences of Government Programs". Paper presented at the National Bureau of Economic Research's Conference on Research in Income and Wealth, Madison, Wisconsin, May 14, 1982.

President's Committee on Urban Housing, A Decent Home - The Report of the President's Committee on Urban Housing. Washington 1969.

The Rand Corporation (Rand), Fourth Annual Report of the Housing Assistance Supply Experiment. Publ. No. R-2302-HUD, Santa Monica 1978.

Rosen, Harvey S., "Housing Decisions and the U.S. Income Tax: An Econometric Analysis". Journal of Public Economics, Vol. 11, 1979, pp. 1-23.

U.S. Department of Housing and Urban Development (HUD) [a], Housing in the Seventies. Washington 1974.

-- [b], Office of Economic Affairs, A Framework for Housing Policy. 1977, unpubl.

-- [c], Office of Policy Development and Research, Experimental Housing Allowance Program: Conclusions - The 1980 Report. Washington 1980.

U.S. Executive Office of the President (U.S. Pres.), Office of Management and Budget, Special Analyses: Budget of the United States Government, Fiscal Year 1982. Washington 1981.

Weicher, John C., "Urban Housing Policy". In: Peter Mieszkowski, Mahlon Straszheim (Eds.), Current Issues in Urban Economics. Baltimore 1979, pp. 469-508.

White, Melvin, Anne White, "Horizontal Inequality in the Federal Income Tax Treatment of Homeowners and Tenants". National Tax Journal, Vol. 18, 1965, pp. 225-239.

Comment

Johann Eekhoff

I. Introduction

The following comments on Olsen's paper do not include a description of the instruments of the German housing policy and of its shortcomings. Instead, I'll make several critical comments on the Olsen paper. This is not easy because of Olsen's excellent reasoning. My statements follow the order of subjects in the paper.

II. Rent Control

1. I can easily accept the clear economic reasoning on rent control. But I hesitate to support the conclusion "that rent control is a policy with no redeeming social value" (p. 206). And I am not sure whether the statement that "the belief that landlords make excessive profits is not supported by any systematic evidence" (p. 200) can be generalised.

At least in West Germany there is a *strong feeling* that landlords *make* high profits and *are* wealthier than their tenants. This feeling might not be the best guide for housing policy in the future, but its causes and effects have to be considered seriously. I think in Germany this belief has a real basis. The experience with two world wars has shown that it turned out to be highly rewarding to have invested in dwelling units, i.e. to investors whose buildings had not been destroyed. The advantages of real capital and a severe housing shortage secured relative and absolute high rents for many years. No politician can neglect this historic experience. Let me call this the inherited problem of economic rents in the sense of excessive profits or the *post-war rents*.

2. Another source of housing shortage and of economic rents of existing dwelling units is the development and growth of urban agglomeration areas. The other side of the coin is the surge in rent for the old

inhabitants of the agglomeration areas, which is considered a social problem. I'll come back to the stated social problem under the subject public housing and concentrate on the aspect of economic rents in agglomeration areas.

3. In well chosen examples the "Deutscher Mieterbund" (German Tenants' Union) pulls together the post-war rent and the agglomeration rent in order to demonstrate the excessiveness of rents, especially in the older stock of housing units. The organisation compares the actual annual rent and the pre-war capital investment, thus keeping alive the belief in excessive profits of landlords.

4. The general feeling that landlords are in a strong market position and are able to claim "unjustified" rents led to the Eviction Protection Law in 1971. The original purpose of this law was primarily the protection of renters against increases in rents above the increase of the average cost of living. During the legislative process, eviction protection was more focussed upon than rent control. But eviction protection is only effective if rents are controlled. So in fact we again have rent control although its main justification is eviction protection. Behind this official justification there is still the desire for rent control. And the German Tenants' Union fears that rents will explode if the Eviction Protection Law would be substantially reduced or abolished. The latest modification of the law was called "Rent Enhancing Law" by the Tenants' Union.

5. Now, what are the main conflicts and problems about rent control and what could be the advice for housing policy? I think we cannot deny the inherited problem of post-war economic rents. The importance of this problem is only slowly diminishing. Once this has been accepted, there is a goal conflict between (re)distribution and efficiency. And my main question is: How can the trade-off between these two goals be kept small? And if there is no acceptable compromise: How can we convince the man on the street and the politician that they can trust in the efficiency and rent-damping forces of a free market? Is it reasonable to argue that the potential investors and renters are living in the same society and that a strong belief in high profits and security against inflation will induce investors to accept very low or even negative real interests on the capital invested in dwelling units? In this case the experience and expectation of investors would be sufficient to squeeze excessive rents out of the housing stock by high investment levels.

6. Another question is whether housing policy has to react to agglomeration rents. A straight answer could be that agglomeration rents are land rents and that land taxation is the adequate instrument. But besides the economic argument that price differences indicate scarcity there remains a social problem of high rents or generally high costs of housing. Those families who have been living in urban agglomeration areas for many years have to bear high housing costs although their income may not have risen and although they may not be able and willing to move out of the area.

If we respect the right of families to stay in an area and not to be uprooted by changing economic conditions or if we only observe this behaviour we have to think about the social net, i. e. the minimum standard of living. The question to which I do not have an answer is whether unconditional cash grants or housing allowances should in some way rise according to the size of cities to offset the higher costs of living or in our case the higher costs of housing. It might be inadequate to connect housing allowances to nominal income, because the same nominal income renders a lower real income in agglomerations than in other areas. But if the difference in housing costs or rents is eliminated by differentiated housing allowances there is no incentive to consume housing services where they are cheap. How can this dilemma be solved?

III. Income Tax Treatment of Homeownership

7. Tax subsidies for homeowners are often regarded as a device to increase the housing supply through a filtering process - and again to keep down rents. Another important justification for them is to redistribute income over the life-span of a family. According to this argument tax subsidies make it easier to carry the high financial burden at the beginning of the earning period when the desire to have a large own home is especially high. Tax subsidies in the home-building or home-buying phase correspond to a higher tax during the rest of the earning phase. Those households that get a large subsidy in one phase pay high taxes in the other phases. The effect of the subsidy is not limited to homeowners. It is partly passed on to renters by the filtering process. So much for this type of reasoning.

8. In his paper Olsen concludes that the income tax provisions in the United States should be eliminated. I agree with this conclusion re-

garding the specific provisions in the United States and also the provisions in Germany. One implicit proposal in the Olsen paper deserves further elaboration. What Olsen calls a neutral treatment of homeownership is also known as the consumption-good model, i.e. the owner-occupied dwelling unit is treated like other consumption goods and not as a source of income-tax-relevant earnings or deductions (losses). Alternatively, the owner-occupied dwelling unit could be treated as an investment good. In this case the difference between a comparable market rent and all costs (depreciation, mortgage interest, etc.) would be tax relevant.

9. How can the consumption-good model and the investment-good model be compared and judged? In the consumption-good model the homeowner pays less tax than in the investment-good model, because it can be assumed that the present value of all net rents is positive. Which reasons justify the treatment of the owner-occupied dwelling unit as a consumption good? What are the criteria to distinguish consumption goods from investment goods?

Do the answers to these questions depend on the tax system? Does the introduction of the consumption-good model imply that all earnings from capital goods are free from income taxes, i.e. that the renter does not have to pay taxes on earnings from his capital assets? Are the services of the homeowner, which he immediately consumes, part of his taxable income? At least one point should be stressed: the time pattern of payments is much more favourable in the investment-good model than in the consumption-good model, because depreciation and interest payments can be deducted from taxable income and taxes on the market rent surpass the tax deductions only after 10 to 15 years.

IV. Housing Subsidies to Low-Income Families

A. Rationales

10. Olsen states that "recipients prefer an unconditional cash grant to a housing subsidy" and that it is therefore "difficult to justify housing subsidies unless taxpayers receive tangible benefits particularly related to the housing of recipients *or* care about recipients" (p. 214). I agree that the external effects of a higher minimum standard of the housing of recipients and the immediate health effects to

the recipients are negligible, because the minimum standard of housing units in the United States and similarly in Germany are already fairly high. Nevertheless, many families still have severe housing problems, for which low income is the main reason. Therefore, it is not astonishing that Olsen calls "paternalistic altruism" (p. 214) the major rationale for housing subsidies. But it has to be explained why the donators and politicians prefer housing subsidies whereas the recipients would rather take unconditional cash grants.

11. It is easy to prove that a recipient reaches the same or a higher level of utility if he gets the money equivalent instead of a certain amount of housing services. But the donator may look at this problem from another viewpoint. He may not only see one recipient but a whole family and he may be very doubtful whether his good money will actually be used for good purposes and not spent on alcohol, cigarettes, drugs or even burglary tools, explosives and guns. The donator might claim the right of the breadwinner in a family and direct his money to similar purposes as in his own family - particularly if he suspects that the head of the receiving household has other preferences. Do not the preferences of donators and tax-payers deserve more attention in economic theory? Can we ignore these effects in a policy aiming at a redistribution of income? Are housing subsidies to be considered an efficient tool of income redistribution, because resistance to this kind of redistribution is relatively weak?

Preference structure of a donator

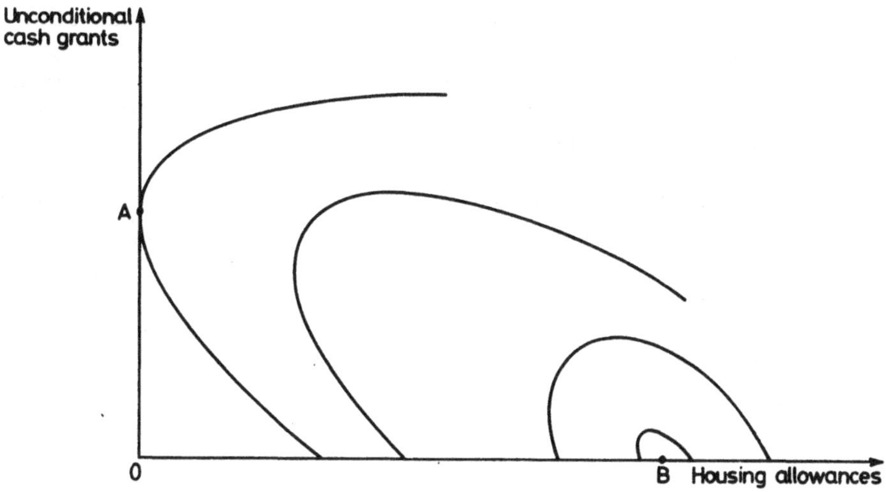

Let us consider the case of voluntary redistribution. This means that a (wealthy) person enhances his welfare or utility by giving part of his income to poor families. The utility structure of the wealthy person may have the form shown in the figure.

Having a given income, the wealthy person donates the amount OA if he is restricted to unconditional cash grants. But he might be willing to give a larger amount (OB) if he can be sure that the money will be spent on housing. In the chosen case the donator reaches a higher utility level if his payment is restricted to the consumption of housing services. The open question is whether his welfare gain by conditioning the money outweighs the welfare loss of the recipient, taken into account that the amount of conditioned money might be higher than the amount of unconditioned money.

12. Another line of reasoning, which shall only be mentioned here, refers to market imperfections. It is often maintained that the supply of low-income housing is inelastic and hardly reacts to cash grants and housing allowances and that problem families are discriminated against in the housing market. From this diagnosis it is only a small step to the supply of public housing.

B. Public Housing

13. Public housing still seems to be an attractive instrument in housing policy. Let me stress only one point. If local or regional scarcities on the housing market arise, public housing can be concentrated in these regions. Public housing is a visible and countable "proof" of the political activity to alleviate housing problems, though the effectiveness might be very low or even negative. Public housing is preferred to housing allowances, because it is believed that the additional supply will help to keep down rents, particularly in the market section of low-income families.

The question is whether public housing is an effective and efficient remedy to *local housing problems* of low-income families or whether it is a self-defeating tool which attracts more poor people.

Can the necessity of regionalisation be denied? Should a limited program of public housing be handled by local authorities and limited to emergency cases?

C. Housing Allowances

14. Olsen refers to the experiments with housing allowances in the United States which did not have a significant effect on rents. The main objection to a shift from public housing to a large-scale housing allowance program with entitlement in Germany is still the fear that the additional demand will raise rents considerably and will have little effect on the number and quality of dwelling units. I do not share this view. But I find it very hard to overcome this objection and to convince discussants in this field. I would be very glad if information on the American experience with housing allowances could be made available not only to economic theorists but also to politicians and interest groups in order to show by empirical evidence that the alleged "market imperfections" are not as strong as often believed.

15. One problem of housing allowances as opposed to public housing is seen in the fact that the amount of allowance, which depends on the number of persons in a household, is reduced when the size of the household shrinks, i.e. when children found their own household or when old members of the family die. If the household made full use of housing allowances when it had many members and little income, the remaining allowance to those members who are left may not suffice to pay the rent and the household is compelled to move. To avoid this dilemma, households will be prevented from making full use of housing allowances, so that this instrument may not be very effective.

Thomas H. Tietenberg

Market Approaches to Environmental Protection

I. Introduction

1. Background

For many years economics as a discipline and economists as the practitioners of that discipline had relatively little impact on environmental policy in the United States. This was true in spite of the existence of a large number of sophisticated economic models which had important policy implications. Various hypotheses have been advanced to explain this resistance of the American policy process to economic analysis, ranging from the lack of realism in the models [Ackerman et al., 1974, pp. 39-53] to the lack of economic training of members of the U.S. Congress [Kneese, Schultze, 1975, p. 116].

Whatever the reasons, there is currently some evidence that this resistance is no longer as strong as it once was, particularly for air pollution control policy. Recent policy initiatives by the U.S. Environmental Protection Agency (EPA) have incorporated economic incentives, albeit to a limited extent, in its predominantly regulatory approach to controlling emissions. The foremost of these is the introduction of controlled trading of the right to pollute among emitters, a clear step in the direction of a transferable discharge permit (TDP).

Although the central concept involved can be traced at least back to Alfred Marshall and Henry George, it seems fair to attribute much of the revival of interest to Dales [1968] for water and Crocker [1966] for air. The concept is a disarmingly simple and powerful one. Its intellectual genesis is to be found in the realization that the behavioral sources of the pollution problem could be traced to an ill-defined set of property rights. The right to discharge pollutants had historically, in the absence of government intervention, been allocated at a zero price to all potential users. While this allocation process *can* be cost-justified when the costs of controlling pollution (including the administrative and enforcement costs) exceed the costs of pollution damage incurred by the absence of control, it *cannot* be justified when the level of pollution damage indicates that some form of control is appropriate. One natural outcome of using this perspective to characterize the nature of the pollution problem is that it suggests a particular policy approach - the establishment of a correctly defined right to discharge.

2. The Policy Context

Although the existing regulatory approach to air pollution control is exceedingly complex, it is possible to capture briefly the essence of both the basic approach and the recent reforms which have moved it further in the direction of an increasing reliance on economic incentives. For those substances designated as "criteria" pollutants, the existing system of air pollution control relies on ambient standards (or concentration targets) defined by the EPA and implementation plans submitted by the states (SIPs) to detail the procedures by which the states intend to meet those standards. Other pollutants such as chlorofluorocarbons are regulated directly by EPA.

In the SIPs, historically the states have chosen to meet the ambient standards by defining maximum allowable emission levels for each source of the pollutant. It wasn't long before this command and control approach created a large regulatory burden. Once the emission standards had been established there was little incentive for existing sources to adopt newer technologies when they became available. Coupled with an increase in the number of sources over time, this implied a degradation of air quality. In recognition of this fact, the pollution control authorities have had to impose even more stringent controls on new sources. This discrimination among sources tends to force an inefficiently high proportion of the control costs on new sources. This in turn lowers the return on the introduction of new technologies designed to raise productivity. According to one estimate a small but non-negligible proportion of the slowdown in U.S. productivity growth can be attributed to this source[1]. When these excess costs are added to those caused by the fact that the allocation of emission standards even among existing sources is not cost-effective, the size of the resulting regulatory burden creates significant pressures for reform.

---

[1] Environmental regulations have been estimated by Haveman and Christainsen [1981, p. 74] to have caused from 8 to 12 percent of the slowdown in U.S. productivity.

Three major reforms have taken place recently which have the effect of reducing some of this regulatory burden by moving current policy closer to a market approach. These are the alternative emission reduction approach (known popularly as the "bubble" concept), the emission offset policy, and emission reduction banking.

The "bubble" concept specifically allows existing emitters to trade a more relaxed degree of control on one source for a more stringent degree of control on another source of the same pollutant as long as total emissions are not increased by the substitution. These trades can, under certain circumstances, occur between plants or even between firms. The object, of course, is to allow a firm to meet its emission reduction goal as flexibly and cheaply as possible while insuring that air quality is not degraded by the trade.

The emission offset policy was originally designed as a means for allowing economic growth in areas which were in violation of the ambient standards (non-attainment areas) while insuring no further degradation of their air quality. It allows potential new entrants to a non-attainment area to procure sufficient reductions from existing firms (over and above their previous legal requirements) so as to offset the increases in pollution which would otherwise occur upon their initiation of production in the area.

Emission reductions banking is a system for allowing sources to reduce their emissions more than required and to bank the excess for subsequent sale. This portion of the program is designed to stimulate a market for newer, cheaper control technologies and to assure the availability of reductions which can be traded.

3. An Overview of the Paper

Most observers would probably agree that some environmental regulation by the public sector is necessary. Yet there probably would be substantially less agreement on the form that regulation should take. The American experience provides a case study of one attempt to introduce economic incentives with their inherent greater flexibility into a regulatory system that was traditionally very inflexible.

Our experience with this social experiment is limited so we can make no pretense of fully understanding all there is to know about how it will work out. It is mature enough, however, that some clear insights are beginning to emerge. The purpose of this paper is to isolate those insights so that we may begin the process of seeing the extent to which they may be generalized to other areas of regulatory reform and other countries.

The paper opens by discussing the theoretical and empirical foundation on which the case for transferable discharge permits rests. This is followed by a section which discusses the principal design challenges which operating TDP systems face. Special attention is paid to the empirical evidence which demonstrates the significance of those challenges as well as the manner in which the challenges can successfully be met. The final two sections discuss the manner in which the existing markets in the United States have responded to these challenges and the possibilities for further regulatory reform.

II. The Analytical Framework[1]

1. Permit Markets and Cost Effectiveness

When it was first proposed by Dales [1968], the transferable discharge permit system was seen as a means by which two objectives could be simultaneously accomplished: (1) the efficient level of pollution could be achieved and (2) the responsibility for meeting that level could be allocated among emitters in a cost-effective manner. Further, it was believed that these objectives could be accomplished even when the control authority had no information either on damage costs or control costs.

As originally conceived the TDP market was a place in which environmentalists and polluters would battle with dollars. Environmentalists would purchase rights and, by denying their use to polluters, use them to obtain clearer air than would otherwise prevail. They would presumably purchase permits until a further purchase would cost more than the benefit they would receive. At that point an efficient level of pollution would be attained. Furthermore, changes in technology, information on the risks of pollution, or other relevant factors would automatically be incorporated in the market allocation.

[1] In this paper the mathematical background is omitted. The reader interested in seeing the mathematical development should consult Tietenberg [1981] and Montgomery [1972].

That turned out to be an overly optimistic assessment. It is now realized that polluters and environmentalists are not on an equal footing when bidding for the permits. For the polluters, a permit is a private good with all the benefits of ownership accruing to the owner. For the environmentalists, however, it is a public good with the benefits accruing to the residents of the area regardless of whether they contributed to the purchase or not. This creates a classic "free rider" problem in which the inability to exclude nonpurchasers creates an incentive to purchase less than the efficient number of permits. Therefore, the normal outcome of such a market would be to allow excess pollution. An efficient allocation would not be achieved.

The other anticipated virtue of a TDP market, the ability to allocate the responsibility for a predetermined emission reduction among emitters in a cost-effective manner, has withstood the test of time and, indeed, has served as the principal motivating force behind the current reforms. The demonstration of why this works occurs in two steps. The first step, due to Baumol and Oates [1971], consists of a proof that the minimum cost allocation of control responsibility among sources for achieving a given desired emission reduction is that allocation where the marginal costs of control are equal for all emitters[1]. The second step consists of a proof that an emission permit market will, in equilibrium, sustain that allocation.

Intuitively it is easy to see why each of these proofs is valid by showing that the assumption it is not true produces a contradiction. Suppose that we were considering an allocation which we believed to minimize costs where the marginal costs were not equalized. It would be possible to take some of the control responsibility away from the high marginal cost source and give an equal amount to the low marginal cost source. Such a rearrangement would achieve the same reduction, but at a lower cost. This contradicts the premise that the initial allocation minimized costs; therefore an allocation where marginal costs differ can not be cost-minimizing.

Emission permit markets can attain and sustain this equilibrium allocation because each source will purchase permits up to the point where the marginal cost of controlling the last unit is equal to the permit price. For a source to purchase either more or less permits than this would raise its costs unnecessarily. Since all sources indepen-

[1] We are excluding here the uncommon case where, due to economies of scale, costs are minimized when only one source reduces emissions.

dently set their marginal cost to the same price, the market guarantees that the marginal cost of control will be equalized across sources. This, of course, is precisely the allocation which minimizes the cost of control.

This permit market allocation is dynamically cost-effective as well as cost-effective at a point in time. Not only does the permit market adjust to changing costs of control, such as would occur with changes in control technology or inflation, it actually helps to stimulate newer, cheaper technologies to control air pollution. It does this by providing an active market for them. Since sources can sell their excess permits, they are constantly searching for new ways to control pollution whenever the marginal cost of the additional emission reduction is less than the permit price.

A permit market is dynamically cost-effective in the additional sense that it responds automatically to new emitters without allowing more emissions. Under the old regulatory system which merely forced new emitters to meet legal emission standards without requiring any compensatory decline from existing sources, the arrival of new sources would always cause the total amount of emissions in the area to rise. Eventually the ambient standard would be reached or exceeded. At that point either all growth would have to stop or the control authority would have to go back and clamp down harder on existing sources. Neither of these alternatives is particularly politically palatable.

The emission permit system transfers this problem to the market. The decision to cut back further by existing sources is a voluntary one, undertaken for the purpose of selling permits. Similarly, new sources may decide to enter an area if and only if they can afford to bid the necessary emission permits away from existing sources. No political decisions are involved.

These are powerful properties which were not shared by the regulatory system prior to the recent reforms. Yet, by themselves, these arguments were not sufficient to motivate the change. It still remained to demonstrate not only that the existing system was not cost-effective, but also that the excess costs were sufficient in magnitude to justify moving the regulatory structure into a new, relatively uncharted territory.

This empirical evidence was not long in coming. In the early 1970s Atkinson and Lewis [1974], both EPA employees at the time, published a study which examined, among other things, the relative costs of the traditional SIP control system and an emission permit system which equalized the marginal cost of emission reduction across sources. Focusing on particulate control in St. Louis, they found that the ratio of the costs of compliance for a traditional command and control approach to that which would result from an emission permit system was as high as 6:1 at lower air quality levels and, although the ratio dropped to 4:3 at more stringent air quality, the cost of the permit system was uniformly and significantly less.

Subsequent studies by Palmer et al. [1980] and by Maloney and Yandle [1979] seemed to confirm these findings for a wider sample of geographic areas and types of pollution. Examining the control of chloroflurocarbon emissions in the United States, Palmer et al. found that, for equal degrees of emission reduction, the present value of compliance costs for the traditional mandatory controls over a ten-year period would be $185. 3 mill. while the cost-minimizing approach would cost only $94. 7 mill., approximately half as much. Similarly, using data from 102 domestic DuPont plants, Maloney and Yandle found that DuPont could reduce its compliance cost by 60 percent if allowed to trade emission reductions within each plant and 85 percent if allowed to trade with sources outside the plant.

Not all of the evidence, however, suggests that emission permit systems are that cost-effective. Anderson et al. [1979] found that for NO_x control in Chicago the required degree of control was so severe and every source had to control to such a high degree (leaving little room for trades) that the difference between the regulatory approach and the emission permit approach was almost negligible ($239 mill. versus $254 mill.). As we shall see below, however, this study also found that a permit of a slightly different design could reduce costs drastically.

2. The Role of the Initial Allocation

Another desirable property of a transferable discharge permit system is that it allows the control authority considerable flexibility as to how the permits are introduced into the market. Montgomery [1972] has demonstrated formally that the manner in which these permits are introduced into the market does not affect the final allocation of control responsibility. A cost-effective allocation would be achieved regardless of whether the permits are auctioned off or given away. Intuitively this result occurs because the initial allocation results in a lump sum endowment to the original holders which does not affect marginal choices. It merely determines who acquires the wealth from the creation of a new asset called the right to pollute.

What is involved is the disposition of the transfer payments associated with the right to pollute. These payments are quite different from the compliance costs (the cost of control equipment and labor) which are real resource costs to society. While the transfer payments are not real costs to society (they represent merely a shifting of resources from one segment of society to another) they are real costs to the agent which has to pay them.

There are many possible ways to distribute these transfer payments. In an auction market where the government sells the permits to the highest bidder these payments become an additional cost to the sources and a source of revenue to the government. In systems where the permits are allocated free of charge among emitters the aggregate value of the payments remains the same but now this value is shared among the emitters in a manner determined by whatever rules are used to distribute the permits. Because it has a large menu of initial allocation procedures at its disposal, the control authority has considerable latitude in choosing the manner in which these transfer costs are allocated among sources without upsetting the final, cost-effective allocation of responsibility.

Several studies have found the transfer costs to be sufficient in magnitude to suggest that these initial allocation rules deserve some particular attention. The deLucia [1974] study of water pollution control on the Mohawk River found the permit costs to be roughly equal to compliance costs. Depending on the particular system being considered, Anderson et al. [1979] found them to represent from 25 percent of compliance costs to roughly twice compliance cost. Perhaps the most striking findings were by Palmer et al. [1980], who found that expenditures on permits designed to control chloroflurocarbon emissions, when they were auctioned off, cost ten times more than the cost of compliance.

One question of interest is how sensitive these estimates are to the degree of required control. Do permit expenditures become more or less important as the degree of required control is increased? Using data from St. Louis, Atkinson and Tietenberg [1982] found that permit expenditures became less important as the degree of control was increased, although over reasonable ranges they were never less than 33 percent of the sum of the permit plus compliance costs. Whether or not this result is robust must be taken up by further studies.

Another question of interest concerns how an average source would fare under these various systems. Would an average source be better off (i.e. face lower costs) under the command and control system (with higher compliance costs but no transfer costs) or under an auction permit market (with lower compliance costs but positive transfer costs)? The *average* source would be better off when the savings in compliance costs exceeds the amount of the transfer costs. A close examination of the results discussed above reveals that this would sometimes, but not always, occur. In the case of chlorofluorocarbons, for example, the sources would prefer to suffer the increase in compliance costs than bear the tremendous transfer costs an auction market would entail.

The reluctance of industry, of course, to accept these transfer costs can be mitigated by giving the permits away. If these are given to sources in the precise amounts necessary to legitimize the amount of emissions they were allowed under the purely regulatory control system the transition to a TDP system could be eased. Under this allocation no existing source would be worse off than it was under the old system, but any source which could complete a successful trade would be better off. This is the allocation system which is implicit in the bubble and offset policies.

This allocation rule (and all others which involve the free allocation of permits to *existing* sources), however, creates another problem - it discriminates against new sources, although probably to a lesser extent than the previous regulatory system. Existing sources acquire the permits at no cost while new sources have to pay for them (by bidding them away from existing sources). Therefore, although the bias is lower than under the pure regulatory system (since existing sources now bear some of the responsibility) it still exists.

The literature on the empirical properties of alternative rules for allocating permits among sources is quite thin. In one of the few existing studies (which relates to water pollution rather than air pollution) David et al. [1980] found that when permits for phosphorus effluent into Lake Michigan were allocated among sources in proportion to their average daily flow most of the smaller sources, on balance, had to purchase a small number of extra permits. Meanwhile, most of the very large polluters (Milwaukee, in particular) sold a large number of permits and experienced large revenue gains. Whether these results also hold for air pollutants in other geographic settings remains to be seen[1]. If they do hold, then the capture of these potential "windfall" gains by large sources is likely to present a difficult public policy problem in a nation which seems somewhat hostile to large business entities.

III. Designing the System: Pragmatic Issues

Up to this point in the discussion we have dealt mainly with the conceptual issues which lie behind the current regulatory reform. Yet the establishment of these markets is by no means a trivial exercise. In this section we shall deal with four more pragmatic, but no less important, design issues. These include the treatment of source location, the timing of emissions, the potential for imperfect competition in permit markets and enforceability.

1. The Spatial Dimension

There are two spatial issues which turn out to be of major importance, at least for some pollutants, in the design of TDP markets. For ease of exposition these shall be referred to as the local pollutant problem and the hot spot problem.

The local pollutant problem refers to the fact that, while for most pollutants (called local pollutants) the equal marginal cost rule results in a given amount of *emissions* being reduced at minimum cost, it does *not* result in meeting the *ambient* standards at minimum cost. Derived independently by Montgomery [1972] and Tietenberg [1973], this result is obtained because the location of the emissions matters and the equal marginal cost rule does not incorporate this information. In essence, emission permit systems result in the over-control of distant sources and the under-control of sources which are proximate to the receptor where the concentration is of concern.

---

[1] Some preliminary work by Atkinson and Tietenberg [1982] suggests that similar results are achieved for particulate control in St. Louis.

Empirically, several studies have found that, compared to the least cost method, the use of a permit system defined solely in terms of emissions to achieve a local pollutant ambient standard causes a significant increase in compliance costs. Atkinson and Lewis [1974] found that, for particulate control in St. Louis, the use of equal marginal cost rule for allocating the control responsibility causes the compliance costs to be twice what they would be in a minimum cost allocation. Furthermore, the study by Anderson et al. [1979] (which study, it may be remembered, failed to find much difference between the conventional regulatory approach and the equal marginal cost approach) did find a huge cost savings to be derived from taking the location of the emitter into account in allocating the control responsibility.

The hot spot problem refers to the fact that, while emission trades hold emissions constant, they do not hold the ambient air quality constant. An emission trade, for example, involving the sale of permits by a source located far from the receptor to a source located near the receptor, and upwind of it, would certainly make air quality at that receptor worse in spite of the fact that total emissions remain constant. The practical consequence of the hot spot problem is that, even when a region is in complete compliance with the ambient standards prior to a trade, an emission trade can cause air pollution at one or more receptors to exceed the standard.

Is it possible to design a permit system which solves the hot spot problem while achieving a cost-minimizing allocation of the responsibility for meeting the ambient standard? A theorem which shows that it is possible was first proven by Montgomery [1972]. The permit system which can fulfill this potential is called an ambient permit system.

Unfortunately the ambient permit system is administratively complex. For each pollutant it involves a separately defined set of permits for each receptor location. Any particular source would have to buy enough permits from each receptor market to justify its emissions. Each permit is standardized to take the location of the emitter into account. Regardless of which source uses the permit, the effect on air quality at the receptor is the same.

Administrative complexity is not the only problem to be faced in the implementation of an ambient permit system. A recent paper by Atkinson and Tietenberg [1982] uncovers another problem with this approach. One of the reasons the ambient permit system can achieve the standard at a lower cost than an emission permit system is that its focus is on selective emission control; it actually has to reduce fewer emissions to achieve the ambient standard. In St. Louis, for example, the ambient permit system controlled roughly one half the emissions controlled by an emissions permit system while meeting the same ambient standard. As we shall see in our discussion of the current system, this is a property which has proven to be a major stumbling block in the evolution of the U.S. reform package.

2. The Timing of Emission Flows

Both the emission intensity of contributing sources and meteorological conditions have a temporal component which could conceivably be integrated into permit design. Compared to the spatial dimension, however, very little work has been accomplished in this area.

Perhaps the most striking finding to date concerns the appropriate way of handling those relatively rare, but devastating, occasion when thermal inversions prevent the normal dispersion and dilution of the pollutants. From a point of view of economic efficiency, the most obvious approach is to tailor the degree of control to the circumstances. Stringent control would be exercised when meteorological conditions were relatively stagnant and somewhat less control when circumstances were normal.

It turns out that a reliance on a constant degree of control - instead of allowing these intermittent controls - raises compliance costs substantially, particularly when the required degree of control is high. In perhaps the earliest empirical study which was soundly based on economic theory, Teller [1970] examined the costs of controlling sulphur dioxide in Nashville, Tennessee through fuel substitution. He specifically examined two strategies: constant abatement which requires the same degree of control over time and forecasted abatement which allows the degree of control to be tailored to forecasted weather conditions. Both strategies achieve compliance with the ambient standards, but forecasted control requires less total emission reduction. His results indicate that constant abatement was five times more expensive than forecasted abatement. Clearly this is an area offering potential cost savings. We shall explore in a subsequent section of this paper the extent to which this potential has been exploited.

3. The Potential for Imperfect Competition

One of the questions which has worried some observers about the transferable permit system is whether or not competition will prevail. The fear is that the introduction of transferable permits will allow some source to use the transferable permit market as a means of gaining market power. Those who express this fear point to the fixed supply of permits as the reason for their concern. The results of microeconomic theory show quite clearly that market power on either the buyer or seller side of the market can cause inefficiencies which could spill over from the permit market into other markets. Because of the manner in which the permit system is defined, market power would not lead to lower air quality. It could, however, cause the cost of compliance to be higher than necessary.

Though most of the studies cited above do not focus on the competition problem, the market shares controlled by large sources in the equilibrium allocations do not seem troublesome. A recent study by the U.S. General Accounting Office [1982, pp. 70 f.] examined the potential for market power for five separate pollutants in the San Francisco Bay area. They concluded that "with the possible exception of SO_2 the potential influence of the 'top ten' stationary sources on prices and quantities of air pollution entitlements traded in the Bay Area appears negligible".

Another author who looks specifically at the possibilities for noncompetitive behavior [deLucia, 1974] concludes that, even though there were only eight polluting sources in his study of the Mohawk River, there was little danger of price manipulation by a single source.

There are markets, however, in which sources are faced with special incentives to exercise a form of strategic behavior. Strategic behavior would occur when a source could use the permit market to turn a short-term loss into a long-term gain. Sources would be presented with this opportunity in markets where many of the participants in the permit market are competitors in the product market as well as in the permit market and the competition in that product market is purely from local firms. In this case, some sources could purchase sufficient permits to deny their competitors the ability to commence or to continue production. Once the competitors were shut down, the sources could recoup their losses by charging higher prices in the product market. Though such markets are rare, they do exist. One possible example is provided by Piceance Basin in Colorado, where all purchasers of permits can be expected to use them to cover the emissions generated by the production of shale oil. Even in this case, however, a single seller could not dictate the price of shale oil since other forms of oil would limit the range of prices available to that seller.

The competitiveness problem may well get worse over time as the demand for permits rises with no compensating increase in the total supply. As the permit prices rise and sources choose to control to a higher degree, the opportunities for further reduction become decreased. This means that the supply of available permits becomes diminished and further price increases will not appreciably affect the supply. At this point it becomes possible to imagine the existence of a single seller which is able to appropriate monopoly rent from the sale of permits. This opportunity will be limited only by the competition offered by alternative locations which are governed by other permit markets. The problem is intensified if restrictions are placed on the number and types of emission reductions which can be traded. As markets mature this is an aspect which will merit further scrutiny.

4. Enforceability

The least cost properties of a transferable discharge permit system are based on the implicit assumption that the terms of the permits can be enforced. It has to be possible to identify sources which are not complying and to levy sanctions on them if the resulting air quality is to approximate the desired level.

There are two reasons why enforceability may be made somewhat more difficult by the replacement of a command and control regulatory system with a transferable discharge permit system of one form or another: (1) it will be difficult to ascertain the amount of reduction which will actually be achieved by a seller of permits and (2) it will be difficult to determine the proper exchange ratio to use in order to ensure that trades hold air quality constant at the desired locations. The former difficulty arises from the fact that markets will open up whole new possibilities for emission reduction which are not well understood, while the latter arises from the lack of precision in air quality modeling.

Before a trade can take place the buyer and seller must agree on what is being traded; in trading the right to pollute, the buyer must also obtain the concurrence of the EPA, which is not always as easy as it sounds. This can be illustrated by examining one type of trade.

In the mid-1970's Volkswagen Corporation negotiated with the State of Pennsylvania to locate a plant in a partially constructed Chrysler Corporation factory in the western part of the state[1]. For employment reasons the state was anxious to secure an agreement. As part of its package of enticements the State agreed to reduce its own emissions of hydrocarbons in order to insure that the increases due to Volkswagen's initiation of production would not jeopardize compliance with the ambient air quality standards. The reductions by the State were to be achieved by changing the type of asphalts used in paving. This change was expected to yield a decrease in hydrocarbon emissions by the state of 1,025 tons per year although there was a considerable degree of uncertainty associated with that number. Whenever control authorities confront a new method of reducing emissions such as this one it is difficult to ascertain with any degree of certainty what the *actual* (as opposed to the expected) reductions will be.

The second element of uncertainty in the enforcement problem lies in the reliability of the air quality models used to relate emissions to ambient air quality. These models must be reliable if one is to implement an ambient permit system or, on a less ambitious scale, to simply ensure that the hot spot problem does not arise.

This problem is not as difficult as it may appear. The caricature of trying to keep track of pollutants in an area with shifting wind patterns and velocity misses the point; it ignores the fact that, through the use of probability distributions, the outputs of simpler, steady-state models can be used to characterize the probabilities of given standards being exceeded.

The problem is not trivial, however, because even the steady-state models are not perfectly accurate. When there are inaccuracies, then the use of these models to define trades which leave air quality constant at designated receptor locations may result in air quality levels quite different than expected. Furthermore, although the EPA's reliance on air quality modeling in the United States has been upheld by the courts, a large amount of time and resources have been expended to defend its position[2].

---

[1] For a more detailed description of this case see Liroff [1980, pp. 13 ff].

[2] The history of the judicial treatment of air quality monitoring can be found in Kramer [1979].

IV. Permit Markets in Practice

In the preceeding sections we have discussed the theory and empirical work which serve as the foundation for the movement to reform the regulatory approach to air pollution control in the United States. The actual policies which have been implemented represent major, but incomplete, steps toward a full discharge permit market system. In this section we shall briefly explore the current system of regulations as it has evolved to grapple with the design challenges described in the preceeding sections.

The U.S. Environmental Protection Agency refers to this regulatory reform package as the "controlled trading program". This label conveys accurately the approach that has been taken - to allow trades to take place among sources as long as these trades satisfy a number of conditions. These conditions are designed to ensure that the new trading system is integrated smoothly with the existing regulatory approach. They have the effect of reducing the number of trades and, hence, increasing the cost of compliance.

1. The Current Policy Structure

The Offset Policy. By the end of 1975 many regions of the country had failed to meet one or more of the primary national ambient air quality standards as required by the Clean Air Act. As a result the EPA faced a difficult problem. The Act prohibited the granting of permits to new sources which would contribute to a violation of these standards. Prohibiting all growth in those areas, however, would have been politically unpopular. The offset policy was conceived in 1976 as a way to permit growth in the area without permitting an increase in emissions[1]. The new sources could locate in these regions provided they procured sufficient offsetting reductions (called offsets) from existing sources.

The offset policy was applied to major new sources which would, by their initiation of production, aggravate the air quality in non-attainment regions. As the policy now stands these sources would receive construction permits providing three conditions were met. First, the

[1] A description of the details of the earliest versions of this program can be found in Liroff [1980]. A more current and more detailed description can be found in del Calvo y Gonzales [1981].

new source would have to install pollution control equipment which has been designated by EPA as producing the "lowest achievable emission rate (LAER)". Second, all existing sources in the region owned by the owners of the new source have to be certified to be in compliance with the law. Third, the added emissions from the new source have to be less than the reduction in emissions procured through offsets so that the total amount of emissions after the entrance of the new source would be less than prior to its entrance. This requirement was designed to insure "reasonable further progress" toward the eventual attainment of the ambient standard.

The manner in which this program has been implemented makes it quite different from a true transferable discharge permit market. The requirement that new sources must adopt a LAER technology, for example, rules out the possibility of adopting a less stringent (and presumably cheaper) technology by purchasing more offsets even when this latter strategy is considerably cheaper.

The "reasonable further progress" requirement has two undesirable side effects. On the one hand, the new sources are forced to bear a disproportionate share of the responsibility for improving air quality in the region. Existing sources may sell offsets and use the revenue to clean up their pollution but new sources can only purchase them. This serves to retard the replacement of old production facilities with new ones. Not only can this lower productivity growth (since newer factories usually embody the latest and most productive technology); it also can frequently retard the replacement of older, more heavily polluting factories with newer, less polluting ones.

This constraint also rules out all possible trades where emissions increase even when the air quality benefits are substantial. Suppose, for example, that a particular trade was envisioned between an existing source in a heavily polluted area and a new source in another part of the same urban area, a part which is characterized by air that is quite a bit cleaner than the standard requires. This kind of trade, if allowed, could improve air quality (by reducing pollution at the location where the consequences are most adverse) even when total emissions increase. The "reasonable further progress" constraint would rule out this opportunity.

These controls on the eligibility of offsets to be considered for trades serve to reduce the set of available offsets. Not only does this raise compliance costs in competitive permit markets; it also increases the likelihood that the markets will be imperfectly competitive.

The Bubble Policy. The bubble policy derives its name from a pedagogic device used to explain to the public how the policy works. It is, the explanation goes, as if an imaginary bubble were placed over many sources of the same pollutant either in the same plant or in proximate plants. Emission trades can take place within the bubble as long as the total emissions leaving the bubble are not increased.

As of November 1981, the Environmental Protection Agency had approved 12 bubble applications. The agency has estimated that these approvals saved some $30 mill. in expenditures on pollution control equipment with no additional pollutant emissions. There are apparently several hundred more bubble applications in various stages of the approval process.

The bubble policy can be used by sources to reduce their costs in two main ways: (1) it allows them to escape some regulation by keeping total emissions under the threshold which triggers a permit review process and (2) it changes the responsibility for meeting the regulations once a source is covered by these regulations. An example of the former use is provided by EPA regulations designed to prevent the significant deterioration of air quality in the parts of the country which are cleaner than required by the standards. In those areas, major new sources and major modifications to existing sources are required to obtain a permit and to adopt stringent control standards only if these changes will result in a net increase in emissions. Thus a plant is free to use the bubble policy to offset possible increases in emissions from an expansion with decreases in emissions elsewhere within the plant, thereby avoiding the permitting process.

The bubble policy can also be used to reduce the costs of meeting regulations for sources that are subject to them. Though most of the bubble activity has involved trades within a single plant, there are examples of external trades. As one example, in the summer of 1981 in Louisville, Kentucky, the Borden Chemical Company purchased 25 tons of hydrocarbon credits from the B. F. Goodrich Company. Borden is using some of the credits in lieu of purchasing more expensive technology-based controls for methanol storage tank emissions and the rest for an unspecified expansion at a later date. The purchase cost Borden roughly $2500 per ton on an annual basis while the cost of purchasing the technology-based controls would have been in the neighborhood of $5800 per ton.

Emissions Banking. The third and final component of the controlled trading package involves emission banking. This portion of the program allows a source to control more than required by law and to bank the excess for subsequent use or resale. Emission reductions achieved when firms cease operations can also be banked.

Until 1979 the EPA did not allow banking. The effect of this, of course, was to severely restrict the supply of possible offsets. If sources could not sell the excess control they purchased, there was very little point in investing in any more control than was legally required. In fact, there was a perverse incentive because any sources which controlled more than they were required to would find the bureaucrats responding by tightening up the standards. The control authorities used excess control as a signal that the regulations were too lax.

Under present regulations banking is allowed although in a circumscribed manner. Generally EPA has left it to the states to decide the manner in which the banking system is to be established and this portion of the program is still in its infancy.

We can see how such systems are evolving by taking a closer look at the systems which have been established by California, one of the states which has been most anxious to apply these regulatory reforms[1]. From an economic point of view the main deficiency of the banking system as it is currently being implemented in California is that the property rights to the banked credits are not well defined.

The problem of ill-defined property rights has two dimensions. First, the title to the banked credits is not always clearly vested in the supplier. Some banking proposals envision that at least some portion of the banked credits become the property of the state, which could then do with these credits as it pleases. Second, these systems also hold open the very real possibility that the banked credits could be confiscated if further control is subsequently deemed necessary. Both of these characteristics tend to inhibit the use of this system by sources and, in turn, to restrict the supply of emission reduction credits to facilitate trades.

This is not universally true, however. Some banking systems seem to be working. For example in Louisville, Kentucky during the sum-

[1] This section is based upon the data in GAO [1982] and Liroff [1980].

mer of 1981, one transaction involving banked credits was completed[1]. The General Electric Company is leasing from the International Harvester Company for $60,000 several hundred tons of hydrocarbon emission credits per year until the end of December 1983. This transaction is being used by GE to meet current regulations until the time it installs its own emission reduction control technologies. This case illustrates how banking can introduce a significant degree of temporal flexibility as to *when* the regulations are met without jeopardizing the objective of the regulation.

2. The Treatment of Time and Space

In the preceeding sections we have examined the manner in which the design of each of the three component parts of the current "controlled trading" program by the U.S. Environmental Protection Agency conforms to the dictates of efficient permit markets. We shall now turn to the question of how the package as a whole compares to a free market in permits.

The Spatial Dimension. The methods used to integrate source location into the trading system in the current controlled trading program are rather crude. We can illustrate this by examining the manner in which trades between spatially separated sources are treated in the Los Angeles area, which in this dimension is governed by one of the more sophisticated control authorities. According to established policy, the purchaser of offsets must purchase X tons of emission reduction credits for each ton of emission it plans to add to the airshed. X, a number greater than 1.0, is determined by the formula $X = 1.2 + b \cdot d$ where d = distance in kilometers between the new source and the offsetting source and b = 0 for values of $d < 8$; or b = .01 for values of $d > 8$ kilometers.

Does this approach provide a reasonable approximation to the ambient permit system described above? It doesn't because it is *source-oriented* rather than *receptor-oriented*. Under this formula, the further away the selling source is from the point where the new source will commence operations, the more offsetting tons have to be purchased. That is appropriate if and only if the only air quality of interest is the air quality at the site of the new source. If, however, the air quality at the selling site is as important (or more important),

---

[1] This case study was obtained from EPA [1981, p. 1].

this system will make a potentially beneficial trade significantly more expensive than necessary. The ambient permit system records air quality impacts at all receptor locations and allows all trades as long as the ambient air quality standards are met everywhere. Some ambient permit trades could well make air quality worse than it was (prior to the trade) at these locations which had higher air quality than required. In essence, if the goal is to achieve the ambient standards at minimum cost, the current system takes an excessively risk-averse approach to the problems of dealing with source location.

The Temporal Dimension. The temporal dimension has not been handled well by the current reform package, either. The current statute that sets the limits within which the package must be defined rules out the major potential source of cost savings. The Teller Study [1970], discussed above on p. 244, demonstrated that major cost savings are possible when intermittent controls are substituted for constant controls. Unfortunately, the current strategy embodied in the Clean Air Act is to require a degree of control at all times sufficient to meet the standards in even the most adverse conditions. The Clean Air Act Amendments of 1977 state unambiguously: "The degree of emission limitation required for control of any air pollutant under an applicable implementation plan under this title shall not be affected in any manner by ... any other dispersion technique. ... For the purposes of this section, the term "dispersion technique" includes any intermittent or supplemental control of air pollutants, varying with atmospheric conditions" [Stat. 721]. The potential for further reductions in compliance cost are clearly there, but is there any practical way to exploit them? The question is whether changes in the degree of control on relatively short notice are possible for sources.

One approach which has been used with success with some natural resources such as natural gas in the East and water access in the Southwest relies on interruptable contracts[1]. As applied to TDP markets, this approach would act to revoke some permits (and, hence, reduce emissions) whenever the meteorological conditions make such a move necessary. When conditions improved, the permits would be reactivated. These revocable permits would generally carry a lower price than permits which could not be revoked and would be purchased by sources which had the capability to react quickly at reasonable cost. Subject to validation of the Teller study for other pollutants and other areas, to the further development of acceptable means of implement-

[1] I first ran across this idea in Howe and Lee [1981].

ing intermittent controls and to a more hospitable treatment of intermittent controls by the Clean Air Act, this appears to be an area where further developments in regulatory reform might usefully occur.

3. Comparison with a Fully Cost-Effective System

We can now summarize and collect the major ways in which the current approach differs from a fully cost-effective system.

(1) The current system works on the basis solely of emissions rather than ambient permit trades, thus eliminating the cost-reducing benefits of separating out the different air quality impacts on different receptor locations and allowing these to be sold to different emitters. As indicated in the studies by Anderson et al. [1979] and by Atkinson and Lewis [1974], the possibilities for cost reduction foregone by this choice appear to be considerable.

(2) For several categories of sources, the existing system allows trades of emission reductions only above the legislatively mandated reductions. For those sources no existing emitter is allowed to exceed these thresholds, even if another firm could achieve the desired reduction at much lower cost. The combination system would allow all possible trades to take place, thereby expanding the set of cost reduction possibilities. The studies both by Anderson et al. [1979] and deLucia [1974] indicate that this is a quantitatively significant restriction.

(3) The current system involves a case-by-case determination rather than a regularized market. A case-by-case determination increases the administrative costs in several ways. One of the most important is that it opens each determination to legal challenge. Because of the increased discretionary power exercised by the control authority in a case-by-case approach, it also increases the possible appearance of discrimination against certain sources.

(4) The current policy excludes reliance on intermittent control measures. Thus the degree of control under constant control has to be sufficiently stringent to ensure compliance even during adverse atmospheric conditions. As the Teller study [1970] points out, this raises the cost of compliance significantly when a high level of air quality is required.

(5) The current restrictions on the market tend to reduce the supply of offset reductions available to any potential buyer. This raises

compliance cost not only because it rules out trades which could save more money, but also because it raises the likelihood of seller market power.

(6) The property rights to banked emission reduction credits are, in many operating systems, not clearly vested in the supplier. Until such time as these property rights are clearly vested in the suppliers, the incentives to bank credits will be severely diminished.

Some of these differences can be removed by a change in philosophy; they are not limited by the state of the art. Possible policy changes would include allowing existing sources to deviate from their legislated minimums - provided they can purchase the compensating reductions, the introduction of intermittent controls and the more careful definition of the property rights to banked emission reduction credits.

Others are limited by the state of the art. The expansion of trading possibilities without jeopardizing air quality requires a resolution of the two enforceability problems discussed on pp. 246 f. Progress is certainly being made on both fronts. Our experience with new sources of emission reduction is growing, as is our knowledge of air quality monitoring. It is therefore not unreasonable to expect that these barriers, too, might someday be overcome.

V. Concluding Comments

Current air pollution policy in the United States represents an interesting case study in potential use of economic incentives to create a more flexible and yet effective regulatory environment. The process started out with an intentional repudiation of economics in the choice of policy targets and policy instruments[1]. The prevailing attitude seemed to be that "the air we breathe is too important to be influenced by monetary considerations". That attitude has changed somewhat as it has become increasingly clear that the quality of the air actually

[1] Note, for example, this statement by Senator Muskie, the Senate sponsor of the Clean Air Act Amendments of 1970: "The first responsibility of Congress is not the making of technological or economic judgements - or even to be limited by what is or appears to be technologically or economically feasible. Our responsibility is to establish what the public interest requires to protect the health of persons " (116 Congressional Record 16091, 21 September 1970).

achieved and the timing of that achievement are very much influenced by monetary considerations.

At this juncture in history, economic theory and the associated empirical work become relevant. This literature points out the requirements for designing a cost-effective system and the costs of choosing various short cuts. Some of these (such as the transferability notion) have been accepted while others (such as the notion of intermittent control) have not.

In response to this policy interest, the theory and the empirical work have become less abstract and more realistic. The treatment of air pollution policy in the economics literature has become more sensitive to the information requirements of policy design (e.g., dealing with cost-effective rather than efficient systems), the physical characteristics of the pollutants (e.g., the different specifications for fluorocarbons and nitrogen oxides) and legal aspects (e.g., the "reasonable progress" constraint).

There is still a long way to go. Simulations are suggestive, not conclusive. The fact that similar results are achieved for different pollutants in different cities suggests that the empirical conclusions are robust, but, it must be admitted, the sample size of studies is distressingly small. This will soon be rectified to some extent as the number of states gaining experience with the operation of actual markets grows.

These experiments with actual markets will, unfortunately, not completely test the concept of a discharge permit market. As has been detailed above, the operating markets are heavily restricted. This is currently leading to the emergence of some problems which seem related more to the restrictions than to the market system itself. Hopefully, the public will not draw the incorrect inference that it is the market approach which is flawed.

At this juncture it seems clear that the market approach to environmental protection has been a useful avenue for regulatory reform to pursue. Demonstrated savings have occurred. Greater flexibility has been achieved.

Yet the current approaches represent but one hesitant step in that direction. The possibilities for further reform are clearly there if we choose to exploit them.

References

Ackerman, Bruce A., Susan Rose-Ackerman, James W. Sawyer, Jr., Dale W. Henderson, The Uncertain Search for Environmental Quality. New York 1974.

Anderson, Robert J., Jr., Robert O. Reid, Eugene R. Seskin, An Analysis of Alternative Policies for Attaining and on Maintaining a Short Term NO_x Standard. Report to the Council on Environmental Quality prepared by MATHTECH, Inc. Princeton 1979.

Atkinson, Scott E., Donald H. Lewis, "A Cost-Effective Analysis of Alternative Air Quality Control Strategies". Journal of Environmental Economics and Management, Vol. 1, 1974, pp. 237-250.

--, Thomas H. Tietenberg, "The Empirical Properties of Two Classes of Designs for Transferable Discharge Permit Markets". Journal of Environmental Economics and Management, Vol. 9, 1982, pp. 101-121.

Baumol, William J., Wallace E. Oates, "The Use of Standards and Prices for Protection of the Environment". Swedish Journal of Economics, Vol. 73, 1971, pp. 42-54.

Crocker, Thomas D., "The Structure of Atmospheric Pollution Control Systems". In: Harold Wolozin (Ed.), The Economics of Air Pollution. New York 1966, pp. 61-86.

Dales, John H., Pollution, Property and Prices. Toronto 1968.

David, Martin H., J. Wayland Eheart, Erhard F. Joeres, and Elizabeth David, "Marketable Effluent Permits for the Control of Phosphorous Effluent into Lake Michigan". Water Resources Research, Vol. 16, 1980, pp. 263-270.

del Calvo y Gonzales, Jorge A., "Markets in Air: Problems and Prospects of Controlled Trading". Harvard Environmental Law Review, Vol. 5, 1981, pp. 377-430.

deLucia, Russell J., An Evaluation of Marketable Effluent Permit Systems. U.S. Environmental Protection Agency, Office of Research and Development, Washington 1974.

Haveman, Robert H., Gregory B. Christainsen, "Environmental Regulations and Productivity Growth". In: Henry W. Peskin, Paul R. Portney, Allen V. Kneese (Eds.), Environmental Regulation and the U.S. Economy. Resources for the Future, Inc., Baltimore 1981, pp. 55-75.

Howe, Charles, Dwight Lee, Innovative Approaches to the Effective Use of Pollution Rights. Colorado 1981, unpubl.

Kneese, Allen V., Charles L. Schultze, Pollution, Prices and Public Policy. The Brookings Institution and Resources for the Future, Inc., Washington 1975.

Kramer, Bruce M., "Air Quality Modeling: Judicial, Legislative and Administrative Reactions". Columbia Journal of Environmental Law, Vol. 5, 1979, pp. 236-264.

Liroff, Richard A., Air Pollution Offsets: Trading, Selling, and Banking. The Conservation Foundation, Washington 1980.

Maloney, Michael T., Bruce Yandle, Estimation of the Cost of Air Pollution Control Regulation. Clemson University, Department of Economics Working Paper, Clemson, S.C., 1979.

Montgomery, W. David, "Markets in Licenses and Efficient Pollution Control Programs". Journal of Economic Theory, Vol. 5, 1972, pp. 395-418.

Palmer, Adele R., William E. Mooz, Timothy H. Quinn, Kathleen A. Wolf, Economic Implications of Regulating Chlorofluorocarbon Emissions from Nonaerosol Applications. Rand Report R-2524-EPA, prepared for the U.S. Environmental Protection Agency, Santa Monica 1980.

Teller, Azriel, "Air Pollution Abatement: Economic Rationality and Reality". In: Roger Revelle, Hans H. Landsberg (Eds.), America's Changing Environment. Boston 1970, pp. 39-55.

Tietenberg, Thomas H., "Controlling Pollution by Price and Standard Systems: A General Equilibrium Analysis". The Swedish Journal of Economics, Vol. 75, 1973, pp. 193-203.

--, "Transferable Discharge Permits and the Control of Air Pollution: A Survey and Synthesis". Zeitschrift für Umweltpolitik, Vol. 3, Nr. 1, 1980, pp. 477-508.

--, "Economic Analysis and Air Pollution Control Policy: Recent Developments". In: Maurice B. Ballabon (Ed.), Economic Perspectives: An Annual Survey of Economics, Vol. 2. New York 1981, pp. 71-103.

U.S. Environmental Protection Agency (EPA), Office of Policy and Resources Management, The Controlled Trader. Washington 1981.

U.S. General Accounting Office (GAO), A Market Approach to Air Pollution Control Could Reduce Compliance Costs Without Jeopardizing Clean Air Goals. Document No. PAD-82-15, Wash-

Comment

Klaus-Werner Schatz

One need not be surprised that pollutant-discharging industries lament environmental policy measures, for such policies impose costs of one sort or another on them. It is interesting to note, however, that - at least in Europe and in particular in Germany - the current basic approach to environmental policies, namely regulation, has hardly been called into question, although resistance to intervention is usually strong. This seems to be all the more puzzling when one considers that - and Tietenberg's paper demonstrates this clearly - market approaches would provide much flexibility for enterprises to meet emission or ambient standards, once these standards are chosen.

In comparison, regulation seems to offer nothing but rigidity. In order to meet standards for regions, individual sources are forced to not exceed certain emission limits; or an installment of pollution control equipment is prescribed which represents the most recent level of technology. But there is not only this command and control aspect. Regulation grants rights also. It entitles polluters to discharge; and the limits up to which discharge is allowed are usually subject to negotiation with the bureaucracy, as is the installment of pollution control equipment. In favourable circumstances, the usage of the environment may even be allowed at no cost or at costs close to zero, namely, when discharge rights are allocated up to the required amount and strict prescriptions with regard to control devices are not made. The incentives to exert influence on the bureaucracy are naturally strongest for enterprises or industries whose waste discharge is above average or whose competitiveness would be endangered by severe discharge limitation. The bureaucrats have little incentive to resist this lobbying because the ability to bear the burdens from regulation usually has to be considered in each individual case. Hence, those sources which in principle are the main target of environmental policies and lament these policies the most will in practice, if such policies are to be conducted at all, tend to prefer regulation.

Detrimental effects on income distribution, which may be seen in the context of the initial allocation of pollution rights under regulation, become even greater when the rights are ill-defined (in the sense of the property rights theory). They are not tradable and hence, in the view of the firm, using the rights is not subject to opportunity costs, whereas refraining from the use and implementing pollution avoidance measures imposes private costs. For this reason, pollution is not reduced at those points where it would be cheapest to comply with target emission or ambient standards, but simply at those points where its reduction is required. The regulatory approach to environmental policy is, therefore, unnecessarily costly to society in a comparative static sense. Tietenberg presents empirical examples which support the notion that it is also unnecessarily costly to the business community taken as a whole.

The most important feature of regulation is that it is dynamically inefficient; it is backward-oriented. Firms will adopt new technologies only in order to reduce the costs of compliance with regulation, but not in order to reduce pollution. This is dynamically inefficient for society, if the marginal costs for reducing pollution relative to other marginal costs decline (which is presumably the case), for this change in relative costs is not reflected in a corresponding change in the use of the environment and other resources. Moreover, regulation tends to discriminate against new sources of pollution which by definition increase the absolute amount of pollution and degrade the ambient quality. The burden of maintaining standards is evidently assigned to an unduly high degree to these new sources. For example, it is primarily the new sources which have to install pollution control equipment that represents the most recent level of technology. Hence, structural change is impeded, and productivity growth is dampened - neither of which would be necessary to meet standards. While this is detrimental to society, it benefits old sources, as competition is lowered, if not on product then on factor markets. Therefore, it is not only the preference of bureaucrats for command and control to which the persistence of regulation in environmental policy has been attributed; in addition, there is an alliance between regulators and those regulated against which market approaches have to be pushed through. Turning to the main questions which are raised by transferable permit approaches such as those advocated by Tietenberg, I would like to concentrate on three issues.

(a) The final allocation of permits will not be affected whether the permits are sold at auction or whether they are given away to present polluters at the required amount. As Tietenberg mentions, the costs to society will be the same in both cases, but they will be borne by the producers if auctioning is preferred. One would expect, therefore, strong resistance to this modus from sources of pollution. If the permits are given away, the government would discriminate against new sources which would have to purchase permits from old sources that received them free; hence, structural change and productivity growth would be impeded (as is the case with regulatory approaches). Should the authorities share in the cost of controlling pollution for new sources, and in what way?

(b) As Tietenberg mentions, transferable discharge permits do not guarantee that ambient standards for regions are met at minimum costs, if the private costs of controlling pollution are the same irrespective of the distance between source and receptor. What should be done? Another spatial problem is across-the-border pollution, which is not subject to local permission, as local ambient standards are not affected. However, if ambient permit systems which require each source to buy permits from each receptor market are too complex for practical purposes and hence subject to high transaction costs, what should be done? Would it be appropriate to tackle the spillover problem by relying on liability rules which would allow receptor markets to claim compensation for damages either directly from distant sources or from the regions where the sources are located?

(c) It has often been argued that transferable permit systems are open to misuse by sources of pollution which compete on the same product market as means of gaining market power. As Tietenberg and others have rightly argued, such misuse would not be caused by permit systems, but must rather be rooted in independently existing imperfections on product or on factor markets which, moreover, have hitherto not been exploited to attain market power. Bonus and others have claimed, however, that the owners of installed sources may be subject to extortion, if the permits which they have used so far expire and if speculators happen to acquire permits which are needed to go on with production. Presumably, this is a real danger. It has therefore been suggested that independent banks (similar to banks of money issue) be created on a regional basis. While the aims of environmental policies, i.e. the definitions of ambient standards, would be fixed by regional political authorities, the banks would have to keep prices for the permits within certain limits - possibly around a trend - by open market policies in order to prevent, among other things, destabilising speculation. The performance indicator for the banks would be the degree of meeting the ambient standard [for details see Bonus, 1981, pp. 54-77]. Presumably, such banks could not only contribute to the solution of problems arising from possible extortion, but they could also improve the dynamic efficiency of the transferable discharge permit approach.

There are a number of additional arguments involved with this approach (many of them are mentioned and discussed by Tietenberg), but as compared to actual regulatory approaches (admittedly not as compared to ideal or "Nirvana" regulation), the advantages of transferable discharge or ambient permits taken together are extremely convincing. I have two other points to make, however, which are connected with liability rules.

First, in the current debate on the prevention of externalities, (net) damages which are feared or really caused for the immediate neighbourhood play an important role, while the benefits for society clearly outweigh these damages. Permit approaches cannot prevent such intra-regional differences in costs and benefits from waste discharge, and, therefore, they may hardly be applicable if equity considerations are important. But why can't permits and liability rules be combined to the effect that damages in excess of - let us say - the regional average generate a claim to compensation? Presumably, this combination would also effect the moving of sources to locations where ambient standards can be attained at lowest social costs.

Second, discussion has recently focussed on individual pioneering projects, for which damages cannot really be specified in advance. In such cases, transferable discharge permits are hardly applicable. As a matter of fact, regulation is supposed to preclude possible damage. To give one example: German law in effect prescribes that during the construction phase of nuclear power plants the most recent level of technology must be applied to protect the population. It has to be certified by bureaucrats that this level is achieved; the certification may be subject to examination by courts. As technology changes and as it is never possible to show that all measures to reduce risk have been taken, the construction of nuclear power plants has nearly been stopped in this country. As a general rule, regulation discriminates against pioneering projects. Liability rules would work much better in this field[1]. Liability forces the investor to concentrate his own efforts on the prevention of damages. Therefore, all the knowledge and the abilities of entrepreneurs and their pioneering technical specialists (and not the wisdom acquired by bureaucrats) could be activated. The present dilemma is not that liability does not in the end rest with

[1] For a discussion of the virtues of liability rules see Buchanan and Faith [1981].

entrepreneurs but that the projects which they want to carry through have to pass regulation beforehand, and the costs of regulation have to be borne in addition. Presumably, neither electricity nor automobiles nor chemicals nor aircraft would have attained the role they play in our present-day society if government regulators had had to permit them.

References

Bonus, Holger, "Emissionsrechte als Mittel der Privatisierung öffentlicher Ressourcen aus der Umwelt". In: Lothar Wegehenkel (Ed.), Marktwirtschaft und Umwelt. Walter-Eucken-Institut, Wirtschaftswissenschaftliche und wirtschaftsrechtliche Untersuchungen, Vol. 17, Tübingen 1981, pp. 54-77.

Buchanan, James M., Roger L. Faith, "Entrepreneurship and the Internalization of Externalities". The Journal of Law and Economics, Vol. 24, No. 1, 1981, pp. 95-111.

Michael W. Pustay

Deregulating Air Transportation: The U. S. Experience

I. Introduction

The United States Congress initiated federal regulation of the U.S. airline industry with the passage of the Civil Aeronautics Act of 1938. The Act established a five-person Civil Aeronautics Board (CAB, the Board) charged with undertaking the economic regulation and development of the then infant domestic airline industry. The Board was granted extensive control over entry into and exit out of airline markets and the prices charged for air transportation. The legislative mandate of the Board remained essentially unchanged until 1978, when the Airline Deregulation Act was passed. The immediate impact of the 1978 Act was to relax significantly CAB control over entry, exit, and prices. The Act also developed a timetable for complete phasing out of all economic regulation of domestic air service.

Pre-Reform Regulation

A critical element in the deregulation of U.S. airline service was the development of an economic theory that accurately explained the nature of competition in the airline industry. The development of this theory allowed deregulation advocates to challenge the then prevailing notion of how the regulatory system worked, to expose its failings, and to predict the performance of the industry under alternative government policies.

A variety of criticisms had developed in response to the effects of CAB policies adopted in the 1950s and 1960s. Carriers complained that they were unable to earn the rates of return authorized by the CAB. Consumer groups asserted that airline prices were too high and pointed to the relatively lower rates charged passengers in non-federally regulated intrastate markets such as California and Texas as proof that federal regulation had gone amiss.

In January, 1970, in response to a variety of such complaints, the CAB initiated the Domestic Passenger Fare Investigation (Docket

21866), or the DPFI as it became known. The DPFI represented the first comprehensive review of CAB fare-setting policies. The DPFI provided a forum for various interests to state their views on the optimal procedures to establish domestic passenger fares. Among the participants were the carriers themselves and representatives of various government agencies.

Two economists testifying for the U.S. Department of Transportation, James C. Miller III and George W. Douglas, played a key role in the DPFI. Douglas and Miller [1974] argued that the natural monopoly-regulated rate of return model then used by the Board was inappropriate and was causing CAB regulation to be misdirected.

Douglas and Miller introduced into the DPFI proceedings a model which provided a coherent explanation of the behavior of the airline industry. The Douglas-Miller model explicitly recognized that major airline markets, inherently and in practice, are competitive, not monopolistic. CAB entry policies had over the years allowed an average of two to four carriers to serve most major markets. Douglas and Miller's model was based on the insight that when prices are regulated in these markets carriers would utilize quality competition to compete for passengers. The CAB did not restrict such competition: once the CAB had certificated an airline on a route, it had no legal control over the supply decisions of the carrier - the number of flights it offered, the size of the aircraft used, and the timing of the flights[1]. Other forms of non-price competition were also available to the carriers: advertising, the friendliness of the cabin attendants, the carefulness of the baggage handlers, etc. However, Douglas and Miller argued that the single most important non-price variable was the frequency of the flights that the carrier offered in the market. In particular, they found that the best explanatory variable of an airline's share of the passengers carried in a market was the share of flights in the market that it offered.

The Douglas-Miller model proved persuasive because it provided rich insights into the nature of airline competition. For example, Douglas and Miller noted that the CAB's allowable rate of return systematically exceeded the rates of return the carriers actually earned over time and was in excess of rates of return earned by firms in comparable

[1] The CAB did develop minimum standards of service to be offered communities. Typically the minimum was one flight per day, five days per week. This consideration will be ignored in the ensuing discussion.

industries. Given this information, their model suggested that the average load factors attained by regulated carriers should decline over time. This should occur as a result of a "ratchet" effect caused by CAB regulation. If in period one the CAB establishes the allowable rate of return in excess of the carriers' opportunity cost of capital, quality-of-service competition among the carriers should cause them to compete away the intended excess profits. If the primary means of quality-of-service competition is flight frequency competition, then one should observe the capacity offered by the carriers to increase relative to the number of passengers[1]. The actual load factor achieved by carriers would then be less than the load factor expected to be attained by the carriers. If in period two the CAB raises prices again in hopes that the higher prices will allow the carriers to earn the rate of return permitted by the Board, the competitive impulses of the carriers will again be triggered and actual load factors will again fall in period two. This prediction of the Douglas-Miller model is consistent with the observed post-war behavior of the load factors attained in U.S. domestic trunk operations.

The Douglas-Miller model also explained the problems inherent in the Board's cross-subsidy policy for long-haul and short-haul operations. The CAB tried to maintain long-haul fares above the costs of providing long-haul service; simultaneously it attempted to suppress short-haul prices below the costs of providing short-haul service. Excess profits gained on the long-haul routes were to be used to subsidize losses on the short-haul routes. Figure 1 depicts the strategy developed by the CAB. It shows that the taper of the fare curve with respect to distance is less steep than the taper of the cost curve, if costs are evaluated at an identical load factor.

Disregarding any philosophical objections, there was one major problem with the cross-subsidy scheme as pointed out by Douglas and Miller: it did not work. It did not work because the CAB had no control over the supply decisions of the carriers. In short-haul markets where the CAB had presumed that carriers would lose money, the carriers simply cut back on the level of service that they offered until they could at least earn the opportunity cost of their capital. In the supposedly highly profitable long-haul markets, carriers would compete for these lucrative markets by adding more flights. This process would continue until the intended excess profits were competed away. Referring

---

[1] This assumes that the elasticity of demand with respect to flight frequency is less than one.

Relationship of Fares and Perceived Costs with Respect to Distance

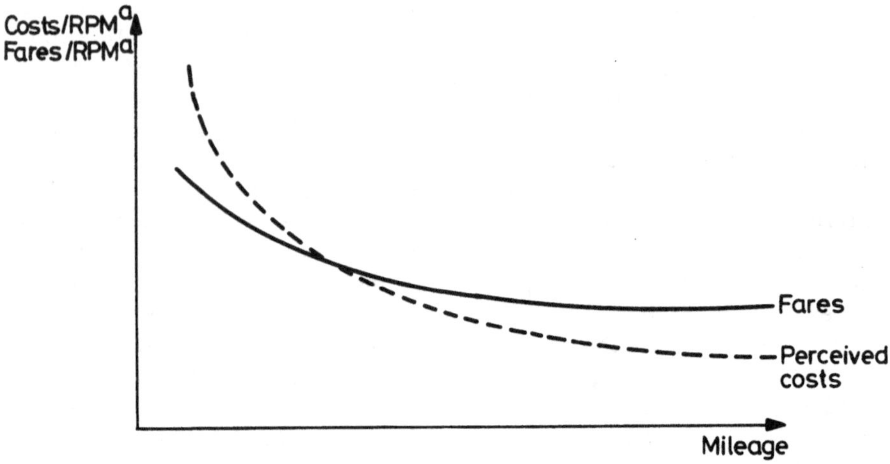

[a]*RPM = revenue passenger mile.*

back to Figure 1, this implies the cost curve measured at a constant load factor will rotate to equal the fare curve as a result of the carriers' capacity decisions.

Equilibrium load factors in long-haul markets will be low and the concomitant quality of service received by long-haul passengers will be high. In short-haul markets, load factors will be high and the quality of service received by short-haul passengers will be low. These implications of their model were empirically verified by Douglas and Miller.

The Douglas-Miller model thus provided a cogent explanation of the impact of CAB regulation on the performance of the airline industry. The model supplied the important new insight that CAB price regulation had the effect of jointly determining the price, the cost, and the quality of service received by passengers in a market. The acceptance by the CAB of the premises of the model - as they were to various degrees in the nine phases of the DPFI - caused it to rethink the underlying logic of the regulatory structure that it had utilized for thirty-plus years. No longer could the CAB merely regulate prices and expect carriers to accommodate its policies by providing the level of service it desired. Rather, it had to consider and anticipate the carriers' supply decisions stemming from their reaction to the CAB's pricing decisions.

Following the DPFI, the CAB initially made some half-hearted attempts to provide travellers with better price and quality-of-service options by modifying its traditional regulatory approaches. However, it soon became apparent that it was difficult within the existing regulatory system to define "better" or "optimal" price-service bundles for consumers. The public policy debate turned to the question of whether the public interest would be better served by the termination of CAB control over carrier entry, exit, and pricing[1].

The CAB itself answered this question in the affirmative. In early 1977, it began to strongly encourage carriers to compete with one another via price competition through its approval of Texas International's "Peanuts" fares and American Airlines' "Super Saver" fares. The Board also substantially relaxed entry into domestic airline markets, announcing in a series of cases beginning with the Chicago - Midway Low Fare Case (Docket 30277) the concept of multiple permissive entry. The Board's administrative deregulation of the airline industry was endorsed by the U.S. Congress with the passage of the Airline Deregulation Act in October, 1978.

II. The Impact of Deregulation in the United States

Less than five years have elapsed since the passage of the Airline Deregulation Act. While this period is insufficient to assess the long-term effects of deregulation, it is sufficient to analyze the initial impact of deregulation on the performance of the airline industry.

1. The Evidence on Fares

Table 1 reports the ratio of the average fares charged by carriers in U.S. domestic markets in 1980 to the fares that would have been charged in these markets had the CAB continued to require carriers to charge the DPFI formula fare. Stratified by size of markets, the ratio of actual to expected fares falls as distance increases. Stratified by distance, fares have generally fallen the most in the larger

---

[1] The work of several economists suggested that competition among unregulated carriers would produce long-run equilibria characterized by consumers being offered optimal price-service bundles. See for example Douglas, Miller [1974], De Vany [1975], White [1972], and Dorman [1976].

Table 1 - Average Fares[a] in U.S. Domestic Markets as a Percent of DPFI Fare Formula, 1980

Market distance	Market size category		
	Top 100 markets	Second 100 markets	Samples of smaller markets
0- 200 mi	92	94	123
201- 500 mi	94	93	112
501-1000 mi	92	91	99
1001-1500 mi	80	87	93
1500+ mi	74	81	91
Average of all distance categories	87	90	112

[a]Weighted average of all fares, excluding first class fares. Weights are based on the number of passengers. The DPFI fare is the average fare for 1980, weighted by service segment traffic of the months the fare was in effect.

Source: [Graham, Kaplan, 1981, p. 25].

markets. Both of these empirical findings are predicted by the Dougles-Miller model. The former finding results from an undoing of the cross-subsidy scheme. The latter finding stems from the fact that in larger markets the utilization of larger aircraft and the greater frequency of flights causes the optimal load factor to rise and the optimal fare to fall. Table 1 also indicates that only in smaller short-haul markets have actual fares risen above the fares that would have been charged under the DPFI fare formula; this finding is consistent with the unwinding of the cross-subsidy scheme induced by deregulation.

2. Capacity Utilization

The effects of deregulation on capacity utilization are also consistent with the Douglas-Miller model. Graham et al. [1981] discovered that load factors rose with distance and density and fell with the number of carriers certificated in a market for 314 sampled markets in 1980. They found the distance-load factor effect to be more pronounced for smaller markets than for larger ones, a result they attributed to the impact of the sluggish 1980 economy. Most interestingly, the distance-load factor curve for 1980 lay above the same curve for 1969 [ibid., pp. 10 ff.].

Additional insights into the capacity utilization problem can be gained by analyzing the intensity of use of aircraft in the pre- and post-regulatory reform periods. Table 2 provides information regarding the revenue block hours and the average seats per aircraft reported by the trunk airlines for six relatively modern aircraft types common to the fleets of many of the trunk carriers. These aircraft were selected because of their relative fuel efficiency. These are the aircraft the carriers would have continued to favor in times of rising fuel prices. Even though the trunk carriers as a group suffered traffic de-

Table 2 - Utilization of Selected Aircraft by U.S. Trunk Airlines in Domestic Operations, 1973-1980

	1973	1974	1975	1976	1977	1978	1979	1980
B-747								
Hours[a]	9.41	8.24	8.08	8.63	9.63	9.40	10.64	9.47
Seats[b]	328.4	342.4	352.6	356.8	357.4	374.3	378.4	378.5
DC-10-10								
Hours[a]	8.06	7.52	7.81	8.05	8.69	9.18	9.28	8.45
Seats[b]	232.2	237.3	233.1	237.4	244.2	254.5	259.4	261.9
L-1011								
Hours[a]	6.82	6.38	6.61	6.96	7.54	8.00	8.62	8.89
Seats[b]	221.8	236.3	242.3	246.6	250.5	268.7	283.9	284.5
727-200								
Hours[a]	7.64	7.43	7.51	7.72	8.00	8.04	8.59	8.05
Seats[b]	124.7	125.6	126.6	129.0	130.8	132.0	131.9	132.6
737-200								
Hours[a]	5.56	5.17	4.97	5.14	5.44	6.11	6.44	5.46
Seats[b]	93.6	95.0	95.7	96.6	95.7	101.9	103.5	105.9
DC 9-30								
Hours[a]	8.15	7.39	7.45	7.59	7.57	7.59	7.52	7.83
Seats[b]	89.9	90.2	90.1	90.6	91.4	90.9	90.8	90.7

[a]Average revenue block hours per day per aircraft. - [b]Average available seats per aircraft.

Source: CAB [c].

clines in 1980, the average daily utilization of these aircraft is generally higher in the transition and post-reform years of 1978, 1979, and 1980 than in the preceding four-year period. Similarly, the trunk airlines increased the seating density of these aircraft, with the exception of the DC-9-30, in the post-reform period. It can be concluded in the post-reform period that the trunk carriers have used their aircraft both more intensively and extensively. Such behavior is consistent with the Douglas-Miller model.

3. Entry

The relaxed entry standards initiated administratively by the Board in 1977 and mandated by the Airline Deregulation Act of 1978 have encouraged existing carriers to expand their operations into new markets. The relaxed standards have also encouraged airlines that had not previously provided interstate scheduled service to enter such markets.

The aggregate effect of the new entry has been dramatic. As Table 3 shows, the relaxed entry standards resulted in a significant realignment of the market shares of the various carriers. If 1977 can be characterized as depicting the status quo prior to regulatory reform[1], we observe that trunk airlines lost nearly seven percentage points of market share in four years.

Four groups of carriers gained at the expense of the trunk carriers. The local service airlines - Republic, U.S. Air, Ozark, Piedmont, Texas International, and Frontier - increased their market share by almost 40 percent, from 8.4 percent in 1977 to 11.6 percent in 1981. The local service carriers took advantage of their well developed short-haul route networks to compete in longer-haul markets.

The second group of airlines to take advantage of entry freedom were four former intrastate carriers, who, because of their single-state operations, had been exempt from federal regulation. These four carriers increased their share of the national market by nearly one percentage point over the period from 1977 to 1981.

---

[1] The CAB had already begun to relax its control of the industry in 1977. However, the effects of these reforms on the 1977 statistics would be minor.

Table 3 - U.S. Market Shares[a] by Carrier Type, 1977-1981 (percent)

Carrier Type	1977	1978	1979	1980	1981[b]
Trunks	88.1	87.7	86.5	84.0	81.3
Local service[c]	8.4	8.8	9.5	10.8	11.6
Former major intrastate[d]	2.3	2.4	2.7	2.9	3.2
Former charter carrier[e]	0	0	0	0.8	1.9
Major new entrants[f]	0	0	< 0.1	< 0.1	0.4
Alaskan and Hawaiian	1.1	1.0	1.0	1.0	1.1
Other[g]	0.1	0.1	0.2	0.4	0.5
Percent total	100.0	100.0	100.0	100.0	100.0
Absolute total scheduled domestic RPM's	160,449	187,200	208,890	200,178	197,189

[a]Share of scheduled domestic revenue passenger miles (RPM's). - [b]Twelve months ending August 31, 1981. - [c]Republic, U.S. Air, Ozark, Piedmont, Texas International and Frontier. - [d]Air California, Air Florida, Pacific Southwest and Southwest. - [e]Capital International Airways and World Airways. - [f]Midway Airlines, New York Air, People's Express. - [g]The coverage of carriers in this category broadened in 1979.

Source: CAB [b], and carrier records.

The third group of carriers consists of two former supplemental carriers who branched out into scheduled operations as a result of the relaxed entry standards, Capital International Airways and World Airways. These two carriers accounted for nearly two percent of the domestic scheduled market in 1981.

The last group of entrants consists of carriers who initiated their service subsequent to the passage of the Airline Deregulation Act of 1978. The most important of these carriers are Midway Airlines, New York Air, and People's Express. They had gained 0.4 percent of the market by August, 1981. Their impact on the marketplace has been disproportionately large relative to their market share. The labor costs of these new carriers are far lower than those of the older carriers. These labor cost savings confer upon these carriers major cost advantages. Southwest's costs per seat of operating a 737 aircraft for a 200-mile flight average 61 percent of Piedmont's costs and 47 percent of United's. This cost advantage has allowed Southwest and its younger brethren to charge rates for air transportation that are quite painful for the older trunk carriers to match[1].

4. Effects on Industry Profits

The first year of regulatory reform was a prosperous one for the airline industry. A variety of discount fares stimulated traffic growth and growth in carrier revenues. Carriers were free to adjust their route structures in ways that reduced their costs.

The second, third, and fourth years of regulatory reform have not been as happy for the industry. The crash of a DC-10 aircraft in Chicago and the subsequent grounding of the DC-10 fleet caused major problems for several carriers. The revolution in Iran set off a chain of events which led to a tripling of the price of oil. The airlines responded to increased fuel costs by raising their prices. These price increases, coupled with two recessions, impacted negatively on the growth of airline traffic. To make matters worse, the air traffic controllers' strike in August, 1981 played havoc with the carriers' ability to schedule their fleets efficiently, forced them to ground some aircraft, and increased the travel time costs borne by travellers.

However, the impact of these events has not been uniform on the carriers. Some airlines - in particular the local service carriers and the former major intrastate airlines - have fared quite well since the passage of the Act. The trunk carriers, on the other hand, have not done very well, as Table 4 reports.

While the past three years have not been prosperous ones for the industry, there is no reason to believe that its problems would have been lessened had regulatory reform not taken place. Decreased profits, lowered real prices, and lower sales are predictable short-term responses to the shifts in demand and supply that confronted the industry. Regulatory reform has allowed the industry to adjust to these changes in the marketplace far more easily than would have been the case prior to the passage of the Airline Deregulation Act.

---

[1] We are unable to obtain relevant data for the three airlines which entered the industry after the passage of the Act. Southwest Airlines initiated its service in 1971 and is thus a relatively young carrier.

Table 4 - U.S. Domestic Operating Profits of Trunk and Local Service Airlines, January 1976-June 1981 (U.S.$ Million)

Year	Quarter	Trunks	Local service	Intrastate carriers[a]
1976	1	- 81.9	2.8	.
	2	214.6	30.5	.
	3	251.3	37.1	.
	4	86.9	25.7	.
1977	1	9.7	2.4	.
	2	158.9	30.7	.
	3	234.4	42.3	.
	4	114.2	53.9	.
1978	1	87.8	6.9	.
	2	285.6	54.3	.
	3	416.2	51.0	.
	4	48.4	26.2	.
1979	1	- 31.3	- 2.0	.
	2	149.2	83.0	.
	3	- 23.1	42.5	24.5
	4	-166.6	5.1	15.5
1980	1	-207.5	- 5.5	15.0
	2	-117.3	37.1	25.2
	3	56.8	60.8	28.1
	4	36.0	68.6	6.3
1981	1	- 84.3	45.8	14.4
	2	22.7	91.0	15.6

[a]Former major intrastate carriers: Air California, Air Florida, Pacific Southwest and Southwest.

Source: CAB [a].

5. The Effects of Deregulation on Concentration

Airline deregulation has led to a decrease in concentration, according to empirical work by Graham et al. [1981]. They regressed in log-linear form the Herfindahl concentration index for 191 markets in the fourth quarter of 1980 against distance, market density, the Herfindahl index for that market lagged by one year, and a dummy for new entry which had occurred in the market in the past year. The dummy for new entry was significantly negatively related to the Herfindahl index. They also discovered that the Herfindahl index in a market for the fourth quarter of 1980 was positively correlated with the logarithm of the Herfindahl index in that market for the previous year. However, the coefficient of the lagged index was only 0.68. Since this coefficient was more than six standard deviations less than one, they concluded "there was a strong tendency for highly concentrated markets to become less concentrated even when entry has not occurred" [ibid., p. 26].

This result, coupled with the information contained in Tables 3 and 4, suggests that deregulation has led to deconcentration in the industry and in individual markets. This evidence lends no support to those critics who claimed that deregulation would lead to domination of the industry by a handful of carriers able to exploit economies of scale.

6. Effects on Labor

The relaxed entry standards have had major impacts on the labor forces of the various airlines, especially those of the older carriers. During the pre-reform period the carriers were insulated from the threat of entry into the industry by new carriers. Freed from the threat of entry, the existing airlines were able to negotiate labor contracts that provided their workers generous pay schedules and favorable work rules[1].

The advent of regulatory reform changed this situation. Competition from new entrants with lower pay schedules, lower seniority workers, and more advantageous work rules threatened the financial viability of the established carriers. Since many of the perquisites to workers of these labor contracts are firm-specific - i.e., tied to seniority with an individual firm - the positions and status of many workers in established firms have been threatened. Workers of nearly all of the trunk airlines have made or have considered pay and work-rule concessions in order to maintain the financial viability of their employers. It is difficult to quantify the economic loss suffered by these workers. Nonetheless, it would appear to be substantial.

---

[1] Under similar economic circumstances, labor negotiations in the trucking industry yielded similar results. See Moore [1978].

7. Summary

In summary, the existing evidence is consistent with the predictions of the Douglas-Miller model regarding the effects of regulatory reform on the performance of the U.S. domestic airline industry. Regulatory reform has allowed carriers to compete using price as well as quality of service. Carriers have responded to this freedom by generally lowering their prices, ceteris paribus. They are also using their inputs more productively. Aircraft, for example, are being utilized more intensively and extensively. Labor agreements are being renegotiated to increase the productivity of the industry's work force.

Given the success of this model in predicting the impact of deregulation on the performance of the airline industry, we now turn to the question of the likely effects of similar reforms on the performance of the European airline industry. We wish to examine the extent to which the U.S. experience is translatable to the European industry.

III. Translating the U. S. Experience to Europe

In its 1979 memorandum on the development of air transport service within Europe, the Commission of the European Communities recognized that certain deficiencies exist in the air transportation industry in Europe:

> "A tendency towards high tariffs for scheduled air transport not only because of the tariffs setting system but also because business and government account for the largest single demand associated with costly requirements as to flexibility and service level.
>
> Limited flexibility for holiday and in particular VFR [visiting friends and relatives] traffic. Low tariffs ... do not exist on all routes and are furthermore associated with restrictive conditions which limit their use.
>
> Limited possibilities for innovation, in particular with respect to tariffs and types of service.
>
> A strict adherence to a bilateral system which works against the creation of some desirable cross border services and which supports concentration of traffic between and to and from the main airports" [Commission, 1979, p. 8].

These deficiencies are similar in nature to the perceived problems of the U.S. domestic airline industry in the pre-reform period. This should not be surprising. The common problems stem from a common source: government policies which restrict the ability of scheduled airlines to compete via price and which insulate existing carriers from the threat of entry by low-price and/or low-cost carriers. The Douglas-Miller model should predict equally well the impact of these policies in Europe as it did for the U.S. market[1].

Begin with the conditions of entry. Most important airline markets in Europe are between cities in different nations. Entry for a nation's airline(s) into such markets is negotiated between the nations in question. Entry in these markets is far more difficult to achieve than was the case in U.S. domestic markets in the pre-reform period.

Price competition is strongly discouraged. The members of the International Air Transport Association (IATA) collectively determine the prices to be charged in European markets. Because collective rate-making is endorsed by the respective national governments - who are in most cases the owners of the airlines in question - the carriers are free to act as joint monopolists in the setting of European air fares.

The utilization of pooling agreements further restricts competition in many European markets. Sometimes the agreements are limited to establishing jointly the schedules of the carriers involved. Being able to act as joint monopolists in the establishment of their flight schedules, these airlines are freed from the temptation faced by the U.S. airlines to engage in flight-scheduling competition.

However, under this arrangement, once flight schedules have been agreed upon, the carriers have an incentive to compete along other service dimensions - the quality of the food, the attentiveness of the passenger service attendants, etc. Non-price competition will continue until the intended monopoly profits are competed away. As was

[1] One major difference between the U.S. airline industry and the European airline industry is that the former is privately owned. The former carriers are motivated by profit considerations; the latter may be motivated by other concerns. It will be assumed, however, that carriers participating in "reformed" European markets will be motivated by profit considerations or that the requirements for participating in reformed markets include a mandate that carriers act as if they are motivated by profit considerations.

the case in U.S. domestic markets, the costs of providing the service will have risen to equal the price charged for the service. The result of this competition in Europe is that travellers are offered high-priced, ill-timed, and crowded service while being wined and dined by attentive cabin crews[1]. Compared to U.S. domestic passengers in the pre-reform period, the European air travellers are worse off: non-price competition in the United States was focused on flight scheduling, which is a quality-of-service dimension which the travelling public values quite highly relative to other aspects of quality of service, whereas European competition is focused on less valuable dimensions of service.

Because of non-price competition, these routes are not particularly profitable for the carriers. As was the case with the CAB in the United States, the reaction of IATA to the lack of profitability is to raise fares in the hopes of generating the intended excess profits. However, the price increases will not be effective in the long run. Higher prices will simply trigger a higher level of quality-of-service competition.

An alternative type of pooling arrangement is the revenue pool. Participants in a revenue pool split the revenues generated on a route according to some predetermined formula. A carrier in a revenue pool has an incentive to minimize its costs of operations on the route since its share of revenues is fixed. Such routes may be profitable for the carrier, but passengers will suffer from high-price and poor-quality service.

1. Proposed Commission Reforms

In the Memorandum, the Commission proposes a set of reform measures that would increase the entry and pricing flexibility of carriers in European markets. The overall goal is to promote innovative services while maintaining the existing "network of reliable services by designated airlines" [Commission, 1979, p. 19].

The Commission recommended changes in the tariff policies of the airline industry. It suggested that the industry create a third class of

[1] An alternative competitive mechanism is illegal rebating. In particular, the extent of illegal rebating should increase with the gap between the ticket price and the marginal cost of providing the service, ceteris paribus.

fares, introduce a basic, no-frills fare, and utilize heavily restricted, capacity-controlled fares. In short, it endorsed the development of innovative fares of the sort initiated in the United States in 1977 when the CAB permitted American Airlines' "Super Saver" fare to go into effect as well as the fares now utilized by Texas International, Southwest, and others.

The Memorandum does not address the means by which these pricing innovations will be stimulated. Presumably the existing pricing structure is already serving the self-interest of the incumbent carriers. Unless some change occurs in the economic or political environment in which the carriers operate, there is little reason to believe that the incumbent airlines will voluntarily adopt new pricing innovations.

One means available to the member states of changing the carriers' environment is to liberalize entry into European airline markets. The Memorandum proposes two programs to liberalize entry. The first proposal is to grant traffic rights to those airlines which are asking to provide service "on a new route between Member States, a new type of scheduled service, or an existing service at a considerably lower price" [Commission, 1979, p. 19]. Traffic rights in this situation would be granted automatically unless incumbent carriers on the route agree to match the service. However, the Commission Memorandum expresses concern that such a policy might prove too disruptive. Thus it suggests that

> "the new carrier might be asked to show that its proposed new activity would be profitable in order to avoid predatory market entry; licensing authorities could keep watch on the ability of the carrier to expand its activity in view of its resources;
>
> a tariff reduction justifying market entry should be of a certain minimum size ... in order to preserve a certain stability;
>
> the number of new traffic rights that a carrier could obtain in each year under these rules could be limited to avoid sudden disruption;
>
> in order to give a carrier, already designated or not, the time to build up a new route, it should be possible to give protected traffic rights for a limited number of years" [ibid., p. 20].

As an alternative approach, the Memorandum suggested reducing entry barriers within the context of existing bilateral agreements: "Another, more radical means that might be considered of opening the way for innovation in scheduled air service between Community countries might be arrangements to make operations under bilateral agreements more flexible in the following way: that if an airline of a Community country were prepared in its own commercial judgment and with the consent of the licensing authorities of the country of its own base of operation to introduce new links with points in another Community country or countries not at present served directly by or through same-flight services, or to offer services of a new type (accompanied by fare and marketing innovation), the receiving Community country(ies) should, after a certain period for consultation, no longer be enabled to reject (except on demonstrable and nondiscriminatory operational, noise and pollution control and airport congestion grounds) those services, which would then be deemed to be permissible in accordance with the relevant bilateral agreements" [ibid., p. 23].

2. Analysis of the Proposed Reforms

The key to improving the performance of the European air transportation system lies in relaxing entry controls for scheduled service. Freedom of entry into airline markets plays a critical role in ensuring that travellers are provided the quantity and quality of air transportation they desire at prices that will compensate the carriers for their efforts. The European industry is likely to continue to perform in the future as well (or as badly) as it has in the past unless it is confronted with new competitive pressures enforced by the discipline of the marketplace.

The first alternative proposed by the Memorandum, however, is unlikely to provide this competitive stimulus. Allowing existing carriers to preempt an innovator's proposal is one sure way to discourage innovation. Entrepreneurs would be dissuaded from expending the resources necessary to investigate possible market opportunities if their efforts and investments could be nullified by a preemptive move by the incumbent carrier on a route.

This proposal also places a large amount of decision-making responsibility in the hands of various bureaucracies, instead of in the hands of entrepreneurs. The bureaucracies are granted authority to determine what constitutes "similar" service or tariffs; to define profitable service; to judge when entry is predatory; to assess whether firms are overly ambitious in their marketing plans; to judge the minimum decrease in fares sufficient to be of value to the public interest; and to determine the optimal duration of the period of monopoly protection for innovators. The Memorandum is vague regarding the process by which these reforms would be implemented and administrative control delegated to some agency(ies). It does not state whether the findings of this agency would be binding on the member states or merely advisory. Moreover, the Memorandum does not recognize the tremendous time delays likely to be created by this institutional arrangement.

The second entry proposal is bolder, more feasible, and more likely to lead to significant improvements in European air transportation. The proposal states that a carrier receiving permission from its own national licensing board would be able to provide innovative service - service on a new route or a new type of service on an existing route. The other country in question would not be able to deny the innovator operating rights after the passage of an agreed-upon time period. This approach confers the benefit of creating competition between the two regulatory agencies. Since this proposal is structured to operate within the context of a bilateral agreement, the definitions of innovative services and other such issues can be resolved within the bilateral agreement itself. The agreement need not require the approval of other member states or of airlines based in other states which might be hostile to a general relaxation of entry standards within the European Community. Dealing with the various definitional issues will be made much simpler if the number of participants is narrowed[1].

3. Outcome of the Reforms

What would be the outcome of these reforms? It is difficult to predict precisely because so much depends upon the extent to which the bilateral treaties relax the entry barriers facing airlines. If the barriers remain high, the reforms will accomplish little.

An interesting scenario would unfold if one bilateral treaty substantially eliminated all entry barriers between the two nations involved. Assuming that the state-owned carriers would enter (or be allowed to enter) only those markets which they find profitable to serve, a variety of events can be anticipated.

---

[1] A multilateral relaxation of entry controls would be preferable to a bilateral relaxation, ceteris paribus. However, given the disagreements among the member states regarding the advantages of deregulation of the trans-atlantic market, it is doubtful that a multilateral relaxation of entry in European markets would be politically feasible.

Between these two countries, a likely outcome would be a duplication of the events that occurred in domestic U.S. markets. Pricing freedom would initially result in the offering of a variety of fares granting substantial discounts to selected types of travellers. These fares would likely to be highly restricted in terms of minimum and maximum stays, advance purchase requirements, etc.

The second, and more critical stage, would occur when new or existing firms enter a market and provide all travellers and potential travellers a low-price, low-quality service as an alternative to the existing high-price, high-quality service. These carriers' ability to offer lower prices will stem from five sources:

- Cost savings attributable to decreases in the quality of services offered passengers - higher load factors, denser seating configurations, less costly meals, etc.
- Increased utilization of aircraft, landing gate facilities, etc. as carriers are induced to provide more off-peak services.
- The lower input prices enjoyed by newer carriers relative to the more established carriers, particularly with regard to labor costs.
- Elimination of the costs associated with the stopover rules of European air tariffs and other cross-subsidies in the fare structure.
- Making explicit and legal any illegal, under-the-table rebating arrangements.

It would be hoped that the success of the reforms introduced under the bilateral agreement would spread to other international markets. The benefits to consumers of improved service and lower prices should create political pressures to replicate the reforms between other member states. Diversion of traffic - especially pleasure traffic - should increase the pressures on airlines serving other markets to agree to the spread of the reforms. Moreover, once the reforms are implemented, it should prove difficult to reverse them as airlines would have to be "uncertificated".

4. The Impact of the Reforms on Community Air Transportation Objectives

In its 1979 memorandum, the Commission identified four objectives for the Community's air transportation system: development of an efficient, low-price, nondiscriminatory air transportation network; promotion of an efficient and healthy airline industry; protection of the interests of airline workers; and improving the conditions of life for the general public.

The impact of these reforms on the attainment of these four objectives can be predicted using the U.S. experience as a guideline. Travellers as a group will be better off with increased airline competition. Most passengers will benefit from the availability of low-price, low-quality air service. A minority of passengers may be worse off if this option is made available; but even most business travellers should benefit from the increase in the number of flights induced by the increase in the quantity demanded of air service as a result of the lower prices[1].

The airlines as a group should not be harmed by the relaxation of entry and pricing controls. However, these reforms do increase the penalties for poor management. Some carriers may suffer because of the relaxation of controls. Increased competitive pressures should result in a decrease in the per unit costs of airline operations and significant increases in the productivity of airline workers and the airlines' capital stock. Some of the measured improvement will come from the movement from high-price, high-quality service to low-price, low-quality service. The remainder will come from "true" productivity increases - i.e., a shifting downward of the airlines' isocost curves as managements utilize the factors of production at their disposal more efficiently.

Relaxation of entry and pricing controls will have a dichotomous impact on airline employees if the U.S. deregulation experience is an indicator. Overall, the relaxation of controls should increase the aggregate employment levels of the European airline industry. Increases in the quantity demanded of airline travel should benefit those persons seeking jobs in the industry. However, existing employees of carriers

[1] These statements are based upon evidence drawn from the behavior of carriers in the United States that, in the aggregate, airline passengers preferred lower-price, lower-quality service to higher-price, higher-quality service. However, the airlines have developed a variety of mechanisms to serve the wishes of both business and pleasure travellers - e.g., first class, coach and economy service; peak-off-peak pricing; conditional reservations; puddle-jumper fares, etc. By no means should the U.S. regulatory reform experience be interpreted as aiding only those customers who prefer low-price, low-quality service.

who do poorly as a result of relaxation of pricing and entry controls will not find such relaxation in their self-interest. Many of their fringe benefits are linked to their seniority with their employer and their economic health is thus tied to the economic health of their employer. Employees of such carriers are not likely to gain as a result of regulatory reform.

The fourth objective is difficult to operationalize: how does one define "improvements in conditions of life for the general public"? If one chooses to define this as maximizing the social welfare function in the market for air transportation services, then the reform measures will promote this objective. Relaxation of entry controls will subject the industry to the rigors of competition and induce it to serve better the needs of existing and potential air travellers.

References

Commission of the European Communities, Contributions of the European Communities to the Development of the Air Transportation Service. Publ. No. COM (79) 311, Brussels 1979.

De Vany, Arthur S., "Capacity Utilization under Alternative Regulatory Restraints: An Analysis of Taxi Markets". Journal of Political Economy, Vol. 83, No. 1, 1975, pp. 83-94.

Dorman, Gary J., Airline Competition: A Theoretical and Empirical Analysis. University of California, Department of Economics, Working Paper No. SL-7603, Berkeley 1976.

Douglas, George W., James C. Miller III, Economic Regulation of Domestic Air Transport. The Brookings Institution, Washington 1974.

Graham, David R., Daniel P. Kaplan, Developments in the Deregulated Airline Industry. Civil Aeronautics Board, Washington 1981, mimeo.

--, --, David S. Sibley, Efficiency and Competition in the Airline Industry. Civil Aeronautics Board, Washington 1981, mimeo.

Johnson, Robert M., "Initial Decision of Robert M. Johnson". Civil Aeronautics Board, Docket 21866-9, Washington 1972.

Moore, Thomas G., "The Beneficiaries of Trucking Regulation". The Journal of Law and Economics, Vol. 21, 1978, pp. 327-344.

U.S. Civil Aeronautics Board (CAB) [a], Air Carrier Financial Statistics. Washington, various issues.

-- [b], Air Carrier Traffic Statistics. Washington, various issues.

-- [c], Airline Operating Cost and Performance Report. Washington, various issues.

White, Lawrence J., "Quality Variation When Prices are Regulated". The Bell Journal of Economics and Management Science, Vol. 3, 1972, pp. 425-436.

Comment

Holger Bonus

What strikes me most upon reading Pustay's impressive paper is why it should have taken 30 years or so for the literature to discover that the market for air transportation is indeed a competitive one, and what this implies if prices are regulated. It is difficult to see how the natural monopoly argument should apply to this market any more than to that for farm machines or computers, say. Thus when Pustay appears to draw some comfort from his observation that here at last is a case where the development of a sound economic theory did away with bizarre regulatory policies, it disturbs me to learn how the Civil Aeronautics Board could get away with such policies for so long a time, apparently not seriously challenged by economic theory.

Pustay's case is straightforward. When prices are fixed in the face of stiff competition while entry is barred to new carriers, so as to grant "fair" rates of return to incumbent carriers, then competition will turn to the next "free" parameter, i.e., quality - a vector composed of such elements as timing and frequency of flights (this one ranking highest among customers), friendliness of cabin attendants, drinks offered, meals served and the like. Given that the majority of customers prefer flights that are inexpensive, to rule out lower-quality but cheaper flights by regulation will produce welfare losses. Competition will then result in excess capacities as the carriers try to outmatch each other by offering tight flight schedules; and as a result, costs will rise until excess profits have vanished. Another factor driving up costs will be expensive arrangements with unions: the high price level granted through regulation permits the carriers both to operate excess capacities and to meet the inflated cost of labor. If regulatory authorities subsequently move to increase prices in order to secure "fair" rates of return, what happens is simply that costs are driven up even further, and excess capacities are increased. Thus prices always appear justified through the cost.

The situation gets even worse when regulation is extended to the most important non-price variable, timing and frequency of flights. Pooling arrangements among European airlines amount to such an extension; and as a result, passengers here are faced with infrequent, high-priced and crowded flights, combined with expensive services which they do not really want.

Pustay shows that deregulation worked broadly as predicted; and he displays some cautious optimism with regard to the European market. However, it is my impression that the U.S. experience will in fact *deter* Europeans from deregulating air transportation.

The reason is that some of the events which followed deregulation fit precisely into the pattern of predictions made by those who oppose deregulation. To many people (economists included), the market appears to be inherently disordered and therefore ought to be closely watched any time, just to keep it from getting out of hand. Thus, once a market is regulated it is tough to get it deregulated; and this sentiment is somewhat stronger in Europe than it is in the United States. The market for apartments in West Germany is an excellent example. Moreover, when West Germany returned to a market economy in 1948, a strong fraction resisted on the grounds that the situation was too serious to be handled by "blind" market forces. The present recession again and again gives rise to calls for rigid state intervention; and it turns out to be extremely difficult to install market approaches into environmental policies here [see Tietenberg, 1983; Bonus, 1982]. The same sentiment might be responsible for the U.S. Civil Aeronautic Board's ability to practice regulation for more than 30 years. At any rate, the U.S. experience is presently used as a proof by which the need for regulation is safely established.

This became quite clear when Braniff went bankrupt. Deregulation had led the market for air transportation straight into chaos, was the line adopted by news media. In the scramble for bigger market shares, the airlines had pushed prices down to levels which could no longer support operations; and behind that scramble was the conviction - or so the reasoning would go - that *economies of scale* would permit the big carriers to push smaller ones right out of business. Thus the natural monopoly argument proved very much alive in the press; and it was clear that the U.S. development was generally used to show that regulation ought to be reestablished in the United States, and certainly not be abandoned in Europe.

Difficulties were in fact to be expected during a period of transition. After all, the trunk lines had erected excess capacities before, and they did have to absorb inflated labor costs that could be met by means of inflated prices only, such as were made possible through regulation. Given that new or intrastate carriers were so much more efficient, some airlines had to run into trouble. True, lower prices were likely to stimulate demand; but some carriers just could not afford much lower prices for long. Exploding costs of oil aggravated their difficulties; and the deep recession which followed did the rest by bringing down overall demand for air transportation. In consequence, more airlines will probably succumb in the close future.

The transition from a market so thoroughly regulated for decades to one completely deregulated is always bound to be an arduous one, as cost patterns evolve from regulation that are not easily adjusted. Grave complications arose from outside factors. Unfortunately, the resulting difficulties for the airline industry will convince many that deregulation cannot work; and such conviction may in turn render the case for deregulation in Europe even more difficult than it is already in view of state-owned carriers and the bureaucratic spirit residing within the European Community. I am afraid it will take decades to come until we get the European market for air transportation deregulated.

References

Bonus, Holger, "Information und Emotion in der Politikberatung - Zur politischen Umsetzung eines wirtschaftstheoretischen Konzepts". Zeitschrift für die gesamte Staatswissenschaft, Vol. 138, 1982, pp. 1-21.

Tietenberg, Thomas H., "Market Approaches to Environmental Protection". In: Herbert Giersch (Ed.), Reassessing the Role of Government in the Mixed Economy. Symposium 1982, Tübingen 1983, pp. 233-258.

Kieler Studien

Institut für Weltwirtschaft an der Universität Kiel

Herausgegeben von Herbert Giersch
Schriftleitung: Hubertus Müller-Groeling

162. Harmen Lehment, Devisenmarktinterventionen bei flexiblen Wechselkursen. Die Politik des Managed Floating. 1980. XIII, 289 S. Broschiert *DM* 57,–. Leinen *DM* 73,–.
163. Egbert Gerken, Arbeitsmärkte in Entwicklungsländern. 1981. XIV, 185 S. Broschiert *DM* 52,–. Leinen *DM* 70,–.
164. Horst Rodemer, Die EG-Agrarpolitik. Ziele, Wirkungen, Alternativen. 1980. XIII, 286 S. Broschiert *DM* 59,–. Leinen *DM* 77,–.
165. Lotte Müller-Ohlsen, Die Weltmetallwirtschaft im industriellen Entwicklungsprozeß. 1981. XI, 265 S. Broschiert *DM* 58,–. Leinen *DM* 76,–.
166. Gerhard Fels, Klaus-Dieter Schmidt und Mitarbeiter, Die deutsche Wirtschaft im Strukturwandel. 1981. XXII, 368 S. Broschiert *DM* 58,–. Leinen *DM* 76,–.
167. Sanjeev Gupta, Black Market Exchange Rates. 1981. XI, 100 S. Broschiert *DM* 31,–. Leinen *DM* 49,–.
168. Rolf Dick, Die Arbeitsteilung zwischen Industrie- und Entwicklungsländern im Maschinenbau. 1981. XIV, 186 S. Broschiert *DM* 57,–. Leinen *DM* 78,–.
169. Asim Erdilek, Direct Foreign Investment in Turkish Manufacturing: An Analysis of the Conflicting Objectives and Frustrated Expectations of a Host Country. 1982. XIV, 303 S. Broschiert *DM* 82,–. Leinen *DM* 99,–.
170. Bernhard Fischer, Egbert Gerken, Ulrich Hiemenz, Growth, Employment and Trade in an Industrializing Economy: A Quantitative Analysis of Mexican Development Policies. 1982. XI, 238 S. Broschiert *DM* 56,–. Leinen *DM* 79,–.
171. Juergen B. Donges et al., The Second Enlargement of the European Community: Adjustment Requirements and Challenges for Policy Reform. 1982. XVI, 247 S. Broschiert *DM* 58,—. Leinen *DM* 79,—.
172. Bernhard Fischer, Liberalisierung der Finanzmärkte und wirtschaftliches Wachstum in Entwicklungsländern. 1982. XII, 222 S. Broschiert *DM* 55,–. Leinen *DM* 74,—.
173. Wilfried Prewo et al., Die Neuordnung der Meere. Eine ökonomische Kritik des neuen Seerechts. 1982. XIII, 265 S. Broschiert *DM* 73,–. Leinen *DM* 93,–.
174. Adolf Ahnefeld, Zur Indexierung von Kreditverträgen. 1982. IX, 177 S. Broschiert *DM* 49,—. Leinen *DM* 67,—.
175. Axel D. Neu, Substitutionspotentiale und Substitutionshemmnisse in der Energieversorgung. 1982. XI, 137 S. Broschiert *DM* 38,–. Leinen *DM* 58,–.
176. Jamuna P. Agarwal, Hans H. Glismann, Peter Nunnenkamp, Ölpreisschocks und wirtschaftliche Entwicklung. Anpassungsprobleme in der Dritten Welt. 1983. XIII, 261 S. Broschiert *DM* 75,–. Leinen *DM* 95,–.
177. Chungsoo Kim, Evolution of Comparative Advantage: The Factor Proportions Theory in a Dynamic Perspective. 1983. XII, 114 S. Broschiert *DM* 42,–. Leinen *DM* 62,–.
178. Thomas Mayer, Instabile Exportmärkte und wirtschaftliche Entwicklung. Der Fall Kolumbien. Im Druck.
179. Frank D. Weiss, West Germany's Trade with the East: Hypotheses and Perspectives. 1983. XI, 108 S. Broschiert *DM* 39,–. Leinen *DM* 59,–.

J. C. B. Mohr (Paul Siebeck) Tübingen
Postfach 2040, D-7400 Tübingen
ISSN 0340 - 6989

www.ingramcontent.com/pod-product-compliance
Lightning Source LLC
LaVergne TN
LVHW011116300926
849160LV00008B/408
9780367300609